D0899906

# Marginal Workers

CITIZENSHIP AND MIGRATION IN THE AMERICAS
General Editor: Ediberto Román

*Tierra y Libertad: Land, Liberty, and Latino Housing*
Steven W. Bender

*No Undocumented Child Left Behind:* Plyler v. Doe *and the Education of Undocumented Schoolchildren*
Michael A. Olivas

*Marginal Workers: How Legal Fault Lines Divide Workers and Leave Them without Protection*
Ruben J. Garcia

# Marginal Workers

*How Legal Fault Lines Divide Workers and*

*Leave Them without Protection*

Ruben J. Garcia

NEW YORK UNIVERSITY PRESS

New York and London

NEW YORK UNIVERSITY PRESS
New York and London
www.nyupress.org

© 2012 by New York University

All rights reserved

References to Internet websites (URLs) were accurate at the time of writing.
Neither the author nor New York University Press is responsible for URLs that
may have expired or changed since the manuscript was prepared.

Library of Congress Cataloging-in-Publication Data

Garcia, Ruben J.
Marginal workers : how legal fault lines divide workers and
leave them without protection / Ruben J. Garcia.
p. cm.
Includes bibliographical references and index.
ISBN 978–0–8147–3221–2 (cl : alk. paper)
ISBN 978–0–8147–3863–4 (ebook)
ISBN 978–0–8147–3862–7 (ebook)
1. Discrimination in employment—Law and legislation—United States.
2. Minorities—Legal status, laws, etc.—United States. 3. Foreign workers—
Legal status, laws, etc.—United States. 4. Labor unions—Law and legislation—
United States. 5. Labor laws and legislation—United States. I. Title.
KF3464.G37     2011
344.7301'133—dc23          2011031462

New York University Press books are printed on acid-free paper, and their binding
materials are chosen for strength and durability. We strive to use environmentally responsible suppliers and materials to the greatest extent possible in publishing our books.

Manufactured in the United States of America
10 9 8 7 6 5 4 3 2 1

# Contents

# Preface

## *The Place of the Law in the Workplace*

In the late 1990s, I worked as a union-side labor lawyer in Southern California. It was work I thoroughly enjoyed for a few years after law school. I was able to work with clients that I respected who were trying to win a modicum of dignity in the workplace. I wanted to be part of the labor movement in some way, but never could see myself as an organizer or rabble-rouser. But I felt that I could use the law as a way to improve working conditions and empower people.

As with most who aspire to be lawyers for a cause (or "cause lawyers" as Austin Sarat and Stuart Scheingold have dubbed them), I wanted to use the law to further long-lasting social change.[1] And as with other cause lawyers, after several cases I began to wonder exactly what kind of impact I was having on the larger cause of worker rights. My cases were the typical diet of a labor side lawyer—workers denied the right to organize, unionized workers with arbitration cases, and the vindication of statutory rights. These cases followed a familiar pattern—employer misconduct, judicial reprobation, and then an inability to collect anything because of employer insolvency or intransigence. Like other labor lawyers before me, I started searching for the larger meaning of what I was doing.[2] I was fortunate to work for a firm that prized sophisticated, ethical advocacy and a client-centered approach, but I wanted to try to have a different kind of impact.

I had always aspired to an academic career, and the time seemed right to make a move to teaching. After a few years of cases that failed to change most employers' ingrained resistance to workers' rights, I did a research fellowship at the University of Wisconsin law school to probe deeper into the relationship between women, people of color, and their unions. The result was a study called "New Voices at Work: Race and Gender Identity

Caucuses in the U.S. Labor Movement."[3] In that study, I found that workers of color and women in U.S. labor unions worked to assert themselves in identity groups, even in the shadow of the union's exclusive role as collective bargaining representative. This research is discussed in chapter 3. There, the law was not an insurmountable barrier to people of color and women finding protection under a union contract. It also showed that statutory labor law did not solely determine the degrees of freedom available to workers to challenge existing majoritarian structures. My time as a Hastie Fellow at the University of Wisconsin cemented the idea that the "law in action" could be very different from the "law on the books," meaning that the realities of the law frequently do not match the ideals.

Even when I was a practicing lawyer, I represented a number of individual workers in statutory claims against their employers. These claims were often as part of union organizing drives, but they so often ended badly for the workers—with employers quashing union organizing drives and firing workers, and then leaving workers with unenforceable statutory claims. Employers often would go bankrupt, leaving workers unable to collect their full paychecks or benefit from statutorily provided remedies. On paper, the statutes were there to protect workers, but they failed to live up to their promise.

At the same time, I participated in local legislative struggles that were part of a broader movement to improve the lives of workers. In the mid-1990s, I worked on the legal theories behind the Los Angeles Living Wage Ordinance. These ordinances generally require businesses that contract with cities to pay at least a specified wage above the California minimum wage, and to provide an even higher wage if the employer did not provide health benefits. This campaign was successfully carried out by dedicated community activists as it was in other cities, such as Pasadena and Santa Monica, where I also provided pro bono legal assistance.[4]

These campaigns were important in laying the groundwork for progressive change in several cities, but they had limited impact on their own terms. First, these laws generally only apply to those employers that contract with the city that passed the ordinance. The Santa Monica ordinance was unique in that it applied to a "Coastal Zone" where most of the tourist attractions and restaurants are located. This made the law more broadly applicable than the ones in L.A. and Pasadena. As such, the law was also more controversial. It was challenged in the courts and ultimately repealed by voters through Santa Monica's initiative process. Despite all of these years, it seems, minimum wage legislation remains a contested concept. There are ongoing debates about the proper level of the wages and even whether a minimum wage is necessary. This book does not aim to resolve these debates, but I hope that some of the insights contained herein contribute to the dialogue.

This is not solely a book about the unrequited promise of law. It is also a book about how the content of law serves to perpetuate its ineffectiveness. I saw this firsthand when a supervisor at a small bakery in Southern California sought help from my firm after he was fired for organizing a union. The only problem was that the potential client was a supervisor—and supervisors are not covered by the statute. This particular supervisor was simply trying to encourage the employees to exercise their rights. Because the client was a supervisor, the employer could be candid and direct in the termination letter about the reason for the firing—assisting the employees in organizing a union—without any fear of legal repercussions. This shows a basic willingness to flout the right to organize, since the statute does not make the conduct illegal. The employer's actions also communicated to the rest of the workforce that they should not think about unionizing.

There will always be those who think that minimum wage and benefits protections are necessary and desirable. Indeed, the minimum wage is an important anti-poverty tool.[5] The economic debates about the minimum wage will continue. But this book will address concepts that go beyond economic debate. First, no person should work in a condition of involuntary servitude. Another foundational principle is that discrimination on arbitrary grounds should not be tolerated—the only question usually is what constitutes unlawful discrimination. Finally, most people should have the right to associate for their own benefit and protection, although like free speech it is subject to limitations. While the scope of these rights may be debated, their existence as a baseline should not be in serious dispute. The problem is that workers' rights are not seen as fundamental in our culture today.

In fact, workers' rights principles are found in the United States Constitution and many international human rights documents. Most of the Constitution applies only to governmental action, but the Thirteenth Amendment applies to both private and public action and prohibits "involuntary servitude" anywhere in the United States. Discrimination by the government is prohibited by the equal protection clause of the Fourteenth Amendment. Many of the civil rights era protections, while ostensibly enacted pursuant to the Commerce Clause, draw much from the Reconstruction Amendments. And the First Amendment provides protection for labor-organizing activity on public property, as well as limited protection for public employees to speak out at work. These principles also exist in many of the international law instruments to which the United States is a signatory.

At a time when less than 9 percent of the private sector is unionized and the remainder is generally employed at-will, which means that they can be fired without any reason at all, statutory remedies are the only backstop of fair treatment for workers. Yet, many workers are unable to utilize these remedies. Immigrants, women, and people of color have an even more difficult time in availing themselves of statutory protections, as this book will show. Thus, the genesis of this and much of my other work is to evaluate the overall effectiveness of these laws and to suggest alternatives.

Foundational labor principles are lost in the current debates about the amendment and enforcement of statutes. This book will show how statutes leave gaps that workers fall through. It is not my intent to end the reliance on statutes. Instead, I hope that it will provide fuel for policymakers and advocates in the arguments that they make for the protection of workers' rights. But I also hope that these arguments move business and labor to seek common ground on certain fundamental principles, even if there is disagreement about the scope of those rights. In the end, it is my desire that once the crisis of workers' rights is seen in the same light as issues such as climate change, financial collapse, and health care, we may see an improvement in conditions for all workers. I hope this volume can contribute to that change, even in a small way.

# Acknowledgments

This book is the product of a long, arduous process that I could not have completed without the support of my wife, Victoria Carreón. Tori has been a constant source of inspiration and "reality," all with loving humor. My family and friends also have been very supportive throughout my career and especially during the writing of this book. In particular, my parents, Robert and Emilia Garcia, have encouraged me at every turn.

There are many other people, too numerous to mention, who helped with the production of this book, but I will try to name some of them. First, my editor Deborah Gershenowitz provided invaluable support and encouragement getting this book from concept to completion. I am proud that it will be part of NYU Press's Citizenship and Migrants in the Americas Series, and I thank Professor Ediberto Román for his guiding editorship of that series. Thanks also to Gabrielle Begue at NYU Press for her editorial assistance. Second, California Western School of Law in San Diego, the institution where I started my tenure track-teaching career and wrote most of this book, was incredibly supportive both morally and financially. I thank all the colleagues at California Western and other institutions who have provided their moral support and suggestions. Thanks to Dean Steven Smith and Associate Deans William Aceves and Janet Bowermaster, who provided financial support at various stages of this process.

I appreciate the community of scholars that have provided their suggestions over the years, not just on the component parts of the book, but also on the larger themes that are a part of this work. These scholars include the law faculties and students at California Western School of Law, Thomas Jefferson School of Law, the University of San Diego, the University of Nevada, Las Vegas, the University of Cincinnati, and Wayne State University. I also benefited from interdisciplinary and international perspectives at the University of California, San Diego and the University of Heidelberg campus in Santiago de Chile.

The library staff at California Western provided constant assistance with everything from electronic databases to ongoing interlibrary loans, most especially library director Professor Phyllis Marion, Barbara Glennan, Linda Weathers, Saad Ali, and Kim Sterner. Faculty Support Services at California Western also provided excellent help, with Stephanie Sanchez taking the laboring oar on most of the work.

Before I went into teaching, I was a union lawyer at Rothner, Segall, Bahan, and Greenstone in Pasadena, California, from which some of the personal anecdotes in this book are taken. I thank the firm for showing me how to be a lawyer and also for the inspiration the work provided me for my later career.

This book is adapted from many of the articles that I have written for law journals since I started my teaching career, and I am grateful for the work of the student editors of those journals. I was fortunate to have a number of California Western students work as research assistants at various stages of this project, including Sara Hoppenrath, Bart Parsley, Amy Osborne, Tracy Jones, Laura Biddle, Justin Prato, Emma Bennett-Williams, Vanessa DeNiro, Nia Rucker, Barakat Alao, and Jaclyn White Simi.

Chapters have been adapted from the following articles: "Toward Fundamental Change for the Protection of Low-Wage Workers: The Labor Rights Are Human Rights Debate in the Obama Era," 2009 *University of Chicago Legal Forum* 421; "From North to South Country: Race, Gender and Immigration and the Role of Unions in the Sanitized Workplace," 29 *Thomas Jefferson Law Review* 55 (2006); "Labor as Property: Guestworkers, International Trade and the Democracy Deficit," 10 *Iowa Journal of Gender, Race and Justice* 27 (2006); "Labor's Fragile Freedom of Association Post-9/11," 8 *University of Pennsylvania Journal of Labor and Employment Law* 283 (2006); "Transnationalism as a Social Movement Strategy: Actors, Institutions and International Labor Standards," 10 *U.C. Davis Journal of International Law and Policy* 1 (2003); "Ghost Workers in an Interconnected World: Going Beyond the Dichotomies of Domestic Immigration and Labor Laws," 36 *University of Michigan Journal of Law Reform* 737 (2003); "Across the Borders: Immigrant Status and Identity in Law and LatCrit Theory," 55 *Florida Law Review* 511 (2003); "New Voices at Work: Race and Gender Identity Caucuses in the U.S. Labor Movement," 54 *Hastings Law Journal* 79 (2002). Thanks to all the editors on those articles.

And finally thanks to my students, who teach me something new every day.

# 1

# Who Are the
# Marginal Workers?

José Castro, an undocumented immigrant from Mexico, worked in a plastics factory in south Los Angeles from May 1988 to early 1989. In fact, "José Castro" is probably not his real name, but that was the name on the birth certificate he used in order to obtain employment at Hoffman Plastic Compounds, Inc.[1] Three years earlier, in 1986, the U.S. Congress passed an amnesty program for undocumented immigrants, and for the first time outlawed the hiring of unauthorized workers. Nevertheless, Castro found employment relatively easily, although he did have assistance from a friend who helped him fill out the paperwork to get a job with Hoffman.[2] Castro was also helped by the de-unionization of the manufacturing industry in Southern California that put immigrant labor in much greater demand.[3]

Castro's story would be unexceptional in many urban areas over the last 40 years had it not been for the fact that he became involved in organizing a union, resulting in an unfair labor practice case that went to the U.S. Supreme Court. After being laid off by Hoffman for supporting the United Steelworkers Union, Castro and the union sought redress from the National Labor Relations Board (NLRB), the federal agency dedicated to protecting the right of all employees to form unions and bargain collectively. The NLRB decided to prosecute Castro's case as a retaliatory firing in violation of the federal law protecting the right to join unions, the National Labor Relations Act of 1935 (NLRA).

The *Hoffman* case sits at the intersection of immigration and labor law. After the case worked its way through the administrative and court systems, the U.S. Supreme Court was to decide whether Castro, indisputably an "employee" within the broad definition of that term under the NLRA, nonetheless should be denied the statutory remedies because of his unauthorized immigration status. Although he was an employee owed protection under the statute (because the definition of "employee" in the NLRA does not distinguish between documented and undocumented workers), the Supreme Court held in a 5-4 decision that Castro nevertheless was not entitled to the standard NLRB remedy of back pay because granting the remedy would "unduly trench upon the federal immigration policy of preventing unauthorized employment."[4]

The Court rejected the NLRB's argument that denying back pay would actually *encourage* employers to hire undocumented workers because the cost of violating workers' rights would be so low it would offset the small risk of fines being brought by the government to enforce immigration law. In 2002, for example, the federal government prosecuted only 25 criminal cases against employers for hiring undocumented workers.[5] As Justice Stephen Breyer wrote in a dissenting opinion for three other justices, employers will hire illegal labor with "a wink and a nod" and then get off "scot-free" when they violate "every labor law under the sun."[6] The Court, in an opinion by the late Chief Justice William Rehnquist, replied that the employer does not get off scot-free—the employer is still subject to contempt proceedings if it engages in similar conduct again, and must post a notice to employees promising compliance with the law.[7]

Castro was caught in the margins of two different statutes, and his story is emblematic of marginal workers. In the chapters that follow, there are more examples of the ways in which courts have construed bodies of statutory law against the interests of workers. These cases raise a basic question about the efficacy of protective labor legislation, and whether or not a different approach to workers' rights needs to be emphasized. I will pursue that question, and find common threads in recent efforts to put fundamental workers' rights above the political processes of statutory change.

Here, I describe how statutory protections have failed to protect many workers besides undocumented workers, typically through judicial misconstruction. The weakness of labor law remedies for all employees has been documented in labor law scholarship.[8] I recount the stories of workers whose protection is compromised by clashing statutory objectives. Castro, for example, was caught between a protective labor law statute that protects employees regardless of their immigration status, and immigration law which requires authorization to work in the United States. The fact that Castro was undocumented further marginalizes him, since undocumented workers are less likely to assert the workplace rights that they have than other workers whose immigration status is not precarious.

Even though Castro asserted his rights, the operation of immigration law affected his ability to receive the same remedies as other workers.

By providing different remedies to employees who work side by side, the *Hoffman* decision, and many statutes, divide workers who should share common interests. The problem in *Hoffman* is not the statute itself, but judicial mis-construction. Some statutes, however, explicitly divide workers into different categories. Sometimes there is a good reason for divisions, such as the division between supervisors and employees in collective bargaining law, but the courts and administrative agencies have not always been correct in determining where the line between employee and supervisor is drawn.[9] This divides workers who should share common interests, and makes collective change less likely.

The gaps left by statutes like the National Labor Relations Act raise questions about the effectiveness of all legislation to protect workers. Even the immigration control statute has failed to live up to its promise. Much research has shown that immigration law has not functioned in keeping with its purpose of preventing illegal employment while simultaneously meeting labor market needs for immigrant labor.[10] Here, however, focuses on the dysfunction of protective labor laws for the most vulnerable workers, and how to improve the protections of those workers. I define "marginal workers" as those who are technically protected by labor and employment laws, but because of competing policy concerns or bodies of law, they lose full protection. This is especially true of more legally vulnerable workers, such as noncitizens, people of color, and women. Despite the additional protections that these workers enjoy on paper, they are often unable to fully enforce their rights. But all workers are affected by the inadequate protection given to marginal workers. In the *Hoffman* case discussed earlier, José Castro's inability to organize a union affected all workers, not just those who were undocumented. These fault lines divide workers and leave them without protection.

There are a number of ways to ameliorate the situation of marginal workers. First, statutes could be modified and clarified to better protect workers. As will become evident, however, labor legislation fails to fully protect workers, and workers are generally too politically diffuse to change the law to their advantage. With regard to marginal workers, this political powerlessness is even more acute, since many of the workers discussed herein are minorities, noncitizens, or low-wage workers.

Second, courts could simply make better decisions. Many times, court decisions can be criticized as a misapplication of the law. And there have been some situations where legislatures have corrected decisions. In chapter 6, I discuss the case of Lily Ledbetter, whose case led to a Supreme Court decision and a legislative change to the Equal Pay Act. In Ledbetter's case, the political process worked to reverse the decision, but a closer examination will reveal that the gains made by Ledbetter do not stem the tide of pay inequity in the United States.

I address a puzzling paradox about labor and employment law protections: Why are workers still poorly protected by the plethora of twentieth-century statutory innovations passed on their behalf in the last century? The reasons are many, but I focus mainly on the way in which most workplace regulation has been accomplished as the primary problem. Workplace law is seen as a political battlefield between labor and capital, with each successive political change leading the pendulum either more toward the laissez-faire or toward New Deal-style regulation. This political see-saw has created a class of "marginal workers"—workers who fall through the margins of different bodies of law that are supposed to protect them, but lack the political power to fix the holes in the legislation. These pendulum swings have produced a statutory framework that has left numerous gaps and incomplete protections for all workers.

In order to better protect marginal workers, I advocate changing the primary framework in which we conceive workers' rights. We have tended to see workplace regulation as a contest between labor and capital—a pendulum that swings back and forth between labor-friendly and business-friendly administrations. Rather than the spoils of political victory, workers' rights should be seen as fundamental human rights, as they are in international law. Indeed, the human rights frame is increasingly being used by scholars, unions, and practitioners to advance the cause of worker freedom. In so doing, I argue that a global constitution of worker freedom is effectively being crafted and should be encouraged through litigation and dialogue to change attitudes and behavior.

Even in the face of the *Hoffman* decision and the threat of deportation, undocumented workers continue to organize in unions and in litigation against their employers. Several scholars have shown the willingness of immigrants to organize in unions.[11] Like other employees who have found resort to the law unavailing, undocumented workers and unions have also continued to use a dialogue of human rights for greater protection. For example, in the wake of the *Hoffman* decision, the AFL-CIO filed a complaint with the International Labor Organization alleging that the decision violated international human rights law. The ILO agreed, but as a matter of statutory construction of the NLRA, the *Hoffman* decision is still the law of the land.

## The Historical Trajectory of Labor Regulation in the United States

The lack of protection in *Hoffman Plastics* described above raises questions about whether the worker protection goals of the progressive movement of the early twentieth century have been fully realized. In the legal realist tradition, law was an instrument for positive social change and a tool to be used with caution.[12] Working hand in hand with progressive movements, legal reformers enacted workers' compensation and state health and safety protections in the early 1900s. Then, in the 1930s, after the beginning of New Deal reforms and mass protests in the streets, the National Labor Relations Act of 1935 became the first modern piece of labor legislation.

In Critical Legal Studies and other jurisprudential movements of the latter twentieth century, law was viewed with suspicion as a necessary evil for social reform. In legal realist movements, legal scholars sought to reform the law through legislative change and administrative agencies. For the early labor movement, however, law and the courts were obstacles to progress because of the labor injunction, which was used to put a stop to even peaceful picketing.[13] Labor was thus more interested in solidarity actions than a resort to law.[14]

Still, the question of what kind of law—statutory or constitutional—confronted the labor movement in its nascent stages. Constitutional doctrine was frequently used against the labor movement in the form of "substantive due process." Thus, the liberty interest in the Fourteenth Amendment due process clause was being used to invalidate state prohibitions of "yellow dog" contracts. These were contracts that employers required before a worker could start employment, promising that the employee would not join a union. It took the passage of the Norris LaGuardia Act of 1932 to reverse the Supreme Court's decision in *Coppage v. Kansas* to outlaw yellow dog contracts.[15] In spite of this, labor activists in the early twentieth century sought to base congressional legislation to protect freedom of association and collective bargaining on the Thirteenth Amendment to the U.S. Constitution, which prohibits "slavery or involuntary servitude in the United States or any place subject to its jurisdiction."[16] Like much of the New Deal, however, labor legislation was enacted pursuant to Congress's constitutional authority to regulate interstate commerce, and survived the legal challenges of business groups that it was beyond congressional authority.[17]

The 1934 passage of section 7(a) of the National Industrial Act and the subsequent National Labor Relations Act in 1935 began a move toward the legal protection of concerted activity through a federal administrative agency. The National Labor Relations Board (NLRB) was one of the first federal agencies created for the protection of labor rights. More than 70 years after its creation, many see the NLRB as an emblem of the ossification of American labor law.[18] The five-member Board that reviews the decisions of NLRB trial judges are appointed by the president. Thus, with each administration, the pendulum swings back and forth between more labor-friendly to more business-friendly decisions.

In the meantime, the protection for union organizing has diminished over the years. Studies have shown that one in 20 workers who support a union is fired for organizing campaigns at their workplaces.[19] Interpretations of the NLRA by the Board and the courts have decimated worker rights.[20] At the same time, there has been a proliferation of statutes to protect workers in the 75 years since the NLRA was enacted. Ironically, the proliferation of statutes has not led to a corresponding level of protection for marginal workers.

The politics of law, the title of a seminal anthology of the work of critical theorists, has not been good to workers. Critical scholars such as Alan Hyde, Karl Klare, and James Atleson have long questioned whether the law really protected workers' interests.[21] These scholars questioned the courts' handling of labor law, but perhaps the heart of the problem lay with the statute itself—born of compromise and unable to be amended quickly.

In contemporary politics, we see this all the time. Health care legislation took years and was constantly critiqued as a choice between incrementalism or omnibus reform, until finally resulting in the Patient Protection and Affordable Care Act in March 2010. Immigration reform similarly has proceeded at a glacial pace. The Family Medical Leave Act, while it was welcomed in 1994 for allowing workers to take off 12 weeks from work to care for sick family members, is now being criticized for not providing paid leave. It also does little to address the instances of family responsibilities discrimination that are now being brought under Title VII, often unsuccessfully, in the absence of a separate statute dealing with such discrimination. Although Congress passed the Lilly Ledbetter Act early in the administration of President Obama, most other business is stalled by the Senate's filibuster rule, including some nominees to the National Labor Relations Board and Department of Labor. The U.S. Supreme Court's 2010 Citizens United decision allowing corporations and unions to give unlimited funds as independent expenditures will further tilt the playing field away from ordinary workers and toward large corporations.[22]

## *The State of Workers Today*

Some of the insecurity workers feel today is economic. Real wages for all workers, or the amount earned adjusted for inflation, have dropped.[23] More and more workers are working part time. From April to May 2009, for example, the average wages of U.S. production workers shrank from $614.86 to $613.67 per week. This reflects the reduced bargaining power of workers over the years.[24] But not all measures of worker insecurity are related to declining wages. Much of it is also related to the insecurity that workers feel in a down economy, without protections from discharge or layoff.

A great deal of worker insecurity is related to the decline of collective bargaining in the latter part of the twentieth century. Previously, protections in union contracts with their grievance arbitration processes provided a shield against unfair treatment. Now, statutory protections are the primary means of seeking this enforcement, but they have been ceded by the federal government to private plaintiffs. In many cases, private plaintiffs have been able to redress wage and hour violations, but there are many other violations against low-wage workers that are not economical for attorneys to take. Recently, a GAO report found that the Department of Labor under the Bush administration had completely failed to enforce wage and hour law.[25] This uneven enforcement, even if corrected during the Obama administration, calls out for fundamental change in the way we look at workers' rights.

Even if we had full enforcement of the minimum wage, for example, studies have shown it to be inadequate to support a family of four above the poverty line. This reality has led many to advocate for a living wage, rather than the minimum wage.[26] Many cities and governmental entities have enacted living wage laws that apply only to contractors. This, however, is a small number of employers in the economy.[27] Only a few municipalities, such as Santa Fe, San Francisco, and Washington, DC, have adopted a local minimum wage ordinance that applies to all employers doing business within the city limits.

But real wages and income levels are only two measures of the status of workers in contemporary America. Workers today face other types of insecurity. Most workers are employed at will, which means that they are working without a contract or union protection specifying that they be terminated only for just cause. Based on current statistics, only about 15 percent of the workforce is unionized, meaning that nearly 85 percent of the workforce is most likely employed at will, without any contractual job protections. This means that statutory protections provide the backstop of fair treatment for most workers. As a safety net from unfair dismissal and discrimination, protective labor laws provide a patchwork quilt with some rather large holes which marginal workers fall through.

With unionization dropping below 10 percent in the private sector in the 2000s, there is a corresponding increase in the number of workers who are employed at will, without contractual recourse for unfair dismissals. The backstop of antidiscrimination law has contracted in significant ways from its initial promise. Indeed, one of the biggest cases in discrimination law in recent years has been a reverse discrimination case in which then-Judge Sonia Sotomayor participated on the Second Circuit Court of Appeals which was reviewed by the U.S. Supreme Court before she joined the Court.[28] There is little concern about whether or not plaintiffs of color and women are able to get their cases heard by courts that are looking for ways to limit their dockets through doctrine that has a disproportionate impact on people of color and women who bring most of the claims.

All of these developments call for a new approach to the protection of the rights of the most vulnerable members of our society. Because the political processes have failed to adequately protect most workers, a fundamental rights discourse must be used to affirm the dignity of work and the moral imperative of certain basic minimum human rights for the protection of workers. This book focuses on a set of minimum workers' rights as human rights.

And yet "rights talk" in the protection of the marginalized has a controversial pedigree. Legal realists, critical legal theorists, and race theorists have all debated the place of rights in the protection and empowerment of minorities.[29] Critical race and feminist theorists have resolved that rights are necessary for the protection of women and minorities but should not be seen as ends unto themselves.[30] Ultimately, rights continue to form the fabric of everyday life.

The debate over rights talk only begins a series of questions with regard to workers: What effect does rights talk have on the empowerment of workers? What is the effect of the counter-rights talk by employers? Has the language of rights had an effect on judges and administrative agencies offering better protection of workers? What *kinds* of rights should be employed? Should they be statutory, constitutional, or international? Does human rights talk lionize individuality and destroy solidarity?

This book addresses these questions in two ways. First, I demonstrate the ways in which statutory methods of worker protection have failed workers in several high-profile Supreme Court cases involving immigrant workers, workers of color in unions, and noncitizen workers. I also describe how guestworkers are caught between the laws of two countries. Then, I describe and endorse a movement toward seeing U.S. worker rights in the framework of constitutional and international rights that is already part of the fabric of social movements. The point is to provide a conceptual framework of baselines from which to accomplish regulation, but also to change attitudes about the imperative of minimum worker protections.

The debate over how to best protect workers' rights has been going on for years, but the question of whether to use human rights dialogue is a relatively more recent phenomenon. I do not claim to put an end to the debate in this book, but I do wish to provide a new understanding of how to best protect workers.

## *Defining "Marginal Workers"*

I discuss workers who are marginalized not solely because of their economic circumstances. In labor economics, the term has a specific meaning: marginal workers are those in irregular employment, because they are part-time, contractors, or disabled.[31] In a broader sense, many workers are marginalized by the lines of demarcation in statutes themselves. The National Labor Relations Act, for example, excludes agricultural workers and those in domestic service. All statutes exclude independent contractors, and cover only those who are considered "employees" who work under the control of an employer.

The problem with the way that labor regulation has proceeded over the last century is that it leaves a number of politically powerless workers behind. Even when workers have made strides, these have been incremental steps. The problem is that many of the most vulnerable workers in American society have little political power to effect change through legislation. With the decrease in the number of unions over the last 30 years, workers' political power has become diluted. Workers with diffuse interests are unable to effectively band together politically for their interests. This leads to legislation that is incomplete, incremental, sometimes at cross-purposes with other statutes, and lacking coherence.[32]

The deficit in democratic participation identified above requires a new approach to workplace regulation that takes into account the fact that many workers, such as undocumented workers, guestworkers, and other noncitizens, are politically powerless in a majoritarian political system. Even in situations where there is some arguable political power, such as for women, people of color, or public-sector employees, the failure of workers to effectively counter limitations on their freedom of association and ability to earn equal pay has been shown in several recent examples.

I argue that a new human rights dialogue is needed to break out of the back and forth movement of the political processes. Progress has been made in the Obama administration to protect workers, but gaps still remain. Change will have to come in the form of changed attitudes among individuals and in administrative agencies and court decisions incorporating international human rights principles.

## *Plan of the Book*

This book tells the stories of marginal workers, so each chapter begins with a different example of workers trapped in the gaps between different legal regimes. In chapter 2, I trace the ground that has been ably covered by other labor scholars who have framed workers' rights as human rights. As stated earlier, I cast my lot on the side of human rights. I also discuss in this chapter the general problems with statutory change in the protection of workers' rights.

Chapter 3 looks at the clash of statutory objectives of the National Labor Relations Act and Title VII of the Civil Rights Act. In the upheaval of the 1960s, the protest activities of two African American department store workers in San Francisco led to the Supreme Court cleaving between the protections of concerted activities and antidiscrimination law. The implications of this split are salient today.

Chapter 4 looks at noncitizen immigrants, who are supposed to have virtually the same rights as citizens for most employee protections. Title

VII even has a protection for discrimination on the basis of national origin. In 1973, however, the Supreme Court held that discrimination against noncitizens because they were noncitizens was not actionable under Title VII. This decision means that an employer can discriminate against employees for no other reason but their lack of U.S. citizenship. In today's immigration climate, noncitizens are stigmatized and are often the victims of discrimination simply because they are not citizens. Even though recent changes to immigration law prohibit citizenship discrimination, these laws are only enforced through the Department of Justice, rather than private parties. This leaves a gap in remedies for noncitizens, who make up a growing segment of the American workforce.

Chapter 5 examines another group of workers who are legally allowed to be in the United States but unable to make full use of the laws that apply to them. Temporary workers from other countries, anomalously named "guestworkers" in today's parlance, have been part of the U.S. labor force for over 80 years. History shows that guestworkers have faced exploitation in many instances, but also have been ignored by both their home governments and their "host" governments. Violations of the domestic statutes that are supposed to protect workers have been the subject of class actions in recent years. In this chapter, I conclude that international standards, and also international litigation, should be the primary means of addressing these violations.

In chapter 6, I again articulate the thread that runs through the book—that there is a movement toward the protection of workers' rights on constitutional and international levels. These principles can provide a "default canon" in favor of workers' rights, when two statutes are in tension with one another. This orientation will require a number of paradigm shifts that are also in the works—one that has been the subject of some controversy is the place of international law in the U.S. courts. By studying the ways in which workers have been marginalized by statutes, I hope to draw out the following three minimum principles as they apply to private- and public-sector workplaces:

1. Freedom of speech and association are overarching principles found in the Constitution and international law, because only through these procedural rights can workers' bargaining power be fully realized.
2. The categorical approach to discrimination in statutes and the Constitution should be broadened to include international principles to which the United States is a signatory.

3. The meaning of "involuntary servitude" in the Constitution's Thirteenth Amendment is broad enough to encompass a number of practices today—from the denial of the right to collective bargaining to guestworker programs.

I argue that judicial decisions *and* legislation should proceed in accord with these principles.

## What Is This Book Not About?

There are a number of workers who are completely outside the labor and employment laws. They include domestic workers and agricultural workers who are not covered by statutes such as the National Labor Relations Act and the Fair Labor Standards Act. These workers are not the subject of this book per se, because it is about workers who are all employees within the statute's definition and theoretically protected by the law. There have been a number of studies of marginalized workers who are treated as independent contractors, when in fact they are employees. The adult entertainment industry, for example, is notorious for this kind of misclassification. Basically, by claiming the worker is not an employee, the "employer" is absolved of all responsibility for workers' compensation, wage and hour laws, and even discrimination laws. Many of these cases have resulted in large judgments and settlements for back wages, penalties, and attorneys' fees.

There has also been a movement among marginalized workers for greater rights. Home health care workers in Los Angeles County fought for the right to have an employer, by making the County the employer of record. This is one of the cases that Jennifer Jihye Chun discusses in her book *Organizing at the Margins*. She discusses battles over the classification of workers as a way to marginalize them, both in the United States and Korea.[33]

While I think the principles discussed here will beneficially inform the many misclassified workers, my aim is not to go deeply into the state of such workers. At its root, though, much of the problem with marginal workers lies in "employee" status itself. We will see that a more universal approach to those who work is embodied in international human rights. It should also be noted that all of the workers discussed in this book are considered statutory employees, yet because of court interpretations, they are unable to get real protection from the law.

When it comes to fundamental labor rights like protection from discrimination and the right to engage in collective bargaining, employee status should matter little. There are going to be some clear examples of contractors, or workers with a lot of bargaining power, but for the most part, misclassification will continue to frustrate even the laws that are supposed to protect "employees." Or, as in some countries, the law protects all who work for another, eschewing the multipart test that is used in the United States to determine whether someone is an independent contractor.

But what is the logical stopping point? I believe international human rights law provides a logical stopping point. The last chapter will address some of the challenges to this approach, including its impracticability, the alleged antidemocratic nature of international human rights, and the possibility that international human rights might themselves be co-opted. Although these concerns are important, I believe that a new human rights strategy should be attempted. As Bob Dylan sang in "Like a Rolling Stone": "When you got nothing, you got nothing to lose."[34] For many workers today, a new approach might be the only thing that seems worth trying.

## *%*  2  *%*

# Framing Workers' Rights

### *The Legal and Theoretical*

### *Underpinnings for the Protection of*

### *Marginal Workers*

To many, the proposition seems uncontroversial: "workers' rights are human rights." To others, and not just those who favor business interests over workers, this proposition is subject to debate. While this question may not preoccupy workers who are just trying to get by, the larger questions about the source of rights at work have preoccupied scholars and also the leaders of the labor movement. Even though people have worked since the beginning of time, legal protections for workers are an innovation of the twentieth century. While there may be few who debate the humanity of workers, the issue of "rights" in the workplace has often engendered debate.

And the debate about rights is not limited to the workplace area. A focus on rights to protect marginalized people has been a subject of discussion in legal scholarship since at least the 1960s. In 1973, political scientist Stuart Scheingold explored the "myth of rights" in his study of public interest lawyers. He called the myth of rights "the idea held by some activist lawyers that rights can provide salvation for dispossessed peoples." Mark Tushnet critiqued the myth of rights in 1984 in "An Essay on Rights." He called rights talk "probably unhelpful, and possibly harmful" to the cause of justice.[1] From a different political perspective, Mary Ann Glendon in 1991 decried the impoverishment of political discourse in her book *Rights Talk*.[2] Glendon points out that the language of rights has sometimes worked to undermine collective rights. "[I]n labor law," she writes, "where Congress firmly committed the nation in the 1930s to a policy of promoting employee organizational activity and protecting collective bargaining, court decisions have elevated individual rights to erode that policy. Judicial adroitness in applying the constitutional principles of liberty and equality is rarely matched by a corresponding skill in implementing the congressionally endorsed principle of solidarity."[3]

Glendon is not alone in questioning whether the emphasis on individual rights has affected the interest of workers to organize for their own interests. Indeed, the U.S. Supreme Court has in numerous cases privileged so-called individual rights at the expense of collective solidarity.[4] Labor law scholars have recently had occasion to debate the place of human rights talk in protecting workers, particularly with the increase in human rights litigation and advocacy in service of worker rights.[5] Skeptics of "rights dialogue" argue that rights can be disempowering at a time when more solidarity is needed.[6] At the same time, human rights advocates argue that a new rights dialogue is necessary to better protect workers' rights.[7] In this chapter, I will look at the framing of workers' rights, and why it matters for the protection of marginal workers.

## *The Connections between Workers' Rights and Constitutional Rights*

There is a historic connection between workers' rights and constitutional rights and liberties. Civil liberties are fundamental to the functioning of a democratic society. These include freedom of speech and freedom of association. Courts have held that these rights are fundamental, which basically means they can only be abridged when the government shows a compelling reason for doing so. Civil liberties were essential to the forming labor movement. Some of the earliest cases granting First Amendment protection, such as the 1939 Supreme Court decision in *Hague v. CIO*, arise in the context of labor organizing. Though the First Amendment freedoms of speech and assembly apply only to actions by federal and state governments, employers' repression of the right to organize has relied upon the cooperation of police forces, such as in the historical cases in West Virginia, Ludlow, Colorado, and the general strike in San Francisco in 1934. This symbiotic relationship has led some to question whether the complicity between employers and state law enforcement may indeed give rise to a constitutional claim.[8]

There is only one part of the Constitution that applies to both public and private employment. The Thirteenth Amendment prohibits slavery or involuntary servitude whether it is carried out in the private or public sectors. A growing body of scholarship argues that the Thirteenth Amendment can be a powerful basis for the right to organize and bargain collectively. James Pope has explicated the Thirteenth Amendment as an alternative to the Commerce Clause, as a constitutional basis for legislating protection of union organizing.[9] Pope shows that basing the NLRA on Congress's power to regulate interstate commerce, rather than the human rights basis embodied in the Thirteenth Amendment, meant that it lost some of the radical impact. It also means that the NLRA, along with other New Deal legislation, was subject to immediate attack on the grounds that the Commerce Clause did not give Congress the power to pass it. It took a court packing crisis, a change at the Supreme Court, and a change in the philosophy of one justice to get the New Deal legislation through.[10]

Maria Ontiveros has argued that the Thirteenth Amendment provides a basis to better protect undocumented workers such as José Castro, mentioned in chapter 1.[11] Despite the value of these theories, it will be a long, hard road to get courts to accept the Thirteenth Amendment as a basis for the violation of the right to organize. Thus, the expansion of rights for workers will be a slow uphill climb.

## Rights Critics: Too Much Litigation?

Some have questioned the recent overemphasis on rights generally, and specifically new forms of employment protection in the workplace. In recent years, protection for the aged, the disabled, and gays and lesbians among others has been added to the civil rights canon. Walter Olson wrote in the 1980s about the "excuse factory" that has been created by workplace law.[12] Yet, the number of employment discrimination claims in the federal courts has decreased over the last decade.[13] Studies estimate that many workers are unwilling to bring all of the claims that they have against an employer. For marginalized workers like immigrants and guestworkers, that number is probably much less. Moreover, some observers feel that it is business and the right wing that has made the United States a "lawsuit nation."[14]

And yet the distinction between rights and litigation should be made clear. A dialogue about human rights does not presuppose a litigation campaign to enforce those rights, although that is one strategy that I advocate here. Human rights can exist without litigation. Nevertheless, litigation is one of the main ways in which values have been transmitted. The debate about whether litigation transmits values has been studied without a conclusive answer. The question is how we should choose among purportedly dichotomous values. It is about values: How do we value a right to freedom of association against the right of employers to have absolute control over the workplace? Those who favor an unfettered free market will obviously favor no regulation and complete dominion over the workplace. This so-called market fundamentalism is a deeply ingrained ideology in American society. Those who think that workers should have the freedom to choose whether to be represented by a union will clearly side with that value. The difference is that the right to choose a union freely is backed up by an infrastructure of international law, while market fundamentalism is not.

### Proto-Labor Legislation: The National Labor Relations Act

Market fundamentalism reigned supreme in the late nineteenth and early twentieth centuries. In the post–Civil War period, rapid industrialization proceeded with little corresponding regulation. The state and federal governments adopted a laissez-faire approach that allowed businesses to treat their workers as they wished. Workers' organizations such as the Knights of Labor sprouted up and challenged the existing order. When workers were able to organize and strike, they were stymied by the courts through the labor injunction. From this experience, labor leaders developed a mistrust of the courts and cast their lot with the progressive movement in crafting worker protective legislation. This occurred in some states, such as Kansas, which passed laws banning yellow dog contracts, in which a worker at the beginning of employment pledges not to join a union during his or her term of employment. The Supreme Court struck down Kansas's law under its due process clause of the Fourteenth Amendment. The substantive component of the due process clause, the Court held, prevented Kansas from passing a law prohibiting yellow dog contracts, since the Fourteenth Amendment prohibits interference with liberty without due process of law. The law that restricted the right of workers to contract away their rights to unionize according to the Court would impinge on the workers' liberty of contract. Thus, the Court struck down the statute. It would be another 28 years, when the Norris-La Guardia Act was introduced, before Congress prohibited yellow dog contracts as part of federal legislation. The Supreme Court later repudiated decisions like *Coppage v. Kansas* and *Lochner v. New York* when it upheld the New Deal legislation.[15]

## Diffuse Coalitions, Few Results

There are some scholars who continue to believe that labor legislation was tilted in favor of labor unions at the expense of individual workers. Public choice theorists use data to show how legislative enactments benefit only discrete groups. They point to prevailing wage laws that discriminate against nonunion workers, who are often minorities or women. This may be a reason to make sure that all workers who want it have access to union employment, but it does not mean that minimum standards legislation should not exist.

Progressive movements for reform must address the lingering criticism of scholars such as David Bernstein who argue that protective labor legislation marginalizes people of color and women.[16] These scholars argue that regulation of the labor market is the source of the marginalization of workers, particularly African Americans. Bernstein argues that labor laws such as the Davis-Bacon Act, which essentially mandates union-scale wages for public construction projects, negatively impacts minorities. And yet there are positive aspects of prevailing wage laws that have also benefited African Americans. In the early years of the Davis-Bacon Act, there was no protection from discrimination. African Americans and other minorities were thereby truly left without any redress. Even after discrimination was outlawed in federal contracts in 1953, discrimination was still rampant. Thus, the answer was not to end the protective labor legislation, but to add antidiscrimination values to the law of the workplace.

In his 2007 study of how civil rights legislation was enacted in the 1960s, Paul Frymer discusses why it is sometimes difficult to get civil rights legislation passed. "Because gains in civil rights will benefit all members of the relevant group regardless of whether they participate, people have an incentive to 'free ride,' not donate money or time to the organization but still benefit without paying any of these costs. Moreover, many problems facing activist groups concerned about such issues as clean air or civil rights are relatively diffuse. Most people can get by day to day without 'cleaner' air or more access to civil rights."[17] This is also the predicament of marginal workers. Very few people worry about the protections they will need if they lose their job until the need for those protections arises. This makes workplace regulation harder to accomplish.

The labor movement was able to obtain a comprehensive set of protections in the National Labor Relations Act of 1935. But now the weakness of the NLRA has been a rallying cry for reform for some time. There have been a number of efforts to reform the law, but so far none of them have been successful. In fact, most would agree that the amendments to the law have gone against the cause of workers. The Taft-Hartley Act of 1947, for example, outlawed secondary boycotts, in which labor unions picket a business that is not their primary employer. Ellen Dannin has argued well that the NLRA can be reformed without statutory amendment through a litigation campaign similar to the NAACP's campaign to end segregation.[18] Dannin's prescriptions for reform are important and necessary, but there are limitations to reform of statutes.

Dannin correctly notes that the preamble to the NLRA contains important language that judges should use to interpret the rest of its provisions, including:

> The inequality of bargaining power between employees who do not possess full freedom of association or actual liberty of contract and employers who are organized in the corporate or other form of ownership association substantially affects and tends to aggravate recurrent business depressions by depressing wage rates and wage earners and by preventing the stabilization of wage rates in competitive industries.

Certainly the preamble to the NLRA should be used as an interpretive guide, but in no case thus far has its language really been taken to heart. The preamble does contain the important "freedom of association" language which may have been borrowed from the International Labor Organization's founding document, which included freedom of association as one of its founding principles. Here again is the problem with protective legislation for marginal workers. The preamble to the statute is rarely seen as binding authority on the courts, or even as an interpretive guide. And yet, the preamble of the NLRA, for one, provides a way of interpreting the statutes where close cases should be decided in favor of the workers' freedom of association. As several examples in this book will demonstrate, the courts have not always utilized these principles to their full potential.

While Dannin is correct that bad decisions under the NLRA should be rolled back, it is not clear that this will be sufficient. It is also necessary to change the minds of employers, in a way that statutes have not done. The change in attitudes about discrimination took place for a variety of reasons, but some would argue that the constitutional rulings began to change the minds of people. Some would argue that the NAACP's greatest accomplishment was to change the constitutional understanding of equal protection. Thus, something more than reforming statutory law is necessary—what is needed is a paradigm shift.

This book falls in line with the advocates of a human rights approach, much in the same way that critical race theorists and feminist theorists argued that rights are needed for the protection of marginalized women and people of color.[19] As discussed earlier, many of the marginal workers discussed herein are women and people of color. Similarly, I argue that for vulnerable workers, rights are necessary for a minimum baseline of protection and may also provide a basis for organizing to protect their interests. Indeed, sometimes protective labor legislation has been counterproductive for marginal workers.

### *The Captive Audience Meeting and How Labor Law Blessed It*

To illustrate how protective legislation can sometimes frustrate progressive workplace goals, let us look at the captive audience meeting. In his 2009 book, *Can They Do That? Retaking Our Fundamental Rights in the Workplace*, Lewis Maltby lists several ways in which employers may legally restrict the freedom of their employees, such as firing employees for their political views, forcing employees to donate to politicians, or firing someone for hanging with the wrong "crowd."[20] But Maltby does not address one of the most common, and legal, workplace restraints on freedom—the captive audience meeting. Although it can be convened for any number of reasons, the usual reason is to dissuade employees from joining a union. Typically, these meetings involve the human resources officer or another company official, but sometimes include paid outside "consultants" who use psychological tactics akin to enhanced interrogations. When I was in practice, I heard of one employer who dressed up in a Darth Vader costume and used loud music and flashing lights to symbolize the union's "evil empire."

Captive audience meetings are not prohibited by any law, and indeed some argue that they are actually protected by the very law that protects union organizing. The source of this "right" is Section 8(c) of the NLRA, which provides:

> The expressing of any views, argument, or opinion or the dissemination thereof, whether in written, printed, graphic or visual form shall not constitute or be evidence of an unfair labor practice under any of the provisions of this Act, *if such expression contains no threat of reprisal or force or promise of benefit.* [21]

As many have pointed out, the text of the provision does not give employers a "free speech" right.[22] It is an exclusionary rule, meaning that noncoercive speech, that which does not carry "a threat of reprisal or force or promise of benefit," cannot be evidence of an unfair labor practice.

But parsing statutory language is not something that many people relish. I can attest that even the law students I teach sometimes see reading statutes akin to reading stereo instructions. They would rather just plug in the law and hear it play! Unfortunately, much of the law is about parsing statutory language. But judges also gloss over much of this language and write opinions using shorthand and labels. So Section 8(c) of the Act is often referred to as the employer's "free speech" provision, supposedly conferring on the employer "the right to communicate the costs and benefits of unionization." But that is not what the statute was ever intended to do. It was not about the employer's "rights" but rather about NLRB procedure. Indeed, as a matter of state common law the employer may have the right to do many things, but the NLRA was not meant to enlarge the employer's rights—it was supposed to protect the rights of employees. In her book *Taking Back the Workers' Law*, Dannin explains this perversion of the statute in more detail.

Thus, in the 75 years since its inception, the NLRA has been used more effectively by employers than employees, who were the originally intended beneficiaries. This effect is not limited to the NLRA. Take, for example, the use of Title VII by white men claiming "reverse discrimination." *Ricci v. City of New Haven*, the high-profile 2009 U.S. Supreme Court case that was a feature of the Justice Sonia Sotomayor confirmation hearings, is a perfect example of a recent Title VII case that will have a chilling effect on the people that the statute was intended to benefit, namely racial and gender minorities who suffer a disparate racial or gender impact because of an employer practice.

There remain several efforts to try to fill the gaps through state legislative initiatives that, however well crafted, will also not be sufficient. One example is the Worker Freedom Act in Oregon. This is a law passed to give workers the freedom to opt out of captive audience meetings where the employer tries to convince employees to vote against a union. The Oregon statute appears necessary in the face of the federal labor act which allows employers to speak their minds on unionization, as interpreted by the courts. This will go to whether or not the legislation is preempted by federal labor law, which the courts have generally found to be necessary in the interest of the uniformity of the "federal common law."

Yet uniformity can be a double-edged sword. Sometimes federal legislation can be interpreted in a way to preclude more progressive changes in the law passed by state and local governments. Even for those statutes that do not have provisions that explicitly preempt state legislation, courts can read into the statute implied preemption, using several interpretive tools. This is what happened when the NLRA was amended by the Taft-Hartley Act in 1947. The Act for the first time gave federal courts the jurisdiction to hear cases arising under collective bargaining agreements, and the courts later found that this jurisdiction created a federal common law. This was accomplished in order to make federal labor policy uniform throughout the 50 states.

The results of this uniformity have been mixed. On the one hand, federal preemption has meant that many of the breach of contract or tort claims that might be asserted against unions are subsumed as federal labor law claims. On the other hand, when states have tried to limit employer use of state funds to hold captive audience meetings, the courts have ultimately struck such legislation down as being preempted by federal labor law.[23] In *Chamber of Commerce v. Brown*, employers challenged the California law which prohibited companies that receive state funds from using them to "promote or deter" union organizing. The Chamber of Commerce challenged a California law on several grounds, including that the law was preempted by the NLRA and that it violated the company's First Amendment right to speak to its employees. A majority of the U.S. Supreme Court agreed. The *Brown* case is one of many examples in which preemption stunted the development of state law innovations that might have prevented some captive audience meetings from occurring.

There are questions, of course, about which strategy will be most effective. Although there are no easy answers to that question, it is possible to critically examine whether the current strategy of statutory amendment has been effective. The evidence in this book shows a very mixed picture of success. The success is most spotty when it comes to the most marginalized workers in our economy. Here, I am talking about undocumented workers, noncitizens, people of color, and women. The book further shows that these effects also touch non-minorities—public-sector workers, white male union members, and well-to-do immigrants. And yet, there are other marginalized workers which I will not address directly in this book, such as domestic workers, agricultural workers, and trafficked workers. This book deals only with those who are covered employees.

## Rights-Crits

The question I ask here is why we should not pursue a constitutional and human rights strategy to protect workers. Here, the warnings of critical theorists should be remembered. Critical theorists cautioned against the overreliance on rights in the service of progressive causes. Mark Tushnet, mentioned above, argued in "An Essay on Rights" that rights can stunt the growth of social movements. Peter Gabel, also part of the Critical Legal Studies movement, argued that rights were ultimately disempowering.[24] Despite the force of these arguments, it is apparent that in the last 30 years the world has continued to trade in the language of rights. With the fall of communism, and the rise of global constitutionalism, rights talk has become inescapable, though it is more often deployed in service of typically conservative causes.

Critical race theorists such as Angela Harris recognized the tension between what critical legal theorists were saying about rights and what critical race and feminist theorists were trying to do:

CLS writers had argued "that rights were malleable and manipulative, that in practice they served to isolate and marginalize rather than empower and connect people, and that progressive people should emphasize needs, informality, and connectedness rather than rights." Patricia Williams, Richard Delgado, and Mari Matsuda, however, all rejected this yearning to go beyond rights to more direct forms of human connection, arguing that, for communities of color, "rights talk" was an indispensable tool.[25]

In keeping with these critical traditions, I will argue that rights are necessary to advance the cause of worker protection in today's society.

The question for the labor movement now is not *whether* to embrace rights, but which rights to embrace. We can look at statutory rights as partially successful. Take, for example, the broad definition of employee—this has allowed undocumented workers to have some protection for union organizing. The *Hoffman* decision discussed in chapter 1 shows that this protection is incomplete.

## Social Movements and Human Rights

In the chapters that follow, I will discuss in more detail a number of other cases in which the Supreme Court has interpreted protective labor statutes to further marginalize vulnerable and low-wage workers. Of course, there have been salutary benefits to many statutes, and statutes like the Fair Labor Standards Act of 1938 and the Occupational Safety and Health Act of 1970 have been important minimum protections for workers. These statutes were the product of social movements without powerful political constituencies, but which accomplished change through grassroots organizing.

Today, I argue that sweeping reforms are less likely because of the weakness of the U.S. labor movement and the changing aspirations and tactics of social movements. Thus, I argue that a new way of approaching workers' rights is necessary—one that views workers' rights as fundamental human rights. There are a number of ways that this can be accomplished, and many of them are already in play. These include international human rights and constitutional strategies. Some of these are already in practice. The International Labor Rights Fund, for example, is a nongovernmental organization (NGO) that has brought a number of human rights lawsuits for labor violations in other countries. As I will discuss in chapter 6, this approach could be used within the borders of the United States for immigrant workers as well. A focus on new strategies for labor rights raises long-standing debates about whether rights dialogue is best to further the interests of marginalized people.

The question for social movements that wish to further workers' rights is what kind of rights will be most effective at changing attitudes. Certainly there are questions about whether or not human rights dialogues will be effective in changing attitudes about workers' rights. Recent violations of human rights in the War on Terror, and the incomplete justice that the perpetrators of torture have faced, suggest that human rights may not be the key to better protection of workers. The labor movement has generally thought of domestic politics as the key to better working conditions. But that strategy has only proven partially successful. So the question of which rights are most effective remains.

The civil rights movements have dealt with these debates for some time. The National Association for the Advancement of Colored People (NAACP) Legal Defense Fund (LDF) adopted a multi-pronged strategy to end segregation in a variety of public facilities. The LDF, with Charles Hamilton Houston and other greats at the helm, attacked segregated employment in *Steele v. Louisville & Nashville Railroad* case.[26] The *Steele* case implied a duty of fair representation in the Railway Labor Act, which meant that unions could not openly discriminate against their members.

Despite the strategy of *Steele* to use a collective bargaining statute to achieve greater justice in the workplace, most of the LDF's plan to remake society focused on the promise of the Equal Protection Clause in the Fourteenth Amendment of the U.S. Constitution. The result obtained in *Brown v. Board of Education* changed the landscape of public education but also reached much private discrimination, through per curiam opinions that desegregated swimming pools and other public facilities.

Whether or not *Brown* was the catalyst for much of what came after has been the subject of some debate. In the book *The Hollow Hope: Can the Law Produce Social Change?* Gerald Rosenberg argues that race relations improved and desegregation occurred in spite of *Brown*, not because of *Brown*. He traces most of the change in public opinion to legislative change rather than the Brown ruling, which indisputably incurred a vigorous backlash and was seen by some as being antidemocratic. Others question whether Rosenberg has understated the importance of Brown. Richard Delgado, for example, questions whether Rosenberg's approach would hurt the cause of civil rights.[27]

Yet these debates are not unique to the cause of workers' rights. Recently, gay marriage advocates have faced this question. Is the right to gay and lesbian marriage a constitutional right, or something that should be legislated in each state? The answer remains elusive, but there are good strategic reasons to favor one route over the other. Moreover, history shows that sometimes it is unpredictable when the opportunity for change will present itself.

But this debate is relatively recent among scholars of workplace law. In 2009, the journal *New Labor Forum* published a colloquy between Lance Compa and Jay Youngdahl, on the question of whether labor rights are human rights. Compa argued that labor rights are human rights, largely because of the international human rights infrastructure that supports the assertion of labor rights as human rights. On the other hand, Youngdahl argued that human rights divert the focus of the labor movement away from solidarity and collective action. Compa was the principal author of a Human Rights Watch report called *Unfair Advantage: Workers' Freedom of Association.* He edited the 2009 edition of the Labor and Employment Relations Association research volume with fellow Cornell professor James Gross, who edited the collection *Workers' Rights as Human Rights,* published in 2003.[28]

As I have made clear, I fall in line with those who think that labor rights are human rights. But there is more to the debate than just the theoretical view of what is best for the promotion of workers' rights. There is also the question of how best to achieve workers' rights. In Youngdahl's vision, law and rights are secondary to the building of collective power. Others have argued that if the law were just changed or tweaked at the edges, workers would be better protected and thus better able to exercise collective power, as Youngdahl would argue. This book is about a paradigm shift in how workers should be protected, but also about whether court or legislative strategies should be favored.

An element of the strategy is to bring more claims in court, whether they are constitutional, or based on international law. Some of those claims and difficulties will be discussed in later chapters. Labor movement strategies, such as boycotts, picket lines, and strikes, have not had the effect needed to produce lasting change for workers. While the National Labor Relations Act (NLRA) of 1935 first protected the right to strike, unions have used the strike more sparingly. Similarly, consumer boycotts have been used less in recent years in favor of the corporate campaigns. Still, not all of these corporate campaigns have been successful. Thus, much energy is put into changing the law.

Even when a focus on greater rights can be agreed upon, questions about the best way to act on those rights will abound. Should advocates focus on legislation or constitutional advocacy? Rebecca Zietlow has written forcefully about the role of Congress in protecting rights.[29] Civil rights legislation, Zietlow argues, better advanced the rights of minorities than the constitutional mandates of *Brown.* While Zietlow is undoubtedly

right that federal legislation played a pivotal role in improving race relations in the United States, it is unclear that the same can be said of the
statutes passed to protect workers' rights. Congress enacted minimum
labor standards legislation in the 1930s, but it seems that these rights are
still contested after all these years. Media scholars have observed several
themes in the coverage of labor disputes in recent years. These include:
(1) the impression that the dispute is a senseless conflict that would be
resolved if the workers were not intransigent; (2) offers made by the company are emphasized, while concessions extracted in return are minimized, making the union seem ungrateful, greedy, and stubborn; (3) the
inconvenience caused by the strike on the general public is seen as being
the fault of the striking workers, and is viewed as equivalent to the struggles of the workers.[30]

The venom reserved for immigrant workers is also readily visible in
contemporary society. Day laborers with a constitutional right to assem-
ble on street corners are targeted for harassment. Cities such as Escon-
dido, California and Hazelton, Pennsylvania passed ordinances that
restricted the rights of immigrants. In the 1990s, changes in federal law
made it harder for even legal immigrants to collect any government benefits. Thus, when the question of workers' rights for immigrants comes
up, many people rail against the immigrants themselves, rather than rec-
ognizing why the rights of all workers should be protected.

Women and people of color also lag on a number of different economic indicators. First, unemployment rates are significantly higher for
African Americans than for other racial groups.[31] Latinos and Latinas are
concentrated in lower paying jobs, causing scholars to label certain job
categories as "brown collar."[32] As the recent Lily Ledbetter case shows, the
pay gap where the average woman earns 78 cents on every dollar that the
average man makes has not been fully addressed by 35 years of litigation
under the Equal Pay Act.[33]

### Flaws in the Political Process:
### Striker Replacement Legislation

Are workers a discrete and insular minority? There are a variety of
answers to this question. Political scientists can and do spend much time
researching and developing models about the political power of groups.
Often the perceptions of union power are out of wack with the reality of

what can be accomplished. This book tells the stories of many Supreme Court cases interpreting labor law that could have been legislatively reversed, but were not. Even construction unions, which have generally been powerful enough to get large public works projects, have been unable to enact changes in labor law to make it easier for them to organize. After the Supreme Court decided the *Denver Building Trades Council* case, it became more difficult for unions to picket construction sites. So the lesson is that even though construction unions have some political power to get certain discrete work projects through, it is much easier to get pork than protection. It is hard to put a value on protection that members may not use.

Political scientists have long discussed the imperfections of the legislative process. Workers are diffuse with competing interests and constituencies. Labor unions traditionally served to marshal these interests, as part of coalitions, in order to pass civil rights and minimum wage legislation. Now that unions do not represent as large a share of the economy as they did in the past, it is much more difficult to pass legislation.

Critical realism, as I discuss it here, is an orientation that takes a skeptical view of the law's ability to accomplish change. At the same time, critical realism seeks to be realistic about the chances for reform. Particularly in this polarized political environment, it is unlikely that major legislative reform packages will pass. Thus, to effect change, proponents of workers' rights must look to other methods besides the legislative process. These methods will include court litigation, filings in international fora, and the linkage of trade standards with labor standards. While this work will not immediately bear fruit, it is needed to change the dialogue about the centrality of several minimum workers' rights principles.

When courts decide cases against a worker plaintiff, judges commonly respond that it is up to the legislative branches to correct any perceived unfairness or fix any ambiguities in the law. In addition, when denying recourse to workers, judges often comment that the worker has other statutory options. These statements, usually in "dicta" not essential to the court's ruling, contain underlying assumptions about the ability of vulnerable workers to change the law through the legislative process.

The labor legislation of the early twentieth century was the confluence of large-scale protests by workers, the Great Depression, and a political coalition that embraced change in the master-servant relationship that had dominated the market for centuries. For various reasons, the conditions that provided fertile ground for reform in the 1930s and 1940s no longer exist today. Direct action and large-scale protest on behalf of workers' rights had faded with what some call the maturity and others would call the passivity, of the labor movement's tactics. The financial collapse of 2008, as bad as it was, did not lead to the widespread deprivation of the Great Depression. The stalling of the Employee Free Choice Act, labor's top legislative priority after the election of President Obama, shows the political weakness of labor even when the political stars are in alignment.

The workforce is also more diverse today, not just with the lifting of exclusionary bars to employment but also the diversity of working situations. An increasing number of workers are working part-time. Workers are in remote locations from one another, which makes political action more difficult. Historians have also pointed to the fading salience of class in the workforce today.[34] All of these factors make it more difficult to join together to pass legislation. This conundrum calls out for a new approach to workers' rights that includes new theories of litigation and forums for advocacy.

Often, the courts use the broad language in statutes to effectively repeal the worker protections of the law. This has often happened in the courts' construction of labor law. For example, the original labor act has a provision that recognized the right to strike should remain protected: "Nothing in this Act should be construed so as to interfere with or impede or diminish in any way the right to strike." As with the Norris La Guardia Act, the plain language of the original NLRA spoke to very broad protection for workers. In 1938, however, the Supreme Court interpreted the NLRA to allow employers to permanently replace workers who are on strike. In *Mackay Radio v. NLRB*, the Court entertained the argument that allowing the employer to stay in business with replacement workers who could keep their jobs indefinitely (permanently) would impede the right to strike. The Court considered and rejected a number of reasons why allowing permanent replacement workers was not a violation of the right to strike. Thus, was born the question: "Would you rather be permanently replaced or fired?" To workers on strike, the legal label does not make much difference.

Although the statute makes striking a protected activity for which the worker cannot be fired, the *Mackay* case simply changed the meaning of "being fired" to "being permanently replaced." While the permanently replaced workers are eligible to be rehired if a job opened with the employer, this is little consolation if you are a wage earner who cannot afford to wait until your old job becomes available. Indeed, the part of *Mackay* that gave the employer the right to permanently replace was "dicta," a passage not essential to the outcome of the case:

> Although section 13(f) of the act . . . provides, "Nothing in this Act (chapter) shall be construed so as to interfere with or impede or diminish in any way the right to strike," it does not follow that an employer, guilty of no act denounced by the statute, has lost the right to protect and continue his business by supplying places left vacant by strikers. And he is not bound to discharge those hired to fill the places of strikers, upon the election of the latter to resume their employment, in order to create places for them. The assurance by respondent to those who accepted employment during the strike if they so desired their places might be permanent was not an unfair labor practice, nor was it such to reinstate only so many of the strikers as there were vacant places to be filled. [35]

The *Mackay* decision represents an example of employers winning the clash of rights. Even though the right to hire permanent replacements is not in the statute, and the right to strike *is* in the statute, the employer's ability to hire permanent replacements trumps the right strike.

The *Mackay* decision has been criticized for years as hollowing out the right to strike.[36] Ellen Dannin criticized the *Mackay* decision in her book *Taking Back the Workers' Law*, where she asks "Who will strike if it means losing a job?"[37] Julius Getman and Thomas Kohler discuss *Mackay* in the context of freedom: "The policies favoring free collective bargaining and freedom of choice are overlapping and mutually dependent. . . . That employees who participate in the process in the manner contemplated by the law do so at the risk of their jobs seems contradictory and indifferent to the interests of the employers whose rights are supposedly at the heart of our labor relations laws."[38] This is the kind of argument that labor has failed to make to support the overturning of *Mackay*.

These are the stories of workers stuck between the gaps of statutes that are supposed to protect them. Most of the time, the cases are presented as a clash of competing policies or rights. Those seeking to lionize employers' prerogatives have deployed the language of rights quite effectively. The next challenge for labor advocates is to make the debate about rights for workers rather than for employers.

Despite the judicial codification of the *Mackay* rule, there have been attempts to overturn it. In 1990, a bill requiring employers to wait 60 days before hiring replacements was passed by the House of Representatives but filibustered in the Senate.[39] In any case, the bill likely would have been vetoed by President George H. W. Bush. When President Bill Clinton took office after 12 years of Republican control of the Executive Branch, overturning Mackay was one of his top legislative priorities.[40] Even though Congress was controlled by Democrats for the first two years of President Clinton's administration, efforts to pass striker replacement legislation floundered from 1992 to 1994, because of the inability to obtain a filibuster proof majority.[41] After the Republican takeover of Congress in 1994, hopes for a legislative reversal of *Mackay* became even dimmer. The strategy thus shifted to affecting areas of the economy which the president could control by executive order, basically any employment under federal contracts. The order made it the policy of the executive branch to not contract with employers "which permanently replace lawfully striking employees."[42] The order was immediately challenged by employers in court, and the D.C. Circuit held that the order was preempted by the comprehensive federal scheme regulating labor relations.[43] In other words, the president had acted beyond his power, or *ultra vires*, to regulate labor relations in this way.

Although the application of the preemption doctrine in the court case discussed above could certainly be challenged, the administration chose not to test the D.C. Circuit's decision in the Supreme Court, fearing an even more devastating rebuke to the Executive Branch's contracting power. This again shows the failure of the legislative system in protecting workers' rights, even when the goals are rather limited and the political stars would seem to be in alignment.

The fact that *Mackay* has been the law on striker replacements since 1938 can be read in several different ways. First, one could conclude that the popular will is to maintain striker replacement law as it is. Or, even if the popular will is there, organized labor does not have the political muscle to change the law. Finally, since legislative change has not been possible, the courts are content to leave the *Mackay* rule as it is. Of these three explanations, the first proposition is the most dubious; the other two are simply a restatement of what history shows. It is more likely that the public has not taken time to consider the issue, and even if they did, it requires so much explanation that it is unlikely to get anywhere legislatively. Perhaps for this reason, the labor movement has all but given up on striker replacement as a legislative priority.

To those not familiar with labor law, the striker replacement issue is not about worker freedom to engage in collective bargaining, to which the right to strike is inherently linked, but instead is a game of inside baseball which is part of a pendulum swing between Republicans and Democrats that happens each election cycle. In 1991, the AFL-CIO filed a complaint with the ILO Freedom of Association alleging that the *Mackay* decision violated international principles on freedom of association. The Committee on Freedom of Association found that the striker replacement rule diminished the rights of employees to engage in strikes.

### *Interpretive Devices that Deny Workers' Rights*

Statutes are prone to certain rhetorical devices that operate to deny workers' rights. When construing statutes, courts often utilize cannons of construction. These default rules of interpretation are not mandated, but are part of common law judging. In theory, these rules are meant to fill gaps in statutes that are left by legislators. Examples of statutory canons include: (1) statutes should be construed to avoid constitutional questions (canon of avoidance); or (2) when a statute may be interpreted to abridge long held rights of individuals or states, or make a large policy change, courts will not interpret the statutes to make the change unless the legislature clearly stated it (clear statement rule).[44] The use of canons by judges has long been the subject of controversy, but they appear to be here to stay.[45]

In recent Supreme Court decisions on the workplace, canons of construction have more often than not been against the interest of workers. In *Circuit City Stores, Inc. v. Adams*, the Court had to decide whether a provision of the Federal Arbitration Act, passed by Congress in 1925, which excluded from coverage all "contracts of employment of seamen, railroad workers, or any class workers engaged in interstate commerce," meant that all employees were excluded. When Sinclair Adams attempted to sue his former employer Circuit City in California state court for sexual orientation discrimination, his case was dismissed by the court because he signed an employment application with a mandatory arbitration clause. Using the textual canon *ejusdem generis*, or, where general words follow an enumeration of specific items, general words are read as applying to other items akin to those specifically enumerated, the court denied the claim. In the *Circuit City* case, the Supreme Court thus used a canon of construction to deny the judicial forum to Adams.

Instead of using canons to deny workers' rights, I propose that courts and legislatures should keep in mind the human rights canon that exists which favors worker protection. This body of law, including many human rights instruments that the United States has signed, requires courts to construe cases which involve competing statutory claims to resolve conflicts in favor of worker protection. In the last chapter of this book, I will go into further detail about the reasons why such a canon is justified, such as the constitutional and international principles on freedom of association, nondiscrimination, and prohibitions on involuntary servitude that underlie American statutory law. The worker protection canon should also be used by legislatures in crafting legislation, but it is less likely that such principles will guide legislators, who are often guided by political expediency.

### *The Perils of Uniform Worker Protection*

Some have argued for one federal law of discharge. Lewis Maltby, president of the Workrights Institute, has argued for a federal law requiring just cause. Jeffrey Hirsch, has also argued for one federal law of discharge and a strong preemptive effect for any inconsistent state law. The reasons for Maltby's and Hirsch's arguments are clear. It would be better to wait for a friendly Congress and president to change the at-will rule. The conditions after the election of Barack Obama and the 58 seats held by the Democratic Party, and after the extreme financial distress that the country faced in 2008 leading to record unemployment, would seem to be ideal for greater protection at the workplace. Still, it is unlikely that just cause provisions will ever be part of federal law. Even at the state level, Montana is the only state that has enacted just cause protection for all employees, and so it is unlikely that there will be such legislation.

Perhaps it is because at-will employment is such a contested concept, which makes it unsuitable for a federal law in any event. The International Labor Organization does not express opinions about whether a country has an at-will or just cause arrangement. This could be a result of the difficulty in determining a standard for just cause, or a willingness to allow national diversity. In either case, it shows that just cause may not be a minimum national standard that is a human right. Nevertheless, a principle that defines discrimination not by categories of people but by arbitrary factors could also be considered discriminatory.

## Employee Status Eludes Many

The misclassification of workers has become a serious problem in the economy. A broader definition of *worker* is necessary. Recent studies estimate that up to 30 percent of companies misclassify workers.[46] Independent contractors cannot organize or get the protection of labor laws. This is one of the ways in which legal fault lines leave many without protection. To deal with this, doubts should be resolved in favor of worker status, rather than employee status. Scholars have identified many workers who are beyond the reach and grasp of the employment laws, such as domestic workers and prison laborers.[47]

Many of the cases that I handled as a lawyer involved workers who were classified as independent contractors when they were really employees. By misclassifying workers, the employers had no obligations in the workers' compensation system, and no threat of discrimination litigation. It is estimated that 25 percent of workers in some industries are misclassified, either through employer mistake or deliberate evasion.[48] While worker misclassification is a problem that marginalizes workers, the thrust of my argument is that workers who are supposed to be covered by the law are not.

## Freedom Is Not a Bad Word

Freedom is not a dirty word. There is a certain cynicism about freedom among liberals, but conservatives have used it effectively. Workers' rights advocates should as well. Of course, even those on similar sides of the political spectrum will have different versions of what freedom means. Civil liberties progressives see freedom as the bundle of rights needed to exercise fulfillment. Socioeconomic progressives believe that true freedoms can only be obtained through decent wages, minimum housing guarantees, and health care.[49] Many of these ideas were reinforced by Roosevelt's Second Bill of Rights, which included the right to a "useful and remunerative job, the right to a decent home, the right to a good education, among other positive rights."[50] Then, there are those who believe in identity freedom and its importance for full participation. This is important as we talk about freedom from arbitrary discrimination. Of course, freedom and rights will always be double-edged swords. The reason that freedom is necessary is that it is seen above the usual politics.

## Conclusion: A Question of Values

The question of whether to continue to seek statutory amendments of labor law presupposes that improvements to the law will encourage employer compliance. The many amendments that were passed in the twentieth century do not show adequate progress in the lives of workers. This is after almost 80 years of the statutory protection to organize unions. One may look at this decline and conclude that it is simply the preference of individuals not to join unions. If unions were desired by the public, the argument goes, we would see a greater number of unionized workplaces. However, the true cause of below-union density in the United States may be attributed to employer resistance. A way to combat employer resistance to all of the labor movement today is to strengthen the National Labor Relations Act. This will not have the effect of improving unionization rates without a fundamental change in values by employers.

If workers' rights are seen as human rights, then employers may be more likely to follow the law. The alternative, trying to encourage employer compliance through increased statutory and executive regulation, has not been successful enough to protect marginalized workers, as the following chapters will show.

# 3

## New Voices at Work

### *Unionized Workers at the Intersection of*
### *Race and Gender*

In 1968, the United States was in upheaval. On April 4, 1968, Dr. Martin Luther King, Jr. was assassinated. The casualties of the Vietnam War were at their peak in 1968, as were the protests against the war.[1] Although the U.S. Congress passed major pieces of civil rights legislation in 1964 and 1965, race relations were still turbulent and rioting broke out following the murder of Dr. King. The labor movement also continued to deal with a legacy of racial division.

In this crucible of events, a storm was brewing in the workforce of Emporium Capwell Department Store in San Francisco that would define the place of minority workers in unionized workplaces. In fall 1968, African Americans working for the retailer joined with a community organization called Western Addition Community Organization (W.A.C.O.) to protest the lack of promotions for black workers. Their union, Department Store Employees Union Local 1100, had been attempting to redress the discrimination through the grievance arbitration system of the union contract. The employees rejected the contractual solution as being too individualized, seeking instead a class-wide remedy. Although there were a number of other employees involved, two employees, James Hollins and Thomas Hawkins, were fired on November 9, 1968 for participating in picketing and leafleting of their workplace that was not authorized by the union.[2]

The discharges of Hollins and Hawkins resulted in a 1975 U.S. Supreme Court case that defined the intersection of antidiscrimination law and workplace solidarity. The Supreme Court in *Emporium Capwell v. Western Addition Community Organization* attempted to reconcile two statutes that could have protected these black workers—the National Labor Relations Act of 1935 (NLRA) and Title VII of the Civil Rights Act of 1964 (Title VII). The fired workers presented a vision of workplace justice at the intersection of race and class, and a question of how to reconcile the protection of concerted activity in the NLRA with the racial protection goals of Title VII. This chapter tells the story of *Emporium* as a way to illustrate the problem of marginal workers.

In an opinion authored by the liberal Justice Thurgood Marshall, the Supreme Court held that the workers' actions were not protected by the NLRA, because their actions were not authorized by the union, the exclusive bargaining representative. Another look at the facts of the case tells a more complicated story. Hollins and Hawkins had gone to their union but were dissatisfied with the union's plan to deal with the promotion grievances serially rather than as a group grievance. They then requested a meeting with the company president, but were never granted one. Their actions were characterized by the Court as "separate bargaining," which is not allowed by the NLRA when a union is the certified exclusive representative at the workplace. Nevertheless, their actions were not protected by the NLRA.

Hollins and Hawkins were caught in the margins of two different workplace statutes with two different goals—in between union solidarity and civil rights. The legal system could have provided a resolution that more effectively balanced these goals. Instead, the law failed to recognize their claims, ostensibly in favor of collective bargaining. Several scholars have argued that the case failed to serve the goals of either statute.[3] In this chapter, I look at the *Emporium* case and what it means for the enforcement of labor law and antidiscrimination law over the last century. The legacy of the split between race and class solidarity in many ways can be traced back to the statutory fault lines between labor law and antidiscrimination law.

*Emporium Capwell* exemplifies the bifurcation of race and labor claims that has left all workers with less protection, and it also provides an opportunity to consider strategies to unify these two policies better than the courts have already done. This chapter also looks at this split in the broader historical context of the law governing labor-management relations, which in its first century has seen few amendments that have benefited workers. In that context, we will also see the struggle of working women, both within and outside of unions, to negotiate statutory rights in the maze of union and employer organizational contexts. These phenomena are also illustrated through the political and social histories of some major Supreme Court labor and employment cases. Through this history, it becomes clear that the liberal paradigm of legislation, executive implementation, court review, and statutory revision does not work in the field of workplace law as well as it should.

### The Historical Trajectory of Statutory Collective Bargaining

Before 1935, there was no comprehensive statutory scheme protecting the right to organize and bargain collectively. The Clayton Act, a major piece of antitrust legislation in 1914, contained a section that exempted businesses engaged in labor negotiations from price-fixing liability, but it did not contain substantive protections. Labor unions were seen as criminal conspiracies and were enjoined even for peaceful picketing. The labor injunction became a reviled symbol of state intervention in the collective bargaining process. Only a few members of the judiciary questioned the dominant ideology and argued that their labor activity should not be treated the same as economic torts. One of these was U.S. Supreme Court Justice Oliver Wendell Holmes, when he was on the Massachusetts Superior Court, who wrote a theory of fair play in dissent of that opinion in the seminal case of *Veghelan v. Gunter*: "If it be true that workingmen may combine with a view, among other things, to getting as much as they can for their labor, just as capital may combine with a view to getting the greatest possible return, it must be true that when combined they have the same liberty that combined capital has to support their interest by argument, persuasion, and the bestowal or refusal of those advantages which they otherwise lawfully control." Holmes represented a vision of freedom in the face of the labor injunction that was based on fairness, but also a sense that workers are engaged in a "free struggle for life."

In response to labor's pleas for relief, Congress passed the Norris-La Guardia Act (NLGA) of 1932, a federal statute that stripped federal courts' jurisdiction to enjoin in peaceful labor disputes. The NLGA was intended to allow unions the leeway to engage in concerted activities to further their own interests. Over the years, however, court interpretations have weakened the effectiveness of the statute. Even though the Act was plain in its command—"The federal courts shall have no jurisdiction in labor disputes"—the Supreme Court in 1970 found an exception to that prohibition in cases involving a collective bargaining agreement. In *Boys Mar-*

*kets v. Local 770*, the U.S. Supreme Court held that despite the language of the statute, the federal courts can enjoin labor disputes if the disputes violate a collective bargaining agreement. Karl Klare has criticized this decision as "vigorously enforcing the waiver of employees' fundamental right to strike."[4]

In his opinion for the Court, Justice William Brennan (no enemy of labor) pointed to the change that the Taft-Hartley Act of 1947 made to the power that workers had been granted by the National Labor Relations Act of 1935.[5] Because the Taft-Hartley Act gave federal courts the power to hear claims arising from collective bargaining agreements, federal courts also had the power to remedy breaches of those agreements through injunctions. Anti-labor provisions of Taft-Hartley such as these have become a stigmata on the hands of the labor movement. Yet there is virtually no chance that they will ever be repealed.

## The Retrenchment of the Taft-Hartley Act of 1947

In the postwar period, there was much concern over the alleged infiltration of unions by communists and communist sympathizers. The infamous McCarthy hearings set the climate of repression against labor and other progressive groups. In this period in which civil liberties were reduced, workers' rights were also targeted. Taft-Hartley was pushed in Congress ostensibly to cut back the power of labor, and so secondary boycotts were outlawed. Secondary boycotts were powerful tools in the early years of the NLRA, used by unions to picket a business that is not their direct employer in order to pressure their primary employer. The secondary boycott prohibitions were accompanied by the possibility of injunctions and large damage awards, because the union could be responsible for all damages resulting from their picketing.

Congress also amended Section 13 of the NLRA and its original text which protected the right to strike from judicial interference, by adding a final clause about the "limitations and qualifications" of the right to strike. After the 1947 amendment, the text of NLRA Section 13 read: "Nothing in this act, except as specifically provided herein, shall be construed so as to impair or diminish or impede in any way the right to strike, subject to the limitations and qualifications on that right."

Later cases have taken the last clause of section 13 to incorporate the concerns that Congress had about sit-down strikes and other "violent" activities. As the Court said in *Insurance Agents v. NLRB*,[6] the legislative history of that language reflected congressional intent to codify the holdings of Supreme Court cases like *Fansteel Metallurgical Company* and *Southern Steamship*. The problem was that the statute never specified what those limitations were, and so the courts, and the NLRB, are free to graft new exceptions and limitations on the right to strike. Even though the court in *Insurance Agents* acknowledged that the "limitations and qualifications" language does not extinguish the rule, the statutory amendment has also served to codify the *Mackay* rule, which allowed employees to fill the places of striking workers with permanent employees.

The right to strike, and possible international implications of the right of association, were present in the *Emporium* case. The workers in *Emporium* could be considered to be exercising their freedom to strike and engage in concerted activities. The first problem with that version is that they were not on strike, since they continued working while engaging in their criticisms of the company's hiring practices. Second, they were not seeking to go on strike but simply to change the company's employment practices, which they found to be racially discriminatory. But the employer's actions and the union's alleged inaction, as well as the legal context in which the employees sought their remedies, must be viewed in the historical context in which they arise.

## Labor Legislation and Its Effects on Marginalized People

Unions have long struggled with a history of exclusion and discrimination in their ranks. The effect that statutes had in changing attitudes and practices is the subject of debate. Like employers, they operated largely without statutory constraint on their racial and gender preferences until a union reform bill called the Landrum-Griffin Act was passed in 1959 and the Civil Rights Act was passed in 1964.[7] Paul Frymer's work is critically important for an understanding of the ways in which union integration occurred across several branches of government, especially in the courts.[8] By necessity, however, Frymer pays less attention to the role that informal activity within unions served to change the practices of unions. Indeed, this has been the tactic of women and people of color for years. In the face of discrimination in the construction trades, women and people of color fought for inclusion. When faced with discrimination in other sectors of the economy, identity groups and caucuses have worked within the given statutory system to engage in collective bargaining.

The employees in *Emporium* were kind of a black caucus within their union, and the 1960s were a time of extraordinary ferment of caucuses. Black caucuses arose from the tension between integrationist and separationist strains of African American thought and manifested the "Black Power" movement of the 1960s. Much of the black unionist activity paralleled urban centers where large steel and auto factories stood. From the start, there was tension between a vision of black power that wanted to separate from established unions and one that sought to create a black workers' organization which was auxiliary to the union. The first manifestation of the latter strategy was the Trade Union Leadership Conference (TULC), organized by black unionists with UAW Local 600 at Ford's River Rouge plant.[9]

At the Dodge plant in Detroit, the Dodge Revolutionary Union Movement, or "DRUM," burst on the scene in the late 1960s.[10] DRUM sought to improve the conditions of black workers in unions. While it was often cited as the prototypical black separatist organization, DRUM was not only concerned with the conditions of black workers in unions. Many whites joined DRUM's wildcat strikes, since workers of any color could feel dissatisfied enough with the union to join in a work stoppage that was not authorized by the union. DRUM also advocated on behalf of Arab immigrants in the plant, and reached out to them by distributing leaflets written in Arabic.[11] Revolutionary Union Movement caucuses soon spread to other UAW-represented plants, such as FRUM at Ford's River Rouge Plant, ELRUM at Chrysler's Eldon Avenue plant, and CADRUM at Cadillac. Militant activity was not limited to the UAW in Detroit. In the late 1960s, the United Black Brothers of the UAW organized wildcat strikes.

Black workers were not the only ones forming caucuses. Latinos and Latinas, Asians, gays, and lesbians were some of the groups that advocated with their union in the system of exclusive representation. These groups started as strains of protest within majoritarian unions. They later became part of the mainstream labor movement in organizations such as the Labor Council on Latin American Advancement (LCLAA), the Asian Pacific American Labor Alliance (APALA), and Pride at Work (PAW). I will discuss these in greater detail later in this chapter.

## Legal Interventions against Discrimination: Statutory and Judicial

*Emporium Capwell* is part of a larger historical continuum of collective bargaining protected by statute. New voices increasingly became part of the workplace after Title VII made race and gender discrimination by employers and unions illegal in 1964. For 20 years before the Civil Rights Act, animus toward women, people of color, and any union member was redressable under a theory of fair representation in *Steele v. Louisville Nashville Railroad*.[12] In *Steele*, the Court interpreted the Railway Labor Act to impose on the union as exclusive representative a duty of fair representation toward its members. While this theory marked a major shift when announced by the U.S. Supreme Court in 1944, it has remained a high standard to meet for those who feel they have been discriminated against. When Title VII first brought explicit statutory protection for race and gender minorities, it was seen as a primary way in which unions would be desegregated.

Certainly, the threat of litigation would remain a powerful incentive for unions to practice racial justice, but as Paul Frymer has written about race in the labor movement, there were a variety of institutional factors at play besides the statutory command that desegregated unions.[13] These factors include the labor movement's need for new members, the need for unions to avoid large damage awards, and administrative action.

As Frymer details in his book, *Black and Blue*, a choice was made to avoid questions of racial justice in the NLRA, thus bifurcating race and class. The NLRA also took most labor disputes out of the courts and put them in an administrative agency, the National Labor Relations Board. This was sought by the labor movement in an effort to get away from the bias that unions had experienced in the courts. Unions were seen as criminal conspiracies and their peaceful activities were readily enjoined. This was one of the main reasons why the NLRB was created.

The choice to bureaucratize labor relations had some positive impact, such as the streamlining of certain kinds of disputes like refusal to bargain cases. But there were costs as well. The public nature of labor disputes was lost in administrative proceedings that are often hidden in plain sight from public view. Fewer people pay attention to administrative proceedings than court processes. Further, the point of the NLRB was not to punish or embarrass employers, but to make employees whole through back pay and reinstatement.

The model followed by Title VII may have also had an impact on the acceptability of antidiscrimination norms throughout the land. But the structure of the NLRB was intended to largely quell the radical elements of the labor movement that were in the streets in the 1930s. The basic route that most charges take is as follows: When an employer, for example, fires a worker for union organizing, the worker, or any involved union, can file an administrative charge in the National Labor Relations Board. An agent or attorney will then investigate the circumstances of the charge, interview witnesses, and decide whether there is cause to file a complaint against the employer. The NLRB will then file a complaint against the employer and allow for an answer and a hearing on the charges. The employer can then appeal an unfavorable ruling all the way up to the U.S. Supreme Court. This can delay the resolution of cases for years, as was the case in *Emporium Capwell*, which lasted six years before its final resolution in the Supreme Court.

The administrative system has certain advantages, however. For one, it allows employees to bring claims representing themselves or with the assistance of lay professionals. Second, there is a possibility that the NLRB process would be faster than a lawsuit in the federal court system, though speed of processing has not been borne out by actual experience. Indeed, Hollins and Hawkins decided that their claim against the Emporium department store, which included allegations of race discrimination, would be better adjudicated in the NLRB. Finally, one of the explicit purposes of the statute is to try to resolve disputes in the administrative forum. Here, too, in my experience, mediation was rarely accomplished in the NLRB, since positions had usually become too contentious by the time the NLRB was serious about a case.

If there ever were administrative benefits of the NLRB in its more than 70-year history, they are not evident today. Former NLRB Chair William Gould lamented the difficulty of keeping case processing times in his book *Labored Relations: Law, Politics and the NLRB—A Memoir*. In his book, Gould complained about the inability to get the resources needed to reduce case processing times, because of the political football that funding the agency had become. While a charge may be processed in a reasonable period of time at the regional levels, the appeal process has been elongated recently because of political wrangling. In 2008, the five-member body charged with hearing appeals from the regional offices was down to two members. The delays at the appellate level only raise the incentives for employers to string out the process and deny workers' rights.

## *The Exclusive Representative Rule in Emporium Capwell*

A central feature of U.S. labor law since 1935 is the exclusive representative rule. The rule is at the center of the NLRB procedure for organizing a union. In brief, if the union wants to petition the NLRB for a secret ballot election, the NLRA requires the union to obtain authorization to bargain on their behalf from at least 30 percent of the eligible employees at the worksite. Once the NLRB determines the threshold showing of interest is valid, and deals with questions relating to the appropriateness of the unit, an election date will be set. If the union wins the support of the majority of the employees in the appropriate bargaining unit, the NLRB will certify the union as the "exclusive bargaining agent."[14] A union may bypass the NLRB procedure provided that the employer voluntarily recognizes the union upon a showing that it represents a majority of workers in the proposed bargaining unit. Because of the cumbersome nature of the NLRB processes, unions are more frequently mounting pressure campaigns to win voluntary recognition from the employer.[15]

*Emporium Capwell* was unusual, but it proceeded, as do most unfair labor practice charges. The employees argued that they were engaging in protected concerted activities, for their own mutual benefit and protection. Hollins and Hawkins had distributed leaflets that had the following warning message to potential shoppers with the incendiary message:

> *\* \* BEWARE \* \* \* \* BEWARE \* \* \* \* BEWARE \* \**
> *EMPORIUM SHOPPERS*
> *"Boycott Is On" "Boycott Is On" "Boycott Is On"*
> For years at The Emporium black, brown, yellow and red people have worked at the lowest jobs, at the lowest levels. Time and time again, we have seen intelligent, hard working brothers and sisters denied promotions and respect.
>
> The Emporium is a 20th Century colonial plantation. The brothers and sisters are being treated the same way as our brothers are being treated in the slave mines of Africa.
>
> Whenever the racist pig at The Emporium injures or harms a black sister or brother, they injure and insult all black people. THE EMPORIUM MUST PAY FOR THESE INSULTS. Therefore, we encourage all of our people to take their money out of this racist store, until black people have full employment and are promoted justly through out The Emporium.
>
> We welcome the support of our brothers and sisters from the churches, unions, sororities, fraternities, social clubs, Afro-American Institute, Black Panther Party, W.A.C.O. and the Poor Peoples Institute.

The appeal to racial solidarity in the community, including to the Black Panther Party, must have alarmed the employer and perhaps also the union leadership. The employees appealed to the public and also held a press conference. Hollins and Hawkins engaged in peaceful picketing of the store with two other employees. They also requested a meeting with the company president. When they continued their activities, they received a warning letter from the company president, which included the following statement: "There are ample legal remedies to correct any discrimination you claim may exist. Therefore, we view your activities as a deliberate and unjustified attempt to injure your employer."

The letter further warned the employees that if they continued their activities they would be fired. And indeed that is what happened. The employees were fired and filed the NLRB charge with the assistance of the Western Addition Community Organization. The NLRB pursued the claim and it went through the administrative appeal system to the five-member board in Washington, which refused to enforce the charge. Then, the D.C. Circuit of Appeals stepped in and said the charge should have been pursued. Emporium Capwell then appealed to the U.S. Supreme Court.

The Supreme Court in *Emporium* construed Section 7 of the NLRA to not apply to "separate bargaining," even though the workers never actually engaged in direct bargaining with the employer. The Court also gave short shrift to the proviso to Section 7, which allows for employees to "present grievances, and have those grievances adjusted, even in the absence of their bargaining representatives." Justice Marshall wrote in a footnote that the proviso was not intended to protect workers who wished to adjust their grievances, but instead to protect workers from unfair labor practice liability for dealing directly with employees. This narrow reading has not been revisited by the court since the Emporium decision was rendered in 1975.

Justice Marshall's opinion represented the accommodation of black power within class politics. This vision is completely defensible as a means for the advancement of African Americans in society, and was part of the philosophy of early civil rights leaders like A. Philip Randolph, who was leader of the sleeping car porters, and Bayard Rustin.[16] The question is whether the decision presented a false dichotomy, and could have been decided in a different way that accommodated both statutes.

This third way may be represented in the test presented by the dissenting opinion in the District of Columbia Circuit Court of Appeals, which was endorsed by the lone dissenter in the Supreme Court case, Justice William O. Douglas. Justice Douglas feared that black employees might be "prisoners of the union."[17] He argued that the standard should be the one applied in the D.C. Circuit: The employees should be freed from the union's exclusive representation unless the "union had been prosecuting their complaints to the fullest extent possible, by the most expedient and efficacious means."[18] Although Judge Charles Edward Wyzanski's opinion was styled as a "dissent," he concurred that the employees should have an unfair labor practice charge, and thus no further remand was necessary. The opinion also contained the following paragraph, which was startling both in its all-capitals typeface, and its candor:

TO LEAVE NON-WHITES AT THE MERCY OF WHITES IN THE PRESENTATION OF NON-WHITE CLAIMS WHICH ARE ADMITTEDLY ADVERSE TO THE WHITES WOULD BE A MOCKERY OF DEMOCRACY. SUPPRESSION, INTENTIONAL OR OTHERWISE, OF THE PRESENTATION OF NON-WHITE CLAIMS CANNOT BE TOLERATED IN OUR SOCIETY EVEN IF, WHICH IS PROBABLY AT LEAST THE SHORT-TERM CONSEQUENCE, THE RESULT IS THAT INDUSTRIAL PEACE IS TEMPORARILY ADVERSELY AFFECTED. IN PRESENTING NON-WHITE ISSUES NON-WHITES CANNOT, AGAINST THEIR WILL, BE RELEGATED TO WHITE SPOKESMEN, MIMICKING BLACK MEN. THE DAY OF THE MINSTREL SHOW IS OVER.[19]

Judge Wyzanski's opinion was notable for how far it went from the standard typically applied in duty of fair representation (DFR) cases, where the union's handling of a grievance must be shown to be "arbitrary, capricious and discriminatory." This standard has proven to be very difficult for most DFR plaintiffs to win. In the *Emporium* case, the union certainly engaged in a number of actions on behalf of the black employees. For example, the union brought in representatives from the California Fair Employment Practices Commission (FEPC) to investigate the employee's claims. Union representatives also tried to find a solution through the grievance process. The union representative Walter Johnson pointed to the no strike clause in the collective bargaining contract that also prevented Hollins' and Hawkins' actions.

The exclusive representative rule played a central part in the *Emporium* case, but the Court rebuffed an attempt to use the proviso to protect their activities. The proviso to Section 9 is a clarification to the exclusive representative rule, intending to ensure that even if there is a union in place:

> Provided, that any individual employee or a group of employees shall have the right at any time to present grievances to their employer and have such grievances adjusted, without the intervention of the bargaining representative, as long as the adjustment is not inconsistent with the terms of a collective-bargaining contract or agreement then in effect.

The only proviso to the proviso is that the bargaining representative must be given the opportunity to be present when the employees try to adjust their grievances. The employees in the *Emporium* case did argue that their actions were protected by the proviso, but the Court rejected the arguments in a footnote: "The intendment of the proviso is to permit employees to present grievances and to authorize the employer to entertain them without opening itself to liability for dealing directly with employees in derogation of the duty to bargain only with the exclusive bargaining representative, a violation of Section 8(a)(5)."[20] Thus, according to the Court, the proviso was intended to be a shield for the employer, not a sword for the employees. Thus, the employees could not argue that their actions were protected by the proviso, even if under the facts all they were doing was trying to adjust their grievance without the intervention of their bargaining representative.

When cast as a battle between the objectives of Title VII and the NLRA, *Emporium Capwell* is a classic example of the workforce being divided along class and race lines. More than that, *Emporium Capwell* seems to have had a profound impact on what it means to bargain with the employer. The proviso to Section 9(a) is rarely invoked since its evisceration in *Emporium Capwell*. As Justice Marshall stated in his opinion in *Emporium Capwell*, the proviso does not confer a "right" on employees to present grievances to the employer "by making it an unfair labor practice for an employer to refuse to entertain such a presentation, nor can it be read to authorize a resort to economic coercion."[21]

Thus, the language of the statute failed to provide protection to workers. One might ask why there have not been attempts to try again to make the language of the proviso an outlet for minorities in an otherwise majoritarian system. The Court's construction of the statute is the end of the road, and yet many commentators, including me, continue to wonder whether Congress really meant to foreclose what the employees did.

Viewing *Emporium Capwell* in a human rights frame might yield different results. First, if we take "freedom of association" as a starting point, we might conclude that freedom of association sanctions what Hollins and Hawkins did even in the unionized context. ILO Conventions require freedom to associate and bargain collectively, but Convention 87 for one requires that freedom of association be exercised in keeping with the rules of the particular organization. While a union may have rules, and can authorize strikes, it does not follow that all activity that the union does not approve should automatically lose protection.

The actions of Hollins and Hawkins may be considered "disloyal" to the union, but in later cases it became clear that even greater breaches would be sanctioned by the Supreme Court under the rubric of the freedom to associate, or its corollary, the freedom not to associate. In *Pattern Makers League of North America v. NLRB*, the U.S. Supreme Court in 1985 held that a union could not discipline its members for resigning immediately before a planned strike, even though the members, including those who resigned, ratified by majority vote. In the opinion, the Court first intimated that a quasi-First Amendment right not to associate existed, that the union's rule restricting resignations might be unconstitutional, since the union was the exclusive bargaining representative with the imprimatur of the federal government. Because the Court generally tries to avoid constitutional questions, it simply found that the union's rules on resignations were not "reasonable" in the language of the statute and struck the rule down. Now, any union member who wants to resign from the union before a strike can do so without penalty, even at the cost of the union solidarity that the labor law was supposed to protect.

Later cases further deepened the idea that the freedom not to associate was part of the statute as well, and that it had constitutional dimensions because of the union's government-sanctioned role as exclusive representative. The "Beck" objector was a result of *Communications Workers v. Beck*, a 1988 Supreme Court case, which gave further rights to those who disagree with the course of their union or its politics.

I discuss these cases not because I endorse the results in them; indeed, I think that they go against the intent of the statute in many ways, but because they show how much the Court has gone toward a quasi-constitutional right not to associate. Whatever the merits of these decisions as a matter of constitutional law, they do not speak to the activities in which the employees in *Emporium Capwell* were engaged. The employee's actions were more akin to the ILO Convention 87 and 98, which more clearly go to the point of collective bargaining and should have been protected. This, coupled with the international protections against discrimination, build a powerful case that what Hollins and Hawkins were doing should have been protected.

In the realm of the statutory construction of Section 7, there is one last hurdle to overcome: the exception to concerted activity protection for actions that are disloyal to the employer. Most concerted activities are those where two or more employees strike, walk out, picket, or otherwise protest in order to improve their working conditions. Although not mentioned at all in the statute, the court has long held that some concerted activity, if it is "unlawful, violent or in breach of contract,"[22] is unprotected even if it meets all the other criteria for concerted activity. "Disloyalty" is also not protected. The Supreme Court has defined as "disloyal" in a way that is "unnecessary to carry on the workers' legitimate activities."[23] These cases generally involve employees who publicly attack their employer in a way unconnected to their collective bargaining demands. One case involved a television station whose technicians were trying to pressure their employer in negotiations. The technicians distributed anonymous fliers attacking the station and its treatment of the town (Charlotte, North Carolina) as "second class." The U.S. Supreme Court refused to reinstate the workers when they were fired.[24]

In *Emporium*, the question of whether Hollins, Hawkins, or any of the employees involved were disloyal and thus not deserving of concerted activity protection was not decided by the Supreme Court. The question had been debated when the *Emporium* case was litigated in the NLRB and the court of appeals preceding the Supreme Court. The D.C. Circuit Court of Appeals proposed a standard that would ask whether the union is most effectively remedying the alleged discrimination, and if not, whether the employees' actions were "so disloyal to their employer as to deprive them of Section 7 protections."[25] The Supreme Court determined that it need not decide whether the employees were disloyal, because their actions violated the exclusivity principle. Nonetheless, the fact that the *Emporium* employees were connecting their grievances in the public mind with the employer's allegedly racist practices was at least more directly related to their complaints than other disloyalty cases.

In the end, second guessing litigation strategy can be endlessly hypothetical and indeterminate. What we know is that the Court adopted an impoverished vision of worker rights, even though the liberal icon Justice Thurgood Marshall wrote the opinion in *Emporium Capwell.* Justice Marshall was also an integrationist, who probably felt that the employees in *Emporium* were taking a wrongheaded approach to resolving their disputes with the employer and the union. In the end, Justice Marshall rightly concluded that the employees were better off with a union than they were on their own. In the process, however, it appears that both labor law and civil rights law were weakened. In the view of the sole dissenter from the Court's opinion, Justice William O. Douglas, that is exactly what happened. Justice Douglas fully agreed with the standard of the D.C. Circuit, and that the employees' actions were protected concerted activity. He answered Justice Marshall's call for closing ranks with the union as follows: "The law should facilitate involvement of unions in the quest for racial equality in employment, but it should not make the individual a prisoner of the union."[26]

## *The Relevance of Emporium and Concerted Activity Today*

What are the lessons of *Emporium Capwell* for the labor movement? Even when a union successfully negotiates a contract, employees retain many of the statutory protections of the NLRA. Section 7 of the Act provides that "employees shall have the right to engage in concerted activities for their own mutual aid and protection." The section also talks about the right of individuals to engage in collective bargaining. Because the exclusive representative rule is in a separate part of the statute (Section 9), there is reason to believe that in the absence of an exclusive representative, the employees can still bargain on behalf of their members only, instead of for all of the employees in the bargaining unit. Under this theory, the employees could not be disciplined for attempting to bargain, as long as there was not a union as an exclusive representative.

This members-only bargaining theory has been persuasively espoused by Charles J. Morris in his 2008 book *The Blue Eagle at Work.*[27] Morris's book begins with a story that illustrates his theory. Seventeen Thai immigrants unrepresented by the union were fired from their jobs after they went to their boss and sought changes in working conditions. The employer, an electronics company, refused to negotiate. Although they were only speaking for about 20 percent of the total workforce, Morris uses the rest of the book to explain why the employer should have been required to listen to them because Section 7 of the Act provides, "Employees shall have the right to . . . bargain collectively through representatives of their own choosing."

When a union has been voted in by the majority of the employees at the workplace, it is the exclusive representative and the minority of employees cannot bargain directly with the employer. Thus, Morris's theory has been put into place by the Steelworkers Union in some recent campaigns. One of those campaigns, at a Dick's Sporting Goods in Pittsburgh, resulted in an NLRB charge when nonunion employees were refused bargaining. The NLRB refused to prosecute the charge on the theory that the Act had not been violated. Morris used the NLRB's refusal to file a motion to compel the NLRB to engage in rulemaking (which I signed along with 46 other labor law professors).[28]

Whether or not the NLRB eventually accepts his theory, Morris squarely places his statutory argument in the context of international human rights law. Despite accepting the correctness of *Emporium Capwell* when there is a union present, Morris argues that the freedom of association and the right to collective bargaining in ILO Conventions and the Universal Declaration of Human Rights allows for members-only bargaining. Morris is not alone in utilizing international human rights instruments to challenge the prevailing wisdom about the interpretation of the NLRA, as a number of scholars and advocates have argued for a human rights approach to labor law problems. (These scholars include Lance Compa, James Gross, Marley Weiss, James Atleson, and Maria Ontiveros.)

While I applaud the efforts at statutory reform by using a human rights frame, it is important to note the glacial pace of statutory reform, and how difficult it can be to get courts to revise long held interpretations of statutory language. With all this difficulty, one might conclude that it would be easier to start over with brand new language. Given workers' lack of political power discussed above, it is unlikely that a new statute authorizing members-only minority bargaining will be passed soon. Thus, in the meantime a human rights frame is one of the last resorts for a members-only bargaining theory, and a way to enhance the power of workers like those in *Emporium* to have a voice with both their employer and their unions. Human rights are not the sole solution of the divisions between race and class that have hamstrung the labor movement throughout the twentieth century, but as we will see in later chapters, it may be the start of a change in attitudes that all people have toward the linkage of labor rights, civil rights, and human rights—as not only a legal imperative, but also a step toward greater freedom for all of us.

There has been much debate about the effectiveness of antidiscrimination law. Critical theorists such as Alan Freeman began critiquing antidiscrimination law in the late 1970s and 1980s, with articles such as "Legitimizing Racial Discrimination through Antidiscrimination Law: A Critical Review of Supreme Court Doctrine."[29] In this article, Freeman criticized the way that the courts manipulated Title VII and left plaintiffs without protection.

Kimberlé Crenshaw also pioneered the ways in which antidiscrimination law failed to protect people caught in the borderlands of protection. In her seminal work "Demarginalizing the Intersection of Race and Class," Crenshaw pointed out the ways in which the bifurcation of race and sex in Title VII's categories make it more difficult for women of color to assert their claims. This is because the prototypical plaintiff in a race discrimination case is a black man, and the prototypical gender plaintiff is a white woman.

In *The Civil Rights Society*, Kristin Bumiller describes how Title VII constricts plaintiffs and disempowers movements. Bumiller argues that the civil rights movement did not fulfill its promises, and serves to reinforce the victimization of women and racial minorities. Many have argued that the NLRA deradicalized the labor movement as well. Statutes sometimes can make movements complacent. One example is the Equal Rights Amendment (ERA), which the feminist movement tried hard to enact in the late 1960s and early 1970s, after statutory improvements like the Equal Pay Act and Title VII. Yet, the statutes and favorable court decisions made it more difficult to argue how the ERA would change things. According to Gail Collins in her book *When Everything Changed: The Amazing Journey of American Women from 1960 to the Present*: "When the Equal Rights Amendment came under attack in the mid-1970s feminists needed to explain, in the most concrete terms possible, how it was going to make the system fairer. The problem was that there were not that many examples."[30] When the drafters of the ERA first proposed it in the nineteenth century, they did not foresee the statutes and court decisions that would increase women's equality, according to Collins.[31]

Although there is no way to know how things would have been different if the ERA had passed, the lack of explicit gender protection in the Constitution might have stunted the progress that the women's movement has made in the last 30 years. In the 1970s, feminists argued that the symbolic function of the ERA was as important as the substantive guarantees that had been won by state and federal statutes. Unfortunately, there were not enough state legislatures that agreed with that, and the ERA narrowly failed to obtain approval of two-thirds of the state legislatures.

The feminist movement's campaign to constitutionalize rights offers lessons for workers' rights advocates. While a constitutional amendment for workers' rights seems a fool's errand, litigation strategies and public advocacy can sometimes transcend the vicissitudes of politics. As I have discussed, the language of human rights can also provide a transcendent basis for labor rights. It is necessary to develop a new strategy to discuss workers' rights.

## How Emporium Capwell Might Have Come Out Differently

If *Emporium Capwell* is such a problematic decision, how should it have come out in keeping with fundamental labor principles? The question can be answered in a number of ways. First, the Court could have interpreted the statute to protect Hollins and Hawkins's activities. In one sense, they were simply asserting their right to engage in concerted activities under Section 7. Despite their requests for a meeting with the company president, their actions seemed a bit removed from "bargaining," which is not protected except through the union when it is the exclusive representative.

A more robust conception of Section 7 is certainly necessary. Throughout the *Emporium* litigation, arguments were made that the NLRB's construction of Section 7 was too restricted. After all, the argument goes, Section 7's capacious language should be construed broadly in favor of concerted activities, even when the union has not authorized a particular course of action. While unauthorized strikes are not protected, it is not clear that Hollins and Hawkins were on strike. So, one can quibble in various ways with the statutory conclusion reached by the Court. In the end, the Court decided that the construction of Section 7 was constrained by Section 9, even though there is no explicit mention of Section 7 in the statute.

Many of the labor scholars who have commented on the *Emporium* decision have viewed the principle of exclusive representation as the culprit in denying the employees' right to air their grievances. Marion Crain has written several important articles on the difficulty for women and people of color because of the exclusive representative rule.[32] In another foundational article, Elizabeth Iglesias discussed *Emporium Capwell* and its effect on the marginalization of women of color.

One way of remedying the court decision in *Emporium* would be to amend the labor law and clarify the ability of workers to protest discrimination directly with the employer even if the union did not authorize the protest. Or, the proviso to Section 9 could have been amended to make clear that employees had the right to request a meeting to adjust grievances.

There are various reasons why the NLRA will never be amended in response to *Emporium Capwell.* First, members of Congress have little interest in the NLRA, and particularly the rather unique factual circumstances in Emporium. Second, the labor movement is not interested in labor law reform that would present a challenge to the exclusive representative rule. Finally, the workers in *Emporium*, like the undocumented immigrant at the center of the *Hoffman* case, were not likely to be the symbols of a political movement to change the statute. There have been only a few times in recent history—*The Price Waterhouse* case leading to the Civil Rights Act of 1991 and Lily Ledbetter's case (discussed in chapter 6) leading to changes in pay equity claims—when the protagonist of a negative Supreme Court decision has been able to successfully symbolize the need for legislative change.

A better idea is to try to find another basis by which Hollins and Hawkins' action might be protected. This might come in the very notions that would protect unionization itself—freedom of association. While the international human rights instruments do not deal specifically with the issue of "separate bargaining," they place a high value on the elimination of discrimination. In the Fundamental Declaration of Rights at Work, the International Labor Organization prioritized the elimination of all discrimination on the basis of race or color, among other categories, "which has the effect of nullifying or impairing equality of opportunity or treatment in employment or occupation."[33] Thus, this command is on a par with the freedom of association and collective bargaining. Those conventions, such as convention 87, do accept that unions can proscribe reasonable rules with respect to membership.

Although there were arguments about whether the union had done enough to remediate the discrimination, the main focus of the *Emporium* case was whether the employees' actions were protected by the law. If their actions are seen as trying to seek "equality of opportunity or treatment in employment or occupation" in the way they found most efficacious, then one might view their actions as justified, as dissenting Judge Wyzanski in the D.C. Circuit argued in the passage quoted earlier.

Even apart from the primacy of discrimination law in analyzing the *Emporium* case, one can argue that they were simply exercising the human right of association and collective bargaining. While the limits of freedom of association can certainly be debated, concerted activity in an attempt to deal with racial discrimination is in keeping with the goals of collective bargaining. We will see that because the United States has signed on to the principles in Convention 111, the statute must be interpreted in keeping with the international principles.

In reconciling the NLRA and Title VII, the Supreme Court could have achieved the balance between the goals of freedom of association and antidiscrimination. Both principles could have been reconciled in favor of protecting association and the workers from discrimination. If the NLRA did not exist, the Court might have analyzed the case as one dealing solely with retaliation for raising complaints about discrimination. Indeed, the lawyers for W.A.C.O. argued in the alternative that the employees were fired for opposing discriminatory practices, in violation of Title VII. Indeed, the employees eventually did file a Title VII claim after the Supreme Court case ended, which was settled out of court.[34]

Two cases decided shortly before *Emporium Capwell* had more of an impact on the direction of future cases than *Emporium Capwell* itself. First, in *McDonnell Douglas v. Green*, the Court set forth the test to prove discrimination in a Title VII case, in a case which was also about a black activist who was fired. There, the plaintiff was Percy Green, a civil rights activist for more than 40 years, who also protested the lack of black skilled workers at the McDonnell Douglas plant.[35] In September 1964, Green organized a "stall-in" on the roads leading to the McDonnell Douglas plant to protest the hiring processes. Green was laid off from his job at McDonnell Douglas, for no apparent reason, before the enactment date of Title VII in July 1965. When Green applied for his old job on July 27, 1965, he was rejected.[36]

The Supreme Court in *McDonnell Douglas* set forth the test for disparate treatment discrimination, and the fact that the plaintiff could show discrimination through circumstantial evidence. This might have helped the workers in *Emporium Capwell*, since they did not have any direct evidence of discrimination. Still, in a case like *Emporium Capwell*, it does not seem easy to show racial discrimination. The employer can always come back with the argument that the employees, such as those in the *Emporium*, were fired for their disloyalty or some other offense. Incidentally, this would be a defense to the NLRA charge as well.

Another case which had an effect on the *Emporium Capwell* case was *Alexander v. Gardner Denver*, decided in 1974. In *Alexander*, the question was whether or not an employee's claim of discrimination could be brought in federal court after it was unsuccessfully prosecuted in a union grievance arbitration proceeding. The Supreme Court in *Alexander* held that the rights in Title VII were not waivable by a union, or a union contract. The Court has retreated somewhat on that absolute rule that the union *could not* waive the individual's right to go to court, but the *Alexander* case had the broader meaning that employees would be able to pursue discrimination claims despite any lack of success they had in the grievance arbitration process or the NLRB.

And this made sense, but it further cemented the bifurcation of racial discrimination and anti-union discrimination that the NLRB and the courts had cultivated in a number of cases, such as *Handy Andy*, where the NLRB ruled that it would not refuse to certify racially discriminatory unions. Frymer notes that this bifurcation would have large implications for the labor movement, even though it might have made sense from an administrative perspective.[37]

Because the employees in *Emporium* did not bring a Title VII claim, they were left to argue that denying them protection under the NLRA would undermine other statutory schemes like Title VII's opposition clause, which forbids employer retaliation for employees who oppose discrimination in the workplace. In his opinion for the Court, Justice Marshall dismissed the idea that the enforcement of one statute was so closely related to another that there could be any of those side effects.

## Labor Rights Are Civil Rights

The dichotomous legal treatment of labor rights and civil rights has led to the questioning of whether labor rights are really civil rights. To many workers, there is little difference. Zaragosa Vargas's study of Mexican American workers in the twentieth century shows that the plight of minority workers, particularly in the farmworkers' movement led by César Chávez, was about more than achieving collective bargaining or decent working conditions.[38] Vargas argues that labor rights were a way to obtain social citizenship when they were excluded from other aspects of full citizenship.

I have already discussed the new human rights frame that many labor advocates are using—but what is the place for civil rights dialogue? At the risk of seeming reductionist, the link between civil rights and human rights is strong. At a most basic level, civil rights are the rights of citizens, but there are many civic rights that do not adhere to formal citizens. The Constitution, for instance, requires equal protection for all persons within the jurisdiction of the United States. Other civic rights such as due process also apply to persons, and not just citizens. These rights include more than just citizens because they are seen as fundamental to a functioning democracy guided by the rule of law. We can see that labor rights are intimately linked to civil liberties, like the right of association and free speech in a number of different court cases and historical struggles. In a later chapter, I will show that labor rights are also closely linked to civil liberties, but the exact characterization is not as important as a change in perspective about labor rights as fundamental.

In all of this, the flaws of statutes on their own are on display. As discussed, women of color should be the most protected because of the various statutory categories which cover them. This book discusses the interplay of statutes which are supposed to protect, but which lead to even more marginalization.

There are large questions about the effect that Title VII had on discriminatory practices vis-à-vis *Brown v. Board of Education.* In her book *Enforcing Equality: Congress, the Constitution and Individual Rights,* Rebecca Zietlow argues that Congress, and not the courts, was instrumental in changing perceptions about race relations. Although this might be true of civil rights statutes, the impetus for this new movement should be the courts. The struggle of politically powerless minorities to win legislative victories is certainly inspiring. The Civil Rights Acts were part of a larger movement that included a variety of nonwhites and elites. Derrick Bell has written that the legal progress came for minorities mostly because of the need to improve the international image of the United States in its treatment of blacks. Bell called this Cold War opportunity an "interest convergence" between blacks and the U.S. government. Mary Dudziak also has documented the correctness of this theory.[39]

Opportunities for interest convergence are rare, and with the end of the Cold War, the United States has often been less concerned with its international reputation. Opportunities for coalition are also present. But these civil rights acts also contributed to the bifurcation of race and class. I am arguing that the labor movement should stop devoting so much of its resources to changing labor legislation and instead focus on changing the conversation—from domestic rights to global labor rights.

The current state of collective bargaining can make one wonder whether labor unions would be stronger if the NLRA had never been passed. There certainly is the possibility that without the NLRA the labor movement would have floundered under the weight of injunctions and employer repression, but there is also the chance that the workers' movement could be flourishing if workers were able to use the secondary pressure that was banned by the Taft-Hartley Act. Or, the heavily bureaucratized NLRB procedure would give way to more voluntary recognition agreements, or more minority bargaining. The statutory duty of fair representation would not exist, but a common law or tort version might have been developed that may have been more effective for plaintiffs.

## Identity Caucuses as Non-Statutory Routes to Reform

The traditional liberal reform pattern goes as follows: Congress passes a statute, the courts interpret it, and Congress returns with correcting amendments. This has occurred several times with the Civil Rights Acts. When the Supreme Court handed down several decisions in the 1980s that gutted the law, Congress returned with amendments to Title VII. Nearly 20 years after the Civil Rights Act of 1991, there is consensus that a new Act is needed, because of the Supreme Court's recent decisions on the meaning of reverse discrimination. There seems to be little will in Congress to change Title VII, however. If anything, in the current political climate, Congress is likely to leave the result in *Ricci* alone even if it does change other decisions that it might find objectionable. Why? Because the statute's broad language of antidiscrimination is perfectly malleable to suit purposes that were not intended.

Reversing the *Emporium Capwell* case was never a legislative priority for the labor movement, and it is not hard to see why the case is read as being solely about the union's position as exclusive representative. If we see the case as being about expanding the scope of allowed concerted activity to include protesting discrimination with upper management, or expanding the proviso to Section 9 to make it a right for the employees rather than simply a protection for the employers, the changes would have benefited all workers, not just black workers. The labor movement might be stronger today for it, but it also might have been weakened. This is another example of the ways in which organized labor might not always represent well the interests of all workers, because interests are so diffuse and diverse that it would be impossible to adequately represent them all in legislative activity.

Organized labor spent $84 million in 2008 to do political work, much of it focused on increasing legislative protections for nonunion workers.[40] While this has inured to the benefit of the vast majority who are not in unions, there have also been benefits for unionized workers who are at the bargaining table and can use legislative guarantees such as the Family Medical Leave Act, and health care minimums as starting points for negotiations.

Some have argued that labor's energies to obtain minimum statutory standards have been counterproductive to their fortunes. If nonunion workers can get all the protections of the unionized sector without joining a union, what is the purpose of paying dues? In its "Voice at Work" strategy, the labor movement has spent a great deal of time and energy to argue that union membership is about more than better work protections and higher wages (though that is part of their pitch too), and that it is about having a greater say with your employer. While this is true, this kind of abstract notion may not be the persuasion that many people need to risk retaliation for supporting a union.

A focus on legislation and political action has also divided the labor movement and led to the well-publicized split between the AFL-CIO and the group of unions that broke away and formed Change to Win (CTW). CTW is comprised of growing unions like the Service Employees International Union and UNITEHERE. CTW felt that the leaders of the AFL-CIO were not devoting enough resources to organizing new workers, and instead were focusing too much of their energies on electoral politics. There was enough truth to this charge that it caused a good deal of soul searching in non-CTW unions and an increase in the organizing budget. On the other hand, the labor movement spent an unprecedented amount in the 2008 elections. The amount of legislative fruit the effort bears remains to be seen, but everyone acknowledges the need to improve organizing.

In order to facilitate organizing, labor law reform has been a major legislative initiative in the last decade. The Employee Free Choice Act

(EFCA) has been a rallying point for labor leaders for several years, and calls for its passage have intensified since the election of President Obama in 2008. But the EFCA may not be the panacea that many people hope it will be. First, the chances of it passing as originally proposed seem very small. Second, although the labor movement is united on the principles of the Employee Free Choice Act, the divisions in the labor movement and within CTW mean that labor's front is much less united than it needs to be in the face of the opposition of organized business interests.

Even if something like the EFCA can pass, former NLRB Chairman William Gould has recently written that the EFCA may not be the answer for labor law reform. He argues that some of the voluntary recognition initiatives tried by other countries may be preferable to a system where the employer is required to recognize the union, and that the NLRB adjudicatory processes can provide relief with reform.[41] This may be the case. A greater concern may be that this and other legislative initiatives will not be enough to change attitudes about workers, particularly immigrant workers, in this country. The EFCA will not reverse the *Hoffman Plastics* decision discussed in chapter 1, mostly because there is no political will to restore employee rights to undocumented immigrants. Yet, protecting the right to organize, as well as to petition the employer for grievances, regardless of immigrant or minority status, would benefit the entire labor movement. The political capital is not available to pull off that kind of legislation.

New strategies are needed to ensure that immigrants and people of color are fully integrated in the labor movement. One of these strategies is the formation of identity caucuses within the labor movement. From 2000 to 2002, I interviewed some of the members and leaders of these caucuses, and found that they have little interest in changing the NLRA to have a greater say in their unions. One union leader I spoke to when doing my masters' in Madison, Wisconsin, illustrates the feeling: "Union members have many legal options if they are dissatisfied with their union, including decertification. But the best option is to change the leadership."

Even members of the most radical caucuses like the Rank and File Exchange of the UAW, though several decades after the heyday of insurgent activity, believed that legislative change was not the key to greater power in the union: "Lack of numbers in our union caucus has inhibited us from having influence with the union leadership and subsequently the negotiation process with the local and international. So the only way to change that is to have more numbers in our rank and file caucuses so they will take us more seriously."

This shows that legislative change may not be what workers want. Indeed, most studies show that most workers would rather deal with workplace problems internally rather than by filing a lawsuit. In fact, most workers would prefer to have some kind of representation at the workplace.[42] In their study, *What Workers Want*, Richard Freeman and Joel Rogers found that most workers, and especially African American workers, had a strong preference for some form of employee representation in the workplace.[43] Other studies have found that immigrants, particularly those from Latin America, have a stronger preference for unions than do native-born workers.[44]

Women have also shown greater interest in unions than their male counterparts, and have also formed caucuses. The Coalition of Labor Union Women was formed in the 1960s out of the Women's Bureau of the Department of Labor.[45] The first national CLUW Convention was held in Chicago in 1974. According to historian Nancy Gabin, CLUW was committed to "advancing the position of women both as workers and as unionists."[46] CLUW feminists placed most of the blame for inequality on employers.[47] Although they educated women in general terms about Title VII, CLUW leaders did not promote the filing of charges against unions.[48]

While CLUW was trying to assimilate into the greater labor movement, some union women did not welcome the advent of the civil rights era. In the 1960s, many of the waitresses in the Hotel and Restaurant Employees Union wanted to maintain separate locals, but this was complicated by the Civil Rights Act of 1964, which made consciously gender-segregated locals illegal.[49] In the end, however, these groups formed internal caucuses within the exclusive representation system. Rather than trying to change the exclusive representative rule, then, workers found ways to work within it.

But not all marginal workers found solidarity in caucuses. The feature film *North Country* tells the story of a young female ironworker in Northern Minnesota, who suffers sexual harassment at the hands of her supervisors and fellow union members. The film is based on the true story of Lois Jensen, who brought one of the first sexual harassment lawsuits to achieve class action status.[50] The movie and the book tell how Jensen attempts to get support from her union, but instead gets pushback from her male co-workers, many of whom are leaders in the union. When Jensen's lawsuit was viable, the employer and the union began to take notice of her.[51]

The different routes that workers take are understandable. Some will wish to work out problems informally, while others choose to use the statutory levers in court. The point here is that legislative change has not turned out to be the panacea for which liberal reforms hoped. Many of the advances for women's rights came at the hands of judges interpreting the law. But at the same time, many women have chosen to work through the union. The problem is when a particular route or strategy has long-term effects for all workers. Much of this cannot be easily controlled, since workers who are fired, like Hollins and Hawkins, were simply trying to get their jobs back and were trying to use any means necessary to get them back.[52] The problem with much statutory litigation is that, for reasons stated earlier, it freezes a particular court's interpretation of the law in place for a longer period of time than many constitutional cases. Courts are generally less willing to revisit questions of statutory interpretation than they are of constitutional rulings. This is based on the principle, true as it is in theory, that the legislature can always change the law if it sees fit. In practice, state and federal legislatures cannot possibly address all the court rulings that are made, even if the will to do so existed.

## The Implications of the Bifurcation of Collective Bargaining and Statutory Rights

Much has changed in the labor movement since *Emporium Capwell* was decided in 1975. Black workers have become an integral part of the labor movement in both the private and public sectors. They have also achieved leadership positions in many large unions.

But the zeal for arbitration has meant the courts have tried to put more and more statutory claims into arbitration. In 1990, the Supreme Court decided *Gilmer v. Johnson/Interstate Lane*, in which it construed the Federal Arbitration Act to allow for the arbitration of individual statutory claims. The straitjacket of arbitration, however, is not only felt by plaintiffs bringing race claims. In a 2009 decision, the U.S. Supreme Court endorsed the waiver of statutory claims through a collective bargaining agreement. In *14 Penn Plaza v. Pyett*, the Court held that age discrimination claims could be waived by a union in a collective bargaining agreement as long as the waiver was "clear and unmistakable" in the text of the agreement.

The decision makes it possible that unions might negotiate away the right of their members to bring statutory discrimination claims. While most unions would prefer not to do that, it may be tempting for some unions to trade wages and benefits for statutory rights. This is where identity caucuses might be necessary to safeguard the rights of minorities. Thus, the court has weakened one of the predicates for the *Emporium Capwell* decision that workers would always have the right to file statutory claims even if their union did not support them.

Once again, people of color and women who are in unions are forced to choose between union solidarity and statutory rights. Ideally, such claims would be worked out through the union grievance system, but that is not always going to work for women and people of color. The statutory claim system functions as a safety net for claims that the union is unable or unwilling to take. Unfortunately, as will be seen in the next chapter, the safety net for statutory discrimination claims is torn and frayed.

## 4

# Across the Borders

*How Antidiscrimination Law*

*Fails Noncitizens and Other*

*Marginal Workers*

When discussing "immigrants" thus far, I have largely been talking about the "undocumented." The story of Cecilia Espinoza shows that marginalization is not limited to those without authorization to work in the United States. Espinoza applied for a job in 1969 at Farah Manufacturing Company, a clothing company with locations in San Antonio and other parts of Texas. Although not a U.S. citizen, Espinoza was a Mexican authorized to work in the United States. Her application to work at Farah was rejected because of her lack of U.S. citizenship. Farah followed the citizenship policy apparently for "security reasons," according to the court of appeals opinion.[1] The policy had the effect of eliminating from consideration for hire a large segment of the Hispanic population in Texas, even though 96 percent of Farah's employees at the San Antonio plant were of Mexican ancestry.[2] Espinoza challenged Farah's policy under Title VII of the Civil Rights Act of 1964, alleging that the policy constituted discrimination based on her Mexican national origin.[3]

Espinoza's case made it to the U.S. Supreme Court in 1973. In an opinion authored by Justice Thurgood Marshall, the Court held that the category "national origin" did not include being a noncitizen, even though there is a high correlation between national origin minorities and lack of citizenship. Although many noncitizens are national origin minorities, not all national origin minorities are noncitizens. Thus, according to Justice Marshall, Congress must not have intended in Title VII to make discrimination against noncitizens illegal. The fact that a "citizens only" policy may have a disparate impact on minorities was not pertinent to the Court because the plaintiffs had not made that kind of claim under the statute.

In the previous chapter, I discussed the ways that antidiscrimination and labor law failed to work well for workers who were clearly within the ambit of the statute. In this chapter, we will once again look at people of color who should be protected by the law and yet are not because of gaps in the law. The legal safety net is torn and frayed.

Although the circumstances of the *Espinoza* case suggest that there was not animus against Mexicans, the citizens-only policy raised the potential for discrimination against a large number of people of color. Despite being a plausible reading of Title VII, the *Espinoza* decision left the victims of citizenship discrimination without a remedy under Title VII. The decision raises larger questions about the effectiveness of Title VII as it relates to noncitizens, many of whom are people of color. Yet much discrimination today, both overt and subtle, takes place not simply because of race, but "foreignness." But Congress has yet to amend Title VII to include citizenship discrimination, and it probably never will, because noncitizens cannot vote and thus there is little incentive for legislators to amend Title VII to include citizenship discrimination.

This chapter takes the *Espinoza* decision as a starting point to discuss how Title VII fails to remedy many forms of discrimination for marginal workers—those who are at the intersection of various legal categories. Intersectional discrimination occurs when there are multiple possible grounds of discrimination for a single plaintiff. Claims on behalf of black women, for example, implicate the race and sex categories of Title VII. Critical race theorists such as Kimberlé Crenshaw, Elizabeth Iglesias, and Paulette Caldwell have written about the ways in which antidiscrimination law has failed to adequately cover women of color as it does black men or white women. These plaintiffs, as Crenshaw has accurately put it, are "marginalized at the intersection of race and sex."[4] The paradigm put in place by the Civil Rights Act, then, was lacking from the start in some notable ways in protecting those whom it was supposed to protect.[5]

In an era of increasing diversity and social antipathy toward immigrants, Title VII's blind spot to citizenship discrimination and immigrants is likely to become more of an issue. Noncitizens can also be the victims of race, national origin, and gender discrimination, and the difficulties that they face in courts have been shown in several cases.[6] In one case, the court noted some of the indignities that plaintiffs have to suffer in order to put their claim into a legal box: "[A]lthough the verbal harassment [suffered by plaintiff] was replete with references to green cards, boats, wetbacks and border patrols suggesting national origin discrimination, this is racial discrimination within the meaning of section 1981."[7] This is the essence of what is known as "intersectionality" theory—the theory that the law fails to address discrimination on the basis of multiple and alternative grounds of discrimination.[8]

Even when there is relief for a marginalized worker, the failure of the courts to recognize exactly what kind of discrimination is occurring means that hybrid discrimination, mostly against Latinos, Latinas, and other intersectionals, goes unaddressed. As I have argued, the 1964 discrimination law paradigm does not take into account the ways in which discrimination actually occurs in the modern workplace. This chapter describes the way that multiple bodies of antidiscrimination law operate to marginalize noncitizens by failing to recognize the complexity of the contemporary workforce. The chapter uses citizenship discrimination as an example in which the nearly 50-year-old paradigm of antidiscrimination law fails to address new kinds of discrimination. In this chapter, I suggest a more flexible antidiscrimination principle in the Work Law area that will encompass more types of discrimination, which eschews a categorical approach in favor of a ban on discrimination on characteristics that have nothing to do with job performance.

There is ongoing debate about whether to add new categories of protection to antidiscrimination law. Besides the Americans with Disabilities Act passed in 1990 to cover disability discrimination, no new categories of protection had been added to Title VII since its passage in 1964, until the Genetic Nondiscrimination Act of 2008. Although several states have passed prohibitions against sexual orientation discrimination, it is unclear whether Title VII will be amended to include some or all of these categories. The possibility of outlawing discrimination against overweight people by expanding the disability category or adding an additional category is being discussed. Before adding new categories to antidiscrimination law, we also look at the ways in which discrimination law fails those who are supposed to be protected. But all of these efforts face uphill battles and, even if some legislation is passed, it is unclear how progressive it will be. Thus, given the difficulty of passing legislation to protect workers, this chapter articulates a new framework for antidiscrimination law that is grounded in human rights.

## Title VII and the Categorical Approach to Discrimination

Federal antidiscrimination law was enacted in 1964 as a major exception to the doctrine of employment at will. Employment at will is a common law doctrine that allows employers to fire employees for no reason at all. Statutes like Title VII for the first time made exceptions to employment at will. Because of the major shift in power from employer to employee, the number of categories of prohibited discrimination would be severely limited. Even the inclusion of sex as a category was an effort to kill the bill. In the end, Title VII contained five categories—race, color, national origin, sex, and religion. The relationship between race and color is a close one, although there are many examples of "colorism," and so these categories are often interchangeable. The addition of national origin as a category was intended to deal with discrimination on the basis "of the country that someone was from, or where their ancestors come from."[9] The religion category was also added to appeal to conservative and southern lawmakers. All of these categories have their limitations in protecting the workers they are supposed to, not to mention how hard it is to expand these categories into other forms of discrimination, such as sexual orientation or gender preference. As a result, successive generations of social movements have had to work to expand the meaning of the statute either through litigation or the amendment process. Some of these efforts have been successful. Sexual harassment, for example, is not specifically mentioned in the statute, but in the 1980s, courts accepted the views of scholars and litigants that sexual harassment was also a violation of Title VII. Nevertheless, sexual orientation plaintiffs have been largely unsuccessful in being covered under federal antidiscrimination law, even though they have managed to get coverage under state antidiscrimination laws.

In its nearly 50-year-history, Title VII has been amended only in three major ways.[10] First, in 1972, public entities were covered by the statute for the first time. Second, in 1978, the Pregnancy Discrimination Act expanded the definition of sex discrimination to include "pregnancy, childbirth, and related medical conditions." Then, in response to Supreme Court decisions that Congress found to be against the purpose of Title VII, the Civil Rights Act of 1991 made punitive damages available for the first time, but also instituted $300,000 damage caps for the first time. Nearly 20 years after these amendments, the jury is still out about whether they have had a positive impact for workers. What is clear is that the 1991 amendments will continue to be litigated into the foreseeable future. In 2009, the Supreme Court also made it clear that the 1991 amendments did not extend to age discrimination. Whatever the conclusion, it is clear that there were many compromises even in getting the 1991 Act, not all of them beneficial to workers. It is also true that enacting three major amendments in nearly 50 years has meant that more often than not the courts are the last word on most of the disputed issues of antidiscrimination law. With three major amendments in 50 years of existence, it is not a stretch to say that Congress has been amended by the judiciary more often than is has by "elected branch." Thus, we need to look at how the courts have treated noncitizens.

### *The Story of Cecilia Espinoza*

The rigidity of Title VII was on full display in the *Espinoza* case. In *Espinoza*, the court had to decide whether the national origin category applied to discrimination on the basis of citizenship. Cecilia Espinoza and her husband brought a lawsuit against the Farah clothing company. She and her husband, a citizen, alleged that the failure to hire her was a violation of Title VII based on national origin. The federal trial court in San Antonio agreed with the Espinozas that Farah's citizens-only policy was discriminatory. The court found discrimination on the basis of citizenship among the invidious categories, and that Title VII was intended to prohibit discrimination against "inherently suspect classifications." In constitutional law, the court reasoned, the lack of citizenship was an inherently suspect category that merits increased constitutional scrutiny. As a result, the court found, alienage discrimination is a category that Congress intended to prohibit.[11]

The appellate court reversed the trial court's determination. The court saw the categories in Title VII as exclusive, and did not see the linkages between national origin discrimination and alienage. Thus, the Espinozas could not sue. As described above, the Supreme Court agreed. Justice Marshall stated that national origin and citizenship are not synonymous. Congress, he reasoned, could have decided to ban discrimination on the basis of citizenship, but chose instead to use the term "national origin," which the legislative history indicated was intended to cover animus against those from a particular nation, or with ancestry from a particular nation. Although this is a reasonable reading of the statutory language,

Title VII's overriding goal of prohibiting arbitrary distinctions in hiring is lost.

## The Difference That Alienage Makes

What is wrong with discriminating against noncitizens? Some will argue there is no problem with excluding people from employment because of citizenship or legal immigrant status as long as no racial discrimination is involved. The problem, as discussed in this chapter, is that there is often an overlap between the nonwhite races and noncitizen status. In 2007, census data show that 53.6 percent of the foreign-born population was from Latin America, and 26.8 percent was from Asia, leaving the rest from Europe (13.2 percent), Canada, and those identifying as "other."[12] Much of the venom toward immigrants from Mexico may affect legal residents from Mexico and those with Mexican ancestry. Further, even though Title VII does not mention citizenship status, it was in part intended to break down artificial barriers to employment. But national origin discrimination has been defined by the courts as animus toward those from the worker's country of origin, or anyone with that ancestry. Even if we take a narrow view of discrimination, citizenship, or lack of it, is a factor with a close relationship to other categories of discrimination. If we look at the history of discrimination against new immigrants, we see a sound basis for concluding that discrimination against noncitizens should raise heightened scrutiny. Indeed, this has been the conclusion of the U.S. Supreme Court when it comes to state-sponsored discrimination against aliens.

## The Porous Borders of Existing Legal Doctrines

Immigrants make up a large and increasing portion of the American community.[13] Each census counts a growing number of immigrants within the United States.[14] Yet immigrants have fewer legal protections than citizen workers. Particularly after the events of September 11, 2001, the rights and protections available to immigrants are tenuous.[15]

This chapter examines some of the ways that existing legal doctrines have failed to protect lawful permanent residents in the United States. Increasingly, formal U.S. citizenship has become a prerequisite for full entry into the workforce and even the touchstone for many other civil rights in the post-9/11 period. This has been the case in many public-sector jobs, since the U.S. Supreme Court has allowed states and localities to limit many public employee jobs to citizens only, without violating the Fourteenth Amendment. This chapter also aims to break down the distinctions between citizens and noncitizens in public employment. As with such distinctions in private employment, there are few valid reasons to distinguish between citizens and noncitizens in most public-sector jobs, and yet many job classifications divide up the workplace between citizens and noncitizens.

As shown in the *Espinoza* case above, immigrants are protected indirectly and incompletely by the laws prohibiting discrimination in the workplace. Under Title VII of the Civil Rights Act, discrimination on the basis of race, color, national origin, and ancestry is prohibited. Discrimination on the basis of immigration status, however, is not prohibited.[16] Immigrants may receive "national origin" protection under Title VII, but only if some animus toward the particular national origin of the immigrant exists.[17] Proving a national origin claim often requires plaintiffs to show that their discriminator bore some hostility toward their particular nation of origin or ancestry, as opposed to a general, undefined animus toward "newcomers" or "illegals."[18] Yet, there are many instances where the two categories overlap.

Although workplace law barely recognizes them, immigrants form the backbone of our economy and are a substantial presence in U.S. unions.[19] Even though immigrants have made some progress in obtaining basic protection under U.S. labor and employment laws despite daunting citizen/alien and legal/illegal distinctions, their access to job rights and remedies is tenuous. Most courts provide immigrants basic coverage under these laws, but deny equal access to the legal remedies needed to fulfill the promise of the laws' protection.[20] As described in chapter 1, however, undocumented victims of unfair labor practices under the National Labor Relations Act (NLRA) may not obtain reinstatement to their former job if their reinstatement would not be legal under the Immigration Reform and Control Act of 1986 (IRCA).[21] Until the Supreme Court decided *Hoffman Plastic Compounds, Inc. v. NLRB*[22] in 2002 (discussed in chapter 1), most courts and the National Labor Relations Board (NLRB) had decided that undocumented immigrants could receive back pay, as long as they were physically present to collect it.[23]

In *Hoffman*, the Court's denial of back pay to an undocumented immigrant fired in violation of the NLRA does not bode well for remedies available to immigrants under other protective statutes, such as the Title VII antidiscrimination protections, and minimum wage and overtime protections under state and federal laws.[24] Moreover, employers will surely use the precedents under the NLRA to try to deny immigrants' rights under other statutes, such as Title VII. Even for those who are here legally and are supposed to be protected by antidiscrimination law, there are various elements of what might be called "immigrant identity" that are not protected by antidiscrimination law. This chapter will look at ways that these identities might be bases to organize in spite of the law.

### *Noncitizens Need Not Apply: Antidiscrimination Law's Blinders to Immigration Status Discrimination*

As discussed earlier, the invisibility of immigrants under Title VII is not limited to the undocumented. This was made clear by the U.S. Supreme Court in its 1973 *Espinoza v. Farah* decision.[25] Plaintiff Cecilia Espinoza was a lawful permanent resident who brought suit against Farah, joined in the lawsuit by her U.S. citizen husband, challenging Farah's policy against hiring noncitizens as a violation of Title VII's ban on national origin discrimination.[26] In affirming dismissal of Espinoza's claim, the Court held that discrimination on the basis of citizenship was not prohibited under Title VII's national origin category.[27] The decision formally bifurcated immigration status and national origin, but in fact the two categories often overlap.[28]

After *Espinoza*, any claim under Title VII based on the alien/citizen distinction will fail. Still, the informal conflation of immigrant status and history with race and national origin discrimination continues.[29] Thus, in many cases, statements such as "wetback" and "go back where you came from," have been considered evidence of race or national origin discrimination against Mexicans and other Latinas/os.[30]

### *How Citizenship Comes Up Today*

When Espinoza was decided in 1973, there was no federal law prohibiting hiring people who were in the country in violation of immigration law. That did not come until 1986, when Congress passed the Immigration Reform and Control Act imposing penalties for the knowing hiring of the undocumented. Employers now have the responsibility for reviewing two forms of identification—one to establish identity and one to establish authorization to work. With this responsibility, some employers have tried to limit their workforce to citizens only, to ensure that they are not running afoul of immigration law.[31]

The state of Title VII law has remained unchanged since 1973, but in the efforts to pass an immigration sanctions bill in the early 1980s, there was a concern that employers would engage in national origin discrimination when trying to enforce the immigration laws. As a result, when Congress passed the Immigration Reform and Control Act of 1986, it included a provision to deal with any discrimination that the sanction's regime created. This legislative victory in an otherwise retrogressive piece of legislation was due to the hardscrabble lobbying efforts of groups such as the Mexican American Legal Defense and Education Fund. But the law is not as strong, or does not carry the same penalties, as it would if Title VII had been amended.

Thus, discrimination on the basis of citizenship status can be unlawful under the antidiscrimination provisions of IRCA since its enactment in 1986.[32] IRCA requires that businesses with citizenship requirements be justified by legitimate business justification. The Office of Special Counsel of the Civil Rights Division of the U.S. Department of Justice (DOJ) is responsible for the prosecution of immigration-related unfair employment practices. A few examples of the settlements that the DOJ has achieved in the last ten years shows the continuing prevalence of citizenship discrimination:

+ In 2000, a food processing plant in Maryland paid $230,000 to settle claims that it had demanded more documents from non-U.S. citizens than it had from other new hires.[33]
+ In 2001, a Las Vegas Hotel settled with a $75,000 civil penalty for demanding extra proof of citizenship for new hires.[34]
+ In 2004, a North Carolina Healthcare Company paid a $3,600 penalty for requiring proof of citizenship from new hires.[35]

The Department of Justice cases highlight several important factors. First, the relatively small size of these settlements compared to many Title VII cases suggests that employers may be less deterred by the possibility of DOJ charges. Second, General Accounting Office reviews of the Civil Rights Division under the George W. Bush administration showed that civil rights cases were down overall, thus leading to the conclusion that these IRCA discrimination cases were not a high priority for the administration.[36] And this is in keeping with the cautionary tale of this book, which is how politics of law can affect the enforcement of statutory rights. In theory, the enforcement of the law should not be dependent on who is in charge of the administration. Indeed, the Office of Special Counsel saw an increasing number of charges brought by South Asian and Middle Eastern workers in the five years after 9/11.[37]

Immigrants traverse many borders to get to their destinations. As Bruce Springsteen sang in 1995 about an immigrant traveling to see his lover, "where the sky goes grey and wide, we'll meet on the other side, there across the border."[38] Once they reach their destination, they find more borders in the workplace. In part, I am talking about the borders between citizens and noncitizens (in legal terms, aliens). But I am also talking here about doctrinal borders. The borders between race discrimination and anti-immigrant sentiment, for example, are policed by provisions that prevent the Equal Employment Opportunity Commission (EEOC) and the U.S. Department of Justice from exercising concurrent jurisdiction over claims on the basis of national origin discrimination.[39] In addition, IRCA's antidiscrimination provisions do not apply to the undocumented.[40] Thus, even though IRCA may prohibit some discrimination on the basis of citizenship status with respect to hiring, firing, and retaliation, it does not provide Title VII's range of protection (e.g., with respect to discipline or discriminatory working conditions not resulting in discharge) or remedies (e.g., front pay, injunctive relief). This patchwork of legal protection for immigration status under various federal statutes calls out for explicit, uniform treatment of immigration status under Title VII and other civil rights statutes. That is, Title VII should be amended to include immigration status as a protected category in addition to race, color, ancestry, and national origin.

The failure of the statutory schemes to provide a sound basis of equal job rights for immigrants gives credence to those who argue that litigation may not be the way to change the world. Even an amendment to Title VII would, of course, only touch those employers who are otherwise covered by the law (those with 15 employees or more), and would be subject to the same distinctions between documented and undocumented immigrants that have divided the workplace, unless the current regime of employer sanctions for hiring the undocumented is also repealed.[41]

Thus, we see the way that traditional antidiscrimination law fails new immigrants in a number of ways. First, it should be remembered that in current debates about immigration, race is taken off the table as a justifi-cation for actions taken against immigrants, whether legal or illegal. Sec-ond, when employers "prefer" immigrants or Latinos in certain "brown collar" occupations, as Leticia Saucedo has written, the traditional Title VII model does not fit.[42] Third, many categories that seem race neutral actually have a disproportionate racial impact. This was recognized by Justice William O. Douglas in dissent, who cited the courts for the propo-sition that Title VII outlawed "practices, procedures or tests neutral on their face" if they "create artificial, arbitrary and unnecessary barriers to employment when the barriers operate to discriminate invidiously on the basis of racial or other impermissible classifications."[43] Justice Douglas's view of the statute is more in line with a vision of antidiscrimination law that seeks to break down irrational barriers to employment.

The problem is that much discrimination against immigrants today is not specific to someone's country of origin, but rather their status as immigrants or children of immigrants. This explains much of the move-ment to deny citizenship to children of undocumented immigrants born on U.S. soil. Although the Constitution says that all persons "born or nat-uralized in the United States and subject to the jurisdiction thereof" are citizens of the United States, some people, including constitutional law scholars, argue that the children of undocumented immigrants are not covered by that clause.[44] Luckily, the Supreme Court's most recent deci-sion on this topic, in 1898, squarely held that even the children of foreign nationals born in the United States are citizens.[45] Nonetheless, in the cur-rent climate and with the current Supreme Court, there may be a move-ment to repeal. Comments like "go back to where you came from" and "illegal" do not speak directly as national origin discrimination. Thus, the antidiscrimination framework set up in the 1960s has failed to address much of the discrimination of the twenty-first century.

## The Mutually Constitutive Nature of Law and Society

This chapter has described legal doctrine that renders obvious harms to immigrants. In addition, it has shown how race and immigration status are conflated under Title VII, and how remedial options for immigrants are inferior to others who suffer discrimination. Scholars have shown that constitutional jurisprudence and immigration law can be outwardly hos-tile toward the construction of immigrants' identities.[46] The question then is how much credit we will give the law's effect on the production of individual and collective identities. Many scholars explore how law shapes consciousness. The question here is how law has constructed the immigrant as deserving few legal protections, except where protection serves the interest of society by regulating the supply of immigrant labor through incomplete protection of labor rights. Law is built on, and simultaneously reinforces, the social idea that immigrants should pull themselves up by their own bootstraps or go home. This story says nothing about the legal/illegal distinction that has been used to make undocumented immigrants completely illegitimate. The hostility of contemporary politics shows that the legal/illegal distinction means little to immigrants seeking government benefits.[47]

As previously discussed, legal categories divide workers by making legal protection under Title VII and the other civil rights statutes dependent on citizen/alien status.[48] These categories simultaneously homogenize workers, treating people of color from other countries essentially the same as U.S.-born people of color. Immigrants certainly share many similarities with the U.S.-born, but it is a mistake to think that immigrants fit into this racial paradigm for all purposes. Indeed, some discrimination against noncitizens can be explicitly nonracial, such as discrimination against white immigrants from England or any other country.

Explicit legal recognition of discrimination based on perceived or actual immigrant status as a category, in addition to race or national origin, would be a step toward protecting a greater number of immigrants. While every immigrant's history is different and should be regarded as such, legal recognition of immigrant status prevents the subordinated from slipping through the cracks of the existing legal categories, and also recognizes immigrant status as an additional basis for subordination related to race and national origin. As race and national origin are independent yet related categories, immigrant status and background could be an independent basis for protection.

In today's political climate, and for the foreseeable future, there is little likelihood that Title VII will be amended to include immigration status as a protected category. This fact demonstrates the central premise of this book, that statutory amendment is an inadequate foundation for many workers, and particularly noncitizens. This is why new forums for advocacy, as well as a return to fundamental constitutional rights, will be necessary. First, we must examine how and why the constitutional protection of noncitizens has been eviscerated by the Supreme Court.

## Citizenship Requirements in the Public Sector

The federal government, and many state and local governments, have requirements that public employees be citizens of the United States. The ostensible reason for these requirements, according to the Supreme Court majority in *Chavez v. Cabell-Salido*, is that public employees represent the citizenry, and the citizenry has the right to expect citizens to represent them.[49] But this logic seems perfectly circular. It also leaves out the large percentage of noncitizens that are part of communities throughout the United States. Clearly, there are some policymaking and elected offices where citizenship might be a reasonable qualification for the job. But as I will discuss, there have been several Supreme Court decisions which make virtually all public employment subject to citizenship requirements.

The Fourteenth Amendment to the U.S. Constitution provides due process and the equal protection of state law to all "persons within the jurisdiction of the United States." The guarantee of equal protection applies to different types of government classifications, such as race, gender, and illegitimacy. Depending on the category used, the government's action must be justified with more exacting levels of scrutiny by the courts. Thus, when a statute classifies by race, the courts put the resulting legislation through the strictest scrutiny, requiring the government to prove that the racial classification is necessary to meet a compelling governmental interest. If the classification is made on the basis of gender, by contrast, the government has a lesser burden to meet, but still must show that the classification is closely related to an important governmental interest.

When it comes to classifications based on alienage made by state and local governments, the government must show a compelling government interest. The fact that race and alienage classifications frequently intersect only further shows the need for strict scrutiny of alienage classifications, particularly when one considers the history of discrimination against immigrants. Since 1938, the U.S. Supreme Court has found that aliens, among other persons, are "discrete and insular minorities." This conclusion, in footnote 4 of the Court's opinion in *United States v. Carolene Products*, held that some classifications like alienage and race require more searching judicial inquiry than most economic legislation. And yet, the federal government, because of its plenary power to regulate immigration, can require its employees to be citizens of the United States.

Despite this history of animus for immigrants, the Supreme Court has generally allowed states and localities to limit public employment to citizens. When states tried to limit welfare benefits to citizens only, these efforts were struck down as incursions of the federal government's exclusive province. In *Graham v. Richardson*, the Supreme Court held that states cannot limit welfare benefits to citizens under the equal protection clause.[50] In 1977, the Court in *Nyquist v. Mauclet* held that the New York statute prohibiting financial assistance to noncitizens was a violation of the Equal Protection Clause.[51]

When it comes to whether or not legal immigrants can be employed by state and local governments, rather than the federal government's exclusive control over the admission and deportation of immigrants, the equal protection clause applies. Nevertheless, the courts have given states and localities a free hand in most cases of limiting public employment to citizens only. In 1978, the Supreme Court in *Foley v. Connelie* upheld the New York Police Department's requirement that officers be citizens. One year later, in *Ambach v. Norwick*, the Court upheld a New York state law that barred aliens from being public school teachers.[52] These cases operated on the assumption that while these employees were not policymakers, they still represented the face of the government in law enforcement and public education, not unlike jurors and voters.

In *Cabell*, the Supreme Court approved of a bar to the employment of noncitizen deputy probation officers. The Court held that California had a sufficient reason for requiring the officers to be citizens. There are a number of other public employee classifications in California that do not require citizenship, such as state judge, district attorney, and teachers. These are jobs that seem to require some public function, and yet they do not require citizenship. This shows that the application of citizenship requirements is uneven and internally inconsistent. Even though attorneys can be said to fulfill a public function, the Supreme Court has held that it is unconstitutional to limit bar admission to citizens only.

## *Intersectionality: Noncitizenship, Race, and National Origin*

As critical race theorists have often argued, the problem with antidiscrimination law is that it tends to be a black and white binary and does not take into account the increasingly diverse society in the law. Further, claimants with multiple intersecting identities have not fared well in the courts, as shown by empirical studies. Citizenship discrimination is one of the grounds that antidiscrimination law ignores, and yet noncitizens often have intersecting identities. Citizenship discrimination can often have a disparate impact on protected categories.

Should Title VII be amended to prevent such discrimination? When we look at the private sector, there are certainly many employers who do not engage in citizenship discrimination. And there are many employers who do not concern themselves with the citizenship of their employees, such as technology firms that hire large numbers of workers through the H1-B temporary visa program. But the Department of Justice regularly fines employers for citizenship discrimination, and the increased tumult over immigration provides a reason to be concerned about how much citizenship discrimination is occurring.

A hallmark of intersectional discrimination is that it is very hard to remedy because the political coalitions needed to do so are diffuse and hard to organize. Note the passage of the Immigration Reform and Control Act in 1986. Here, immigrants' rights groups were successful in getting an amnesty program with the aforementioned discrimination measures and a program to regularize the status of approximately three million immigrants. The price for these benefits was the employer sanctions regime that ensnared José Castro, the undocumented worker who was the subject of the *Hoffman* case in chapter 1. On balance, then, the IRCA antidiscrimination provisions were obtained at the price of the employer sanctions regime, which many labor activists claim is the reason that it is so hard to organize immigrants.[53]

## Public Norms and the Private Sector

Since Title VII applies to public employment, changing the doctrine will open up more public employment to noncitizens. As described earlier in this chapter, the constitutional rules do not apply to private-sector employment. Private-sector employment is regulated by the Department of Justice Office of Immigration Related Unfair Employment Law Practices. These overlapping legal regimes leave gaps through which workers will fall. Clearly, changes are needed to administrative enforcement regimes.

On a more fundamental level, however, there is a need to question citizenship requirements and other non–work performance related characteristics. U.S. citizenship, or lack of it, has very little relevance to most jobs. Further, as discussed earlier in this chapter, citizenship has historically been used as a proxy for discrimination on an already protected category, such as race or national origin.

Thus, there is not only a need for constitutional protections but also a change in attitudes about citizenship itself. Citizenship is a formal process that governments use to determine political community—only citizens can vote and only citizens can serve on juries. Generally, immigrants have to be lawful permanent residents for five years before being eligible to become citizens. Recently, citizenship status has been used to ration government benefits, such as aid to the disadvantaged and health care. And employment restrictions may be another way to manage scarcity. The pernicious possibilities of citizenship discrimination require a legal regime that is responsive to intersectional discrimination.

Instead of a response to scarcity, however, citizenship requirements often seem to be a way to ferret out disloyalty and dissent, as well as to limit jobs to those who can speak English clearly, even when that is not really a job requirement. A unified framework would see citizenship rules as arbitrary barriers to employment in most places in which they are used. Luckily, many private employers do not have these rules. Nevertheless, there has been a steady increase in the number of claims with the Department of Justice over citizenship and national origin discrimination.[54]

## The Problems with Categories

Let us think now about the expansion of categories. The Civil Rights Act of 1964 set forth five categories for protection against discrimination—race, sex, color, national origin, and religion. In 1967, the Age Discrimination in Employment Act was passed. Twenty-four years later, in 1991, the Americans with Disabilities Act made disability a protected category, even though various aspects of disability discrimination had been made illegal by the Rehabilitation Act of 1973. Although sexual orientation has been added to the list of categories of protection in many states, this provides little solace to those who do not live in the 38 states that do not have protection. This is why the Lesbian Gay Bisexual and Transgender (LGBT) movement has recently moved to pass the Employment Non-Discrimination Act (ENDA). The question facing that legislation is whether or not it will cover transgender or gender identity discrimination. These categories may be compromised in the legislative process, since that process is all about compromise. Current efforts to expand protection to gays, lesbians, and transgendered are running into opposition in part because some people ask where the list of protected categories will end. As overweight people embrace fat as a category, and localities are pilloried for ordinances protecting against "lookism," many question whether the goals of antidiscrimination law go too far.[55]

The very debate about how much to expand antidiscrimination statutes shows the limits of legislation.[56] Any time a new category is added, critics ask, "where will it end?"[57] "Is discrimination against people with pets next?" One stopping point may be found in international law, which has prohibitions against discrimination on many of the same grounds that have already been prohibited by statute, but also include political opinion. But there is another answer to the question of where it all should end. Perhaps employers should refrain from hiring and firing people for "irrational" reasons, or anything that is not performance related. That would subsume many of the categories that could be added to the list of discriminatory reasons, including citizenship status as I have discussed above.[58]

There are some who will say that this is simply the next step toward the elimination of at-will employment, and it may be, but it is also an attempt to develop a coherent framework for discrimination claims. It seems fundamental that people should not be denied a job simply for being fat, or not a citizen, if it does not bear a rational relationship to their abilities to perform a job. We may also add an idea of irrational animus—that is, discrimination against someone because they are not citizens or because employers find them less loyal to the government. These kinds of proxies have been shown to be false in a number of different contexts.

Should immigrant or citizenship status be protected? Social reality shows us that citizenship status is extremely important to many people. Legal immigrants who have lived in the United States for more than the five years required for naturalization are encouraged both by social pressure and public policy to become citizens. Media pundits such as Linda Chavez regularly argue that immigrants should learn English and become citizens.[59] Many governmental benefits, including public employment as discussed above, are limited to those who are citizens. Nevertheless, there might be reasons why immigrants wish not to naturalize, and reasons that might affect their citizenship in their home country (for example, their home country may not allow dual citizenship). There are people who will choose to remain in this state of legal limbo, for a variety of reasons that are personal to them, and yet there is very little legal sanction for discriminating against them.

The point of this discussion is to get away from arbitrary distinctions that divide people against each other. The choice not to become a citizen should be respected, and protected from discrimination. The reason is rooted in the freedom inherent in human rights, and that discrimination is irrational. ILO Convention 111, for example, challenges all forms of discrimination that are based on "national extraction or social origin."[60] This has been interpreted to include "nationality," which has a broader meaning than the courts have given to national origin. In its Preamble, ILO Convention 111 also makes clear that the goal of the discrimination provisions is to assure that "all human beings, irrespective of race, creed or sex, have the right to pursue both their material well being and their spiritual development in conditions of freedom and dignity, of economic security and equal opportunity."[61] While there are categories in the definition of discrimination, Convention 111 also states that other forms of discrimination, "which has the effect of nullifying or impairing equality of opportunity or treatment in employment may be determined" by member countries in conjunction with employers and workers' organizations. Thus, the intent of the Convention is to try to remedy disparate treatment in employment, and also to deal with the effects of that treatment.

It may be time to rethink our categorical approach to discrimination law. The recent expansion of federal discrimination law to include discrimination on the basis of genetics is a welcome sign, but is also an example of the ways in which most innovations in law will not benefit the marginal workers in this book because of their relative lack of political power. Generally speaking, discrimination laws operate to prevent discrimination based on genetic profiles. This mostly affects workers who already have health insurance and are part of the politically diffuse middle class.

Employers have not been the only problem when it comes to discrimination against noncitizens. Some unions have discriminated against noncitizens for years, when immigrants were scapegoated in times of economic trouble. Even today, some public-sector unions have provisions in their constitutions limiting membership to citizens, while other unions have welcomed noncitizens. The American Federation of Government Employees, on the one hand, has a provision limiting membership to U.S. citizens, while the Service Employees International Union has a nondiscrimination clause prohibiting discrimination on the basis of a number of grounds, including citizenship.

Discrimination against noncitizens almost returned to the Supreme Court in a case involving the Carpenters Union of America in the late 1990s. Linden Anderson, a citizen of Jamaica who immigrated to the United States in 1968, had worked for the Carpenters Union as a business representative since 1973. Although he had apparently been a good employee of the union for over 20 years, he was fired when the president of the union discovered that he was not a citizen of the United States, citing the provision in the union's constitution. Anderson sued under a number of theories, including a Reconstruction era statute entitled Section 1981, which provides:

> All persons within the jurisdiction of the United States shall have the same right in every State and Territory to make and enforce contracts, to sue, be parties, give evidence, and to the full and equal benefit of all laws and proceedings for the security of persons and property as is enjoyed by white citizens.[62]

The Second Circuit Court of Appeals based in New York held that this plain language meant that the union's citizens-only employment policy violated Anderson's civil rights.[63] The Carpenters' Union appealed the decision to the U.S. Supreme Court, but the case settled soon thereafter.

The *Anderson* case reflects the divisions that have plagued organized labor for years. But it also says something about the unsettled nature of antidiscrimination law's protection of noncitizens. The law fails to protect noncitizens and other hybrids well.[64] The Anderson case itself was settled by the parties before Supreme Court review. And yet, several courts have decided that section 1981 does not apply to citizenship discrimination.[65]

Thus, the other statutory avenues that exist are blind alleys for many workers. This only highlights the need for a new approach to discrimination. Instead of seeing categories of discrimination as fixed and never changing, we should see categories as merely illustrative examples of an approach to employment that questions any arbitrary discrimination. The goal should not be adding new categories, but instead outlawing all forms of job discrimination that are completely unrelated to particular jobs.

## A Floor, Not a Ceiling

I want to emphasize that the antidiscrimination principle I articulate here is intended to be a floor and not a ceiling. In the future, we are likely to see new forms of discrimination against new social groups. I hope the principle that I advance here is flexible enough to encompass types of discrimination as our society progresses. The reason that Title VII does not have sexual orientation protection is because in 1964 there was no gay and lesbian movement to obtain that protection. While gays and lesbians have certainly come a long way since 1964, it remains to be seen how much they will win through the political process, being a minority of the U.S. population. The debate about the Employment Non-Discrimination Act (ENDA) and whether it will include protections for transsexuals or "gender identity" shows how difficult comprehensive change, rather than piecemeal reform, will be.

Even in the absence of explicit legal protection, workers will continue to organize for equal treatment as they have done in the past, sometimes across the borders of race and national origin. There have been a number of examples from the recent past. In Smithfield, North Carolina, for example, black and Latino/a workers banded together in an attempt to obtain Martin Luther King Day as a paid holiday.[66] The campaign was part of a prolonged 16-year effort to try to unionize the plant, which ultimately led to a union contract.[67] In the late 1990s, an organizing drive at a Holiday Inn Express led to the deportation of eight immigrants in Minneapolis. In bargaining for a new contract in the summer of 2000, Hotel and Restaurant Employees Local 17 adopted an explicitly pro-immigrant stance in negotiations.[68] Thanks to a multiracial organizing drive and the use of a special administrative status for immigrants to testify against law violators, the eight workers were able to get a special status that forestalled deportation.[69]

And it should also be remembered that many immigrants are politically active even though they are not citizens, particularly those who are in unions. There were large marches for immigration reform that took place in many cities in the spring of 2006, which included thousands of immigrants whether they were documented or not. In political campaigns, noncitizens in unions often engage in get-out-the-vote activities even though they cannot vote. Immigrants in unions get a kind of virtual citizenship that is tied to their work. Even if these workers choose not to become citizens, they are still participants in our democracy.[70]

Noncitizens are not only disadvantaged by the failings of antidiscrimination laws in this country, but also abroad. As part of the 1991 Civil Rights Act, Congress aimed to change the result in *E.E.O.C. v. Arabian American Oil Co.*, a Supreme Court decision which ruled against the extraterritoriality of Title VII for employees of multinational companies working abroad.[71] The case prevented an employee of a multinational oil company in Saudi Arabia from recovering under Title VII because, as the Court stated: "It is . . . reasonable to conclude that if Congress had intended to apply overseas it would have addressed the subject of conflicts in foreign law and procedures."[72] Thus, Congress amended the Civil Rights Act in 1991 to expand the definition of employee to include "with respect to employment in a foreign country, [employee] includes an individual who is a citizen of the United States."[73]

Thus, while U.S. residents who are noncitizens may be covered by Title VII, at least for national origin and if they are in the United States, if they work overseas they are not covered at all. What are the reasons for this disparity? It is hard to see any other reason besides a disadvantage being imposed on noncitizens because of their status and their inability to use the political process to complain. If, as in other international antidiscrimination instruments, the word nationality was used, there might be relief for other grounds for discrimination.

In the end, the limitations of the national origin category highlight something about the U.S. legal system that is different than the international legal system. In the U.S. judicial system, the focus is on private parties and their alleged wrongdoing, but the systemic forces that create discrimination are missed. In the international system, by contrast, government's role in ending discrimination is highlighted. For example, in the North American Free Trade Agreement's labor side agreement, nondiscrimination is one of the principles that each government is supposed to "strive to promote." In Principle 7, each country should work to eliminate employment discrimination:

> on such grounds as race, religion, age, sex or other grounds, such as, where applicable, bona fide occupational requirements or established practices or rules governing retirement ages, and special measures of protection for assistance for particular groups designed to take into account the effects of discrimination.

This language provides a basis for an expansive view of discrimination, even though it does not reference national origin or nationality at all. Instead of seeing categories as the outer limit of discrimination, we can see them as merely illustrative beginnings on the road to discrimination norms which disfavors irrational discrimination on any number of grounds, not just the standard categories of race, sex, and religion.

## *Across the Borders of Citizenship*

This chapter has traversed the borders between the legal regimes that are intended to protect. The bottom line is that current race and national origin paradigms in antidiscrimination law fail to appreciate animus against immigrants not only because of the color of their skin, but because they are immigrants. I believe that an appreciation of that fact will lead us to consider the "anti-newcomer" or "anti-outsider" dimensions of discrimination that harm not only immigrants but the native-born as well. The more we conceptualize immigrant status and identity as independent and related to racial, gender, and other identities, the closer we will get to crossing the borders between us.

# Labor as Property

## *Guestworkers at the Margins of*
## *Domestic Legal Systems*

In the middle of World War II, a group of Mexicans made their way to the United States to work in the fields and on the railroads. They did not surreptitiously cross the Río Grande or the Arizona desert. Instead, they were brought by buses and trains at the behest of agricultural employers, the Mexican government, and the U.S. government. The ostensible reason for the "importing" of labor was a shortage of agricultural workers because of World War II. The Mexicans were called "braceros," which in Spanish means "those who work with their arms." Although they were concentrated in a number of Southwestern states, 32 of the 48 continental states had braceros working in the fields.[1]

Legal permanent residents are not the only noncitizens working at the margins of the law. Throughout U.S. history, temporary worker programs led to the exploitation of noncitizens, but the Bracero Program ("the Program") was the largest such endeavor.[2] The Program, in effect at various times from 1917 to 1964, formalized a temporary labor system for agriculture. It began during World War I with approximately 77,000 workers for agricultural labor shortages.[3] The Program ramped up again during World War II, but even after the war was over, growers' purported needs for agricultural workers continued.[4] From 1942 to 1964, over 4.6 million Mexicans were brought to the United States through the Bracero Program.[5] Although the braceros were promised transportation and minimum wages, they rarely obtained all of these rights.[6]

Moreover, the bracero agreement between the United States and Mexico encouraged workers to return to Mexico by deducting funds from their paychecks in the United States and holding the money in "savings accounts."[7] The problem was that many of the workers were not able to obtain access to these accounts and later brought litigation to recover the monies. Former braceros thus brought suit a lawsuit titled *Cruz v. United States*[8] to federal court in 2002 to recover the withheld funds. Their claims against the United States, Mexico, and the various banks were met with a variety of defenses such as the respective government's sovereign immunity, the limited duties owed by banks to depositors, and the time limitations on various claims.[9] The federal court in Oakland, California dismissed the braceros' lawsuit in 2003, but many of the claims based on state law found new life in legislation to extend the statute of limitations in the California state legislature.[10] The legislation showed the braceros' effectiveness in the democratic system well after the Program had been terminated, but it was not until many of the participants in the Bracero Program were citizens in the United States that they had the ability to enforce basic rights.[11]

Guestworker programs like the Bracero Program have been part of immigration policy in the United States for nearly a century.[12] These programs represent the horns of the dilemma presented to guestworkers in the global economy. On the one hand, the prevailing norm enshrined in American law since 1914 is that a person's labor is not a commodity to be bought and sold, like wheat or grain on an open market. The Clayton Antitrust Act, in Section 14, states, "the labor of a human being is not an article of commerce or an article to be traded." On the other hand, in an economy that commodifies everything from foods to ideas, a person's labor is often one of primary things to trade for value. This is the choice that workers in poor countries face as they decide whether to immigrate to richer countries, either illegally or through legal guestworker programs.

The impulse to survive led many braceros to leave their homes and families to go north. According to some braceros, even the trip to their new home made them feel like commodities, since they were transported in cargo trains, not passenger trains, to their new homes. Braceros were also treated like animals when they were sprayed with the chemical DDT upon arrival. According to one oral history, "They sprayed us like rats, like insects. We left covered in powder," said Isaias Sanchez, an ex-bracero.[13] Upon arriving in the United States, however, braceros found the work and income that they lacked in Mexico, but many of the promises that were made to them were not kept. In some cases, they lacked the housing and wages that they were promised. A portion of their wages was also withheld from their paychecks and held by the Mexican government to incentivize their return to Mexico. Unfortunately, however, the workers did not receive the withheld wages upon their return.

The story of the braceros tells much about how current and new temporary worker programs might work in the future. In the current political debate about immigration reform, the term "guestworkers" has been given various meanings, including providing temporary status for undocumented immigrants already in the country.[14] This chapter focuses on "guestworker" programs that seek to bring unskilled workers into the United States on a temporary basis.[15] It describes the lack of bargaining power and voice that guestworkers have on the global labor market—and how this lack of bargaining power leads the workers to be treated like commodities in international trade, widening the democratic deficit both globally and within the United States. International labor agreements and human rights instruments may provide some protection for guestworkers, but the best solution is to have fewer guestworker programs, rather than to expand them as current legislation proposes.

Guestworker programs exacerbate the commodification of labor and widen a deficit of democracy for the noncitizen workers. Guestworkers are commodified because they are without bargaining power or voice in the substantive transaction governing their working conditions. Their inherently temporary nature makes guestworkers unable to enforce their legal rights. Further, they are unlikely to leverage their collective bargaining power to obtain better working conditions or the ability to stay in the United States permanently. Temporary workers have no political voice in their new country, less influence in their country of origin, and no voice at work if they are unable to enforce their rights. This is why any guestworker program that cycles workers through on a temporary basis—even one that purports to grant workers the same rights as U.S. residents—is bound to commodify guestworkers and exacerbate the democracy deficit.

The legal framework for guestworkers is tenuous. Although in theory guestworkers are afforded the same legal protections as any other workers in the host country, in reality guestworkers have been among the most vulnerable workers in the U.S. economy, and have been exploited in several countries. The transitory nature of guestworkers' employment and their tenuous immigration status means that if even if these workers have rights on paper, they will be unable to enforce them, as shown by several recent examples provided later in this chapter.

## Labor Is Not a Commodity

Traditionally, a commodity is a good or material that can be bought or sold in the market.[16] As trade between countries began in earnest in the late 1700s, economist David Ricardo posited the theory of comparative advantage.[17] Comparative advantage holds that increased trade in commodities benefits all countries in the world because each nation has a comparative advantage in some commodity over another. Thus, countries that did not have certain types of raw materials could trade things that they did have with other countries. In the end, so the theory goes, everyone is better off.[18] This theory underlies much of international trade today.[19]

Commodification is the idea that in a market economy everything, from body parts to knowledge, can be bought and sold.[20] Indeed, in the current economy it is hard to think of anything that is not commodified, including pain and suffering.[21] Under the law, labor is one thing that should not be commodified. Yet, developments in law and society in the last 50 years have chipped away at the statutory de-commodification of labor that aimed to give workers greater agency and bargaining power in transactions regarding their own labor.[22] Laws protecting collective action are now swimming upstream in a globalized economy where workers, particularly immigrant and foreign workers, are seen as articles of commerce without bargaining power; thus, labor is being re-commodified.

On a global scale, workers have lost significant bargaining power over the last 50 years as barriers to trade have been removed.[23] With work so mobile, employers can more easily find workers to work for less, and thus workers are less able to command better wages. Historically, the concept of comparative advantage in international trade referred to commodities such as natural resources or raw materials that countries could trade with each other in the global marketplace.[24] The new source of comparative advantage in the global economy is cheap labor.[25] Recent interest in the United States in an expanded guestworker program exemplifies this commodification of labor. Countries jockey for position in the global marketplace to offer the cheapest labor to multinational corporations.

Trade agreements such as the North American Free Trade Agreement (NAFTA) privilege the protection of investment over the protection of labor.[26] This is evident in the fact that the penalties for trade violations in NAFTA are more than those for labor violations. Many trade agreements have been passed on the model of NAFTA, with little input from the guestworkers that are actually affected by the policies. Commodification of labor mutes the voice of the workers who will be most affected by these trade negotiations. This can be seen in the recent negotiations between the United States and Mexico for a guestworker program.[27] The potential guestworkers are treated as commodities without agency or an interest in the outcome of agreements between countries.[28] Theories of virtual representation may close the "democracy deficit" between the workers' interests and the imperatives of international trade and politics, but they have yet to work in practice.

Because of their impoverished status in their home countries, guestworkers have little bargaining power in determining their employment conditions. Specifically, they have the choice between destitution in their home countries and temporary work in the United States. The material benefits of working in the United States should not be underestimated, but these benefits do nothing to provide guestworkers with a say in their employment conditions. In order for workers to have bargaining power in the inevitable global market for labor, they must be given a voice in the negotiations over trade agreements through representatives of their own choosing. Further, in this chapter, I argue that guestworker status is fundamentally incompatible with the ability to exercise meaningful bargaining power at work.

The typical way that workers in the United States have a say in their working conditions is through collective bargaining protected by the National Labor Relations Act (NLRA). In previous chapters, I have discussed the defects of the NLRA for women, people of color, and undocumented immigrants. Guestworkers are in a different posture—legally in the country, but not citizens like many people of color and women in unions. Instead, their right to work in the country is legally tied to a single employer, which only heightens the potential for exploitation. Like many labor and employment laws, the NLRA would apply to guestworkers because they are employees under the statute. In theory, guestworkers would be entitled to all the rights and remedies that would be available to other employees.

In reality, though, most guestworkers cannot effectively enforce the statutory rights to which they are entitled. First, guestworkers' employment is often sporadic and seasonal. There are several months a year that they are back in the sending country. When I was a lawyer representing immigrant workers, there were times when we were not sure if our clients would be available for depositions because they were visiting their home countries. This is even more pronounced when the workers are temporary, which makes it more difficult to enforce rights, if workers can even find an attorney to represent them. Second, the right to organize is hollow if workers are not there long enough to establish common cause with fellow employees. As José Castro's story in chapter 1 demonstrates, the administrative process of the NLRB can take as many as 13 years, far longer than would be necessary to complete a successful organizing drive. Once again, differing citizenship status in the workforce leads to legal fault lines which destroy solidarity.

Finally, if there is any advocacy with government officials to enforce the law, as with opportunities to bring claims under the NAFTA labor side agreement, noncitizen guestworkers will have little political power with elected officials. Without access to remedies and voice at work, the rights available to guestworkers are illusory. Thus, their labor is commodified.

The commodification of labor is a long-term historical process that extends directly from slavery and moves through the history of the labor movement with its goal of de-commodification. Globalization complicates de-commodification precisely because knowledge and intangible labor are so highly valued today.[29] In the global economy, workers would have more freedom of movement if they were considered to be goods rather than people. The democracy deficit refers to the global institutions, such as trade agreements, that are negotiated by governments, often without the input of the people who are most affected by them. Recently, scholars have argued for the creation of global administrative legal institutions to close the democracy deficit.[30] On the domestic front, guestworkers are by nature unrepresented in their new country, and their home country representatives often have little incentive to fully represent their interests. Thus, increasing the presence of a large number of noncitizen workers will only exacerbate the democracy deficit.

Congress is currently considering proposals for a guestworker program in comprehensive immigration reform.[31] Potential guestworkers in countries other than Mexico, however, are unable to influence democratically these legislative proposals. Instead, the workers are treated as commodities to be traded between countries. The commodification of workers adds another dimension to the moral problems inherent in guestworker programs. These moral objections, as well as the economic, policy, and historical problems with guestworker programs, are examined below.

One of the conditions for the enforcement of labor rights is democratic participation. Unions can only flourish if there are engaged citizens, particularly in the public sector. There may be ways to make these programs more responsive to workers as a means to narrowing the democracy deficit, but unquestionably there are ways in which guestworker programs can be improved.[32]

The history of the labor movement in many respects is the struggle to obtain the maximum price for labor that the market will bear.[33] Labor history is also the story of the movement for greater voice and respect in the terms and conditions of employment, essentially for greater bargaining power in labor transactions.[34] This is the story of labor de-commodification. This chapter examines three modern, interrelated phenomena about guestworkers: (1) the commodification of labor, (2) globalization, and (3) the democracy deficit.

History shows workers progressively gaining more bargaining power over the terms and conditions of their employment during the last two centuries.[35] That progress has been threatened in recent years by increased trade and manufacturing in areas where economic deprivation has decreased workers' bargaining power. Further, collective bargaining to increase wages is complicated by a lack of protection for freedom of association.[36]

In the contemporary labor context, commodification is about the lack of voice in the political sphere and in the workplace.[37] This lack of voice in the political sphere widens the democracy deficit. Another immediate consequence of the lack of voice is the inability to change working conditions either with the employer or with the government. The lack of voice at work has been exacerbated by the declining number of workers represented by unions in the United States.[38] The large number of workers who are marginalized because they are undocumented or lacking full-time employment is lessening the bargaining power for all workers.[39]

Workers, and guestworkers in particular, face difficulty in maximizing the full value of their labor, as will be shown in the following section. Nevertheless, the bargaining position of workers in the global economy will be affected by the basic laws of supply and demand. Because there is a large supply of workers globally, wages have stagnated.[40] But, based on the apparent need for guestworkers to fill jobs within this country, temporary workers would seem to have a great deal of bargaining power. Given the public discourse of immigration reform, it would seem that guestworkers are badly needed in the American economy.[41] Nevertheless, guestworkers have little leverage to negotiate terms and conditions of employment, which might include permanent residency in the United States.

The law has progressed in a trajectory from simple commodification to having a voice at work. From the post–Civil War Reconstruction Era through the mid-twentieth century, American law formally rejected the idea of human labor as property, an idea that had existed since the founding of the country in the form of slavery.[42] The Constitution's Thirteenth Amendment ended slavery and involuntary servitude in 1865.[43] Nearly 50 years later, in 1914, the U.S. Congress declared that "the labor of a human being is not a commodity or article of commerce" in the Clayton Antitrust Act.[44] While the practical reason for this section of the Clayton Act was to exempt labor negotiations from antitrust liability, the Clayton Act was also a component of the legal rejection of the commodification of human labor that began with the abolition of slavery in the 1860s.[45] The National Labor Relations Act (NLRA) of 1935 also rejected the commodification of labor by protecting the right to associate and bargain collectively.[46] Since 1919, the United States has also assumed obligations as a member of the International Labor Organization, which has a preamble that rejects the idea that labor is a commodity.[47]

## Globalization Heightens the Marginalization of Workers

Globalization is not a new process, but it is marked in the modern era by an increasing income inequality between countries.[48] The global income gap has led many to seek work in the developed world, even while many opportunities are being shipped out of developed countries.[49] The neoliberal paradigm assumes that everything can be freely traded.[50] Guestworkers fit into this paradigm as another article to be traded. The rise of free trade agreements marks the global economy in the twenty-first century.[51] These trade agreements aim to break down trade barriers, eliminates tariffs on imports, and increase global competition among unskilled workers.[52]

In his book, *The World Is Flat: A Brief History of the Twenty-First Century*, Thomas Friedman heralds the "flattening" of the world, or the leveling of the playing field through technology, which has allowed billions of new workers to compete for the jobs of U.S. workers.[53] Through call centers in Mumbai and in other parts of the world, workers in developing countries are competing with American workers, who must either "skill up" through improved education and training or be left with fewer opportunities.[54] Contrary to Friedman's "flat world," guestworkers find many barriers to mobility and residency in the global labor marketplace.[55] Thus, while the value of immigrant workers to the economy may be high, this value is not reflected in the actual bargaining power of guestworkers in their working conditions or the ability to gain residency in the United States, as this chapter will show.

State and federal domestic labor regulation has historically affected the bargaining power of workers in two ways. First, the NLRA mandated the procedures that would have to be followed by workers and employers.[56] The NLRA requires American employers to bargain in good faith with representatives of employees.[57] Second, the Fair Labor Standards Act (FLSA) of 1938 set minimum wage and overtime laws, which creates a baseline for labor negotiations.[58] Neither the NLRA nor the FLSA explicitly applies to work relationships that take place outside the country.[59] Although the International Labor Organization conventions reasonably further freedom of association, the global economy is notable for its lack of enforceable procedures and standards governing collective bargaining.[60] Instead, multilateral trade agreements such as NAFTA and the Central American Free Trade Agreement (CAFTA) presume that there will be no enforceable standards in labor transactions between countries; instead, these agreements only require that countries enforce their own labor laws.[61]

Trade agreements are also increasingly becoming part of the global economy. The signing of NAFTA in 1994 started a series of free trade agreements that attempted to open trade of goods and services across the borders.[62] NAFTA did not deal with the issue of migration. It did, however, commit the United States, Canada, and Mexico to provide migrant workers in each country's territory with the same legal protection as that country's nationals with respect to working conditions.[63] Unfortunately, undocumented immigration from Mexico into the United States has only increased since NAFTA has been enacted.[64]

In the global economy, trafficking also is becoming an increasing problem.[65] One of the ironies of the global era is that the world has focused increased attention on the fight against human trafficking, while the terminology used in the immigration debate tracks the idea that immigrants can be traded or imported like goods.[66] Several significant pieces of legislation have been passed to combat the spread of human trafficking, in which humans are smuggled like contraband.[67]

At the same time that trafficking is seen as a major problem, trading workers as commodities has been looked upon as commonplace, a necessary by-product of the global economy.[68] The debate about a new guest-worker program has also used the language of "importing workers."[69] Several commentators on all sides of the political debate have decried the "importing of guestworkers" embodied in various legislative proposals.[70] In the context of legal guestworker programs that are in place in the Northern Mariana Islands, government officials criticized the "importation of guestworkers" that was occurring instead of a regulated immigration scheme.[71] Thus, the connection between temporary labor programs and imports is firmly rooted.

### The Democracy Deficit: Workers Lacking Voice in Politics and at Work

The "democracy deficit" is a concept that has been used to describe the increasing importance of unelected institutions in the global environment. Many argue that the increasing importance of institutions such as the World Bank and the International Monetary Fund are displacing the democratically elected institutions in poor countries. Many believe that the democracy deficit legitimizes and increases the wealth deficit between rich and poor countries.[72] The democracy deficit also applies to the large number of people, both legal and illegal, who do not currently have the right to vote in the United States. While the right to vote might legitimately be granted or withheld based on an individual's immigration status or past crimes, a growing gap between the represented workers and the right to choose their representatives should be cause for concern.[73]

There may be ways to close the gap between people with little political power and their governments. One of these might involve representative international institutions and nongovernmental organizations, such as the International Labor Organization (ILO) and the UN. There are limitations on the democratic nature of the ILO, however, since it is an unelected, three-part structure that involves governments, workers, and employers.[74] This tripartite structure can sometimes lead to the absence of workers' voices, unless they are virtually represented by unions and governments. Unions generally will represent the interests of workers, but with only about 13 percent of workers in the United States represented by unions, a significant democracy deficit remains.[75]

In analyzing guestworker programs, it is important to exercise caution about the limitations of democratic participation. The right to vote, for example, is not the *sine qua non* of democratic participation. In spring 2006, more than one million people, including many noncitizens, marched in reaction to various congressional proposals to change immigration laws.[76] Their activism may have had a major impact on the shape of the bill that was passed by the Senate, which included an earned legalization program and lacked many of the most draconian components of the House of Representatives' immigration bill. It remains to be seen whether the large public demonstrations will have an overall positive or negative impact on any immigration legislation. The influence of the recent demonstrations, despite the inability of many immigrants to vote, shows that there are many ways to influence policy democratically.

In addition, foreigners living abroad may be "virtually represented" by their governments through the foreign policy actions of their leaders. In the case of guestworkers, virtual representation has not worked very well because low-wage workers usually lack political power in their home countries.[77] In theory, virtual representation might work, but with the realities of geopolitics today, world leaders will pay little attention to workers who are living between two countries.

Nevertheless, the failure of immigration reform shows the limits of political activism on behalf of immigrants. When immigration reform actually happens, it will be the product of complex political calculations and elections, and the hope of each political party to court the growing clout of Latinos and Latinas in the electorate. Further, guestworkers, who may come from a number of different countries, may not have their interests adequately represented by U.S. Hispanic citizens. Thus, there is little chance for guestworkers to influence labor policy.

International institutions also can do little to remedy the nonresponsiveness of government officials to their own people. In Mexico, for example, the access that poor workers have to their government is defined by the history of one-party rule in that country.[78] The PRI ruled Mexico for 83 years until the PAN won the presidency in 2000.[79] Throughout that time, Mexico became increasingly neoliberal and, in 1994, entered into NAFTA.[80] When investors have the ability to trump national laws, the voice that citizens have in their government is diminished.

With regard to immigrants and guestworkers, the democracy deficit is even more pronounced. These workers have the right to vote in their home countries, unless those countries do not give expatriates the right to vote.[81] There are many ways, however, that individuals can engage in political action besides voting. Immigrants and citizens, for example, took to the streets throughout the country in May 2006 to make their voices heard on immigration proposals in Congress.[82] Nevertheless, noncitizens are ineligible to vote in the United States and thus have little ability to influence legislation.[83] There may be some opportunities to influence legislation through unions and other activism, but by and large, the political arena is dominated by large corporate interests, further exacerbating the democracy deficit. Indeed, immigration reform will likely be shaped by business needs, thus ensuring expanded guestworker programs into the future.

Generally, representative democracy presumes that governments respond to the interests of their people through representative institutions. This theory is embedded in many of the institutions of representative democracy.[84] Congress and other institutions are intended to represent voters. Most immigrants are unable to vote and influence their representatives in their new or home countries.[85] Foreign visitors, for example, are only here for a limited amount of time and rarely need to be protected by elected representatives.

There are fundamental differences between students, tourists, and workers. A guestworker's stay in a country can implicate many more legal rights and remedies than will tourists' or students' stays. Further, because the State is much more entwined with labor as regulator, employer, and enforcer, as it was during the Bracero Program, there is a need for workers to be able to influence legislation that will directly affect the terms and conditions of their employment.[86] Guestworkers have limited ability to influence legislation in workplaces that are heavily regulated by the government.

In response to the need to have a politically active workforce, many make the argument that workers have freely consented to be guestworkers and thus there is no need for political participation.[87] There are several responses to this argument. First, the bargaining power of guestworkers is likely to be significantly less than that of students or technology workers. Further, students and highly skilled workers have a greater ability to change their status. Finally, these workers have more powerful, organized constituencies to look after their interests than do large, diffuse groups that might advocate on behalf of guestworkers. The agricultural lobby notwithstanding, temporary labor advocates have been relatively less successful in efforts to increase the caps on temporary labor programs for non-farm employment.[88]

There may be guestworker models that provide better protection for guestworkers. Jennifer Gordon has proposed a model of transnational labor citizenship.[89] Gordon looks to unions to provide protection for guestworkers. Unions would certainly provide a good framework for the kind of "global hiring hall" that Gordon proposes, but the ability of stretched unions to provide enough protection to the hundreds of thousands of guestworkers in the proposed federal program is subject to debate. Nevertheless, Gordon is right to see the need for third party enforcement of workplace protections, rather than relying on state enforcement.

## The Problems with the Bracero Program

In the current debate about immigration reform, the term "guestworker" has been used to mean many different things. In order to have a palatable legislative proposal containing what many see as "amnesty" for undocumented workers, a path to citizenship for unauthorized workers has been called a "guestworker" program.[90] Under various versions of these proposals, unauthorized workers in the country would be required to register for a temporary worker program that might lead to legal residency if the worker met certain conditions, such as paying a fine and back taxes and learning English.[91] Unauthorized workers in the United States also face commodification and the democracy deficit. Ironically, though, these workers face fewer obstacles to enforcing their rights than do guestworkers. First, they are more likely to be members of unions because they often have long-term ties to the United States.[92] Although they face the constant possibility of deportation, unauthorized workers are probably aware of the low likelihood of actual worksite enforcement. Finally, unlike workers under current temporary programs, unauthorized workers are not tied to the employer who sponsored them into the United States.[93] Thus, while unauthorized workers certainly face a democracy deficit, the historical evidence shows that temporary worker programs are even more problematic for enforcing rights.

Throughout U.S. history, there have been examples of temporary worker programs that exploited different racial groups.[94] The Bracero Program, as discussed above, formalized a temporary labor system for agriculture. It began during World War I with approximately 77,000 workers needed to address agricultural labor shortages.[95] The Program ramped up again during World War II, but even after the war was over, growers' purported needs for agricultural workers continued.[96] From 1942 to 1964, more than 4.6 million Mexicans were brought to the United States through the Bracero Program.[97] Although they were promised transportation and prevailing wages, they rarely obtained all of these rights.[98]

Moreover, the agreement that was reached between the United States and Mexico encouraged workers to return to Mexico to receive "savings accounts," which was money deducted from their paychecks in the United States.[99] The problem was that many of the workers were not able to obtain access to these accounts and later brought litigation to recover the monies. As described earlier, former Braceros brought suit in federal court in 2002 to recover the withheld funds in a lawsuit titled *Cruz v. United States*.[100] Their claims against the United States, Mexico, and the various banks were met with a variety of worthy defenses such as sovereign immunity of nations, the limited duties owed by banks to depositors, and the statute of limitations.[101] The federal court in Oakland, California dismissed the lawsuit in 2003, but many of the claims based on state law found new life in legislation to extend the statute of limitations under California law.[102] The legislation showed the Braceros' effectiveness in the democratic system well after the Program had been terminated, but it was not until the participants in the Bracero Program were citizen participants in the United States that they had the ability to enforce basic rights.[103]

The Bracero Program and the ensuing litigation display the democracy deficit in plain sight. The Program was a negotiated compromise between the United States and Mexico, with those directly affected by it having little or no say in the process. Both the United States and Mexico had reasons for favoring a temporary worker program, with little thought about how the plan would work in practice. Once conditions failed to meet promised expectations in the United States, the Braceros had no option to exercise their rights.[104]

## H-2A, H-1B, and H-2B Workers

Even though the Bracero Program formally ended in 1964, various temporary labor programs sprouted from the Immigration and Nationality Act of 1965.[105] The most often used of these programs are the H-2A and H-1B programs.[106] The H-2A program is intended to bring workers on a temporary basis to work in agriculture.[107] The H-1B program is intended mostly for technology workers. H-2A programs have been more prone to abuse because of the lesser bargaining power that agricultural workers have compared to other workers in society.[108]

By definition, guestworker programs are temporary and respond to actual labor market needs.[109] Yet, several historical and current guestworker programs have satisfied neither of these conditions.[110] The Bracero Program has been one of the most prominent examples. There also continues to be debate about whether there is an actual shortage of agricultural labor.[111] In the absence of a Bracero Program, Congress enacted a patchwork of temporary labor programs in the Immigration and Nationality Act of 1965 with an alphabet soup of designations (H1-A, H1-B, H2-A, and H-2B) corresponding to the different sections of the Code.[112] Even in these programs, the labor certification process managed by the Department of Labor has been criticized for overstating actual labor shortages.[113] Temporary labor programs to address labor shortages thus have rarely been temporary and rarely in response to actual labor shortages.

The abuses in these contemporary guestworker programs have been highlighted by recent NAFTA complaints. In February 2003, the Farmworker Justice Program filed a complaint under the North American Agreement on Labor Cooperation, the side agreement to NAFTA that protects labor rights.[114] The complaint alleged that federal and state authorities "have failed to implement and effectively enforce the labor laws applicable to agricultural workers under the H-2A program."[115] In April 2005, the Brennan Center for Justice and the Northwest Worker Justice Project filed a NAALC complaint, alleging that H-2B workers had been denied the right to counsel.[116]

The complaint process under NAFTA has had mixed results in enforcing labor standards in North America.[117] Some unions and nongovernmental organizations have given up on the NAFTA process because the labor side agreement merely requires NAFTA countries to enforce their own labor laws, which does not always offer adequate protection to workers.[118] Indeed, the Farmworker Justice Fund complaint floundered because the United States responded that federal law provided little coverage to agricultural workers.[119] The NLRA's guarantees of freedom of association and collective bargaining, for example, do not apply to agricultural workers.[120] Further, many of the protections for H-2A workers in North Carolina were based on state law.[121] As a result, the NAFTA complaint did not get past the U.S. Labor Department.[122]

Possible remedies to address the lack of worker protection might include allowing workers to choose their own representatives in negotiations. Legal alternatives might include bringing a claim under the NAFTA labor side agreement or an international labor rights claim. The theory of this claim would be that, in the negotiations over the guestworker program, the United States and Mexico are failing to protect the freedom of association of guestworkers "to establish and join organizations of their own choosing to further and defend their interests."[123] By not affording guestworkers a voice in the negotiations over the terms of their work in the United States, the United States and Mexico also are not promoting the right of guestworkers to "freely engage in collective bargaining on matters concerning the terms and conditions of their employment."[124] Other international labor rights claims might be brought if the working conditions of the guestworkers fall below accepted international labor standards.[125] In these ways, international labor rights standards could serve to de-commodify labor in the global economy. The commodification problem, however, is only one aspect of the challenge of raising and enforcing labor standards for workers in the global economy.

The Northwest Workers Justice Complaint alleging that the H2-B workers had been denied their statutory right to counsel has been under review by the DOL for more than five years.[126] The NAFTA complaint process provided formidable challenges.[127] Despite the obstacles presented by the NAFTA complaint process, H-2B workers have utilized other avenues to challenge deprivations of worker rights.[128] The Southern Poverty Law Center (SPLC) in Montgomery, Alabama has brought several cases to vindicate the labor rights of H-2A and H-2B workers in recent years, primarily challenging abuse of seasonal forest workers in Montana as well as violations by the Del Monte food company against H-2A agricultural workers.[129] These lawsuits, and numerous personal interviews of H-2B workers conducted by the SPLC, tell a story of exploitation and threats of retaliation or harm.[130] Several workers stated that they were told that they would not be recruited to work again in the United States if they refused to drop the lawsuit.[131]

Although the DOL never acted upon the Northwest Justice Workers' Project complaint, the controversy did spur Senator Bernie Sanders from Vermont to introduce a bill requiring the right to counsel for all employers who utilize the H-2B program.[132] In winter 2008, the bill was referred to committee, where no further action was taken.[133] This episode highlights several of the negative features of guestworker programs. First, the workers are not able to get counsel to enforce their rights. Second, it shows the difficulty that guestworkers have in achieving legislative change, even when they partner with domestic public interest organizations. Finally, the use of international labor tribunals, particularly when they are controlled by presidential administrations which are not friendly to workers, rarely results in rulings favorable to workers. Nonetheless, the workers were able to gain significant moral support from engaging in the NAFTA project.

But a larger question remains. First, should guestworker programs be abolished? All of these abuses exist in temporary programs that, in theory, have worker protections.[134] These programs show the inherent difficulty in enforcing rights of guestworkers because of their lack of voice in their own working conditions. In considering expanding guestworker programs, the lessons of the existing H-2A, H-1B, and H-2B programs should be closely examined. While there may be a place for a truly temporary and seasonal worker program, the reality of the abuses of these programs shows that they are more often used to maintain a cheap, compliant workforce. If the United States has true labor needs in certain occupations, employers in these occupations are likely to persist and call for workers with residency, if not citizenship, so that the workers have a political voice. If actual labor needs exist, then governments should try to fill those needs through expanding the number of lawful permanent resident permits.

Modern temporary worker programs in agriculture have been rife with abuse. Many of the promises made to the workers, such as medical benefits and decent housing, are not kept. The program has sometimes led to the trafficking of workers, including a group of Thai workers brought to North Carolina in 2005. According to Kevin Bales and Ron Soodalter in their book, *The Slave Next Door: Human Trafficking and Slavery in America Today*, a labor contractor in North Carolina calling itself "Million Express Manpower, Inc." brought 30 workers from Thailand to the United States on H-2 visas. When they arrived, the labor contractor confiscated their visas and passports and trafficked them to New Orleans shortly after Hurricane Katrina to aid in the reconstruction of that city.[135] At the same time, in 2007, President George W. Bush suspended competitive bidding in the Gulf Coast, which encouraged a number of unscrupulous contractors to exploit workers.

Even when workers complained about working conditions, there were allegations that the North Carolina Growers Association blacklisted them. This led to a complaint under the labor side agreement to NAFTA. Again, though this NAFTA complaint did not result in a decision, the complaint raised awareness of the problems facing workers in temporary programs. While blacklisting has been outlawed by many states, foreign temporary workers are much more prone than most workers to blacklisting because their employment is often linked to a single employer, or a group of employers. Thus, blacklisting statutes have little impact for temporary workers.

The simple fact of these programs is that the workers in them are considered disposable by employers, and often by other members of society as well. Although complaints with international tribunals have shown few concrete results, as will be discussed later in this chapter, they remain an important element in bringing a human rights orientation to guestworkers.

## Objections to Expanded Guestworker Programs

The language of the current debate makes it clear that guestworkers are being viewed as disposable workers. What Edward R. Murrow said about migrant workers in his 1960 documentary *Harvest of Shame* is also true of many temporary workers: "They are the slaves we rent."[136] This quote highlights the moral problems with "importing" predominantly nonwhite workers into the country to do jobs that predominantly white Americans will not do.[137]

A number of policy and economic objections to guestworker programs can also be raised.[138] In the following sections, I will briefly survey these objections and the arguments used to oppose them. In his administration, President George W. Bush sought comprehensive immigration reform that included a three- to six-year temporary program subject to all labor and employment laws.[139] Here, I turn to how guestworker programs, even those subject to labor protections, are inconsistent with treating workers as full participants in society.

Guestworker programs have often been criticized as bad policy.[140] Along these lines, many scholars argue that such programs do not fulfill their stated objectives.[141] Besides not always working properly, guestworker programs also represent a failure of the political process.[142] Often, labor needs have been addressed based on the political power of the various constituencies rather than actual labor needs. Hence, agricultural worker programs are one of the few sectors of the economy to have temporary worker provisions.[143] Thus, the programs represent capture of the machinery of government by powerful moneyed interests. Further, the interests of workers, both in the United States and in other countries, are lost in the equation. In this way, these programs further the democracy deficit between workers and their governments. When the programs skew actual labor market needs, they negatively affect the workers in the host countries. When the actual conditions of workers are not as promised, the workers in the sending countries suffer. Guestworker programs thus represent a failure of the vision of the political system as more than a plutocratic process for doling out benefits to powerful corporate interests.[144]

The end of the Bracero Program resulted in many of the workers involved in the program working illegally in non-agricultural areas of the economy.[145] This might show that a new, expanded guestworker program would reduce the flow of undocumented workers into the United States. Or, it might mean that workers hired into the United States for one purpose might eventually be working for an entirely different employer than the one for which they were originally hired. Unfortunately, the phenomenon of migration is complex and belies easy solutions. There is no guarantee that new guestworker programs would prevent people from trying to immigrate if they found the requirements too onerous, or if the limits of the program are reached, as has been the case with the H-1B and H-2B workers.[146]

### The Thirteenth and Fourteenth Amendments: Consent and Full Personhood

The Thirteenth Amendment to the Constitution states: "Neither slavery nor involuntary servitude . . . shall exist within the United States, or any place subject to their jurisdiction."[147] The Amendment was passed in 1865 to end the practice of chattel slaveholding by private parties, but it had a much more expansive promise.[148] First, the Thirteenth Amendment applies directly to private action.[149] Further, even with consent of the worker and payment for the worker's labor, the Thirteenth Amendment may still be violated if the worker feels coerced into a state of servitude.[150]

The end of chattel slavery in the United States under the Thirteenth Amendment represented the legal de-commodification of labor by giving workers a voice in their conditions of work and the opportunity to exit oppressive relationships.[151] The importance of the Thirteenth Amendment was not lost on the progenitors of the modern labor movement when they argued that Congress could protect freedom of association and collective bargaining under the authority of section two of the Thirteenth Amendment.[152] While Congress instead used the Commerce Clause as the basis for the right to collective bargaining in the NLRA, labor's broader vision of the Thirteenth Amendment today is again being considered as a means of redressing the conditions of some of the most aggrieved workers in the global economy.[153]

The Thirteenth Amendment challenge to guestworker programs also faces substantive obstacles. First, it does not explicitly protect the right to associate and bargain collectively, although many of the progenitors of the NLRA sought to ground those rights in the Thirteenth Amendment.[154] Second, the Supreme Court has held that the threat of deportation is not sufficient to constitute "involuntary servitude."[155] Nevertheless, several scholars are arguing for a broadened concept of the Thirteenth Amendment to include these concepts, and constitutional history shows that their interpretation may eventually prove correct.[156]

Another frequent justification of guestworker programs is that the participants in such programs freely choose to be part of them.[157] The consent of desperate workers in the global economy should be closely investigated. While the prospect of working in the United States for some period of time and then returning to their home countries might be appealing to some workers, other potential "guestworkers" have many family members in the United States and would like to immigrate permanently. In either case, adding workers without rights can only increase the democracy deficit.

There are also many questions about whether guestworker programs are really needed in the labor market today, and how they will manage future flows of undocumented immigrants.[158] Further, there is reason to wonder how further flows of migrants will be adequately dealt with by future guestworker programs. More importantly, the guestworkers in any program will not be able to exert the influence needed to enforce the laws. They rely on an increasingly taut network of social service and immigrant rights organizations to protect their interests.[159] This was also the case when Congress passed the IRCA, and millions of undocumented suddenly became eligible for citizenship. Eventually, many of those granted residency by the 1986 law became naturalized citizens. A legalization program is unlikely in the current political climate, however, meaning that the guestworkers in the United States will likely remain withou t protecti-ton and a voice in their workplace or in the larger democracy.[160]

As many have discussed, the merits of any guestworker program include a possible decrease in the number of migrants who die while attempting to cross the inhospitable Arizona deserts.[161] It is not clear, however, whether all of the would-be illegal crossers would use a guest-worker program, nor whether a program could accommodate them all. Despite implementation of a guestworker program, the most important variable in border deaths would likely continue to be the ways that border authorities push migrant flows to areas where the chance of capture is smaller.[162] Thus, the effects of a guestworker program on border enforcement are hard to quantify.

### International Labor Rights: The (Missing) Link between ILO Principles and Guestworker Programs

Guestworker programs may violate international labor standards, but there has been little thought about how to square guestworker programs with international labor standards. In one sense, only domestic standards are relevant because the guestworkers will be working entirely within the United States. Nevertheless, the international nature of these transactions calls for more attention to the international standards to which the United States and Mexico have agreed. First, both the United States and Mexico are members of the ILO.[163] In 1998, the ILO promulgated four major freedoms that were conditions of ILO membership in its Fundamental Declaration. These rights are: (1) freedom of association and collective bargaining; (2) freedom from forced labor; (3) freedom from child labor; and (4) freedom from discrimination.[164] These rights are also protected in various ILO conventions, which members can choose to ratify.[165] Conventions 87 and 98 protect freedom of association and collective bargaining, and though the United States has not ratified either of these conventions, Mexico has ratified both of them.[166] The United States has also committed itself to the principle of freedom of association in other conventions that it has ratified, such as the International Covenant on Civil and Political Rights.[167]

NAFTA agreement also contains freedom of association and collective bargaining as principles that each of the three NAFTA countries shall "strive to promote."[168] While the precise nature of this obligation is unclear, it seems to lay the groundwork for a North American labor law regime. Other principles that the countries should strive to promote are directly relevant to guestworkers. Article III of NAFTA requires the three countries to treat migrant workers the same as native workers with respect to labor law enforcement.[169] These rights are directly relevant to guestworkers, but it is very unlikely that the federal or state governments will be able to effectively enforce these laws as required by the NAFTA labor side agreement.

### Recent Guestworker Proposals and the Prospects for Reform

In the current debate over immigration reform, the question of what labor rights would be afforded to guestworkers has gone largely unanswered. In proposing a temporary worker program on January 7, 2004, President George W. Bush stated that he wanted to see Congress pass a temporary worker plan because it would be a more "compassionate" way for immigrants to work legally in the United States: "Decent, hardworking people will now be protected by labor laws, with the right to change jobs, earn fair wages, and enjoy the same working conditions that the law requires for American workers."[170] As history shows, however, even when rights are granted on paper, they are often not available in practice. The failures of the Bracero Program are evidence of the gap between law on the books and law in practice.[171]

The House of Representatives took the opening salvo in immigration reform in December 2005 by passing H.R. 4437.[172] The bill did not contain a temporary worker program, nor did it contain any way for the estimated eleven to twelve million unauthorized migrants in the country to regularize their status.[173] Instead, it called for mass deportations, a fence running the length of the U.S.-Mexico border, and for making all undocumented migrants in the country felons. The House bill was the product of many Representatives acceding to the concerns in their districts about the impact of illegal immigration.[174] Massive street protests took place in cities throughout the country in spring 2006, focusing on the draconian impact of H.R. 4437 and calling for broad-based immigration reform.[175]

In the wake of the House bill, various senators crafted bills that attempt to do more than the enforcement-only approach of the House.[176] The Senate passed Senate Bill 2611 on May 25, 2006, which included an "earned legalization program" that would lead to citizenship for many of the estimated eleven to twelve million unauthorized workers in the country.[177] The Senate bill ultimately went nowhere in the then-Republican controlled House.[178] As passed by the Senate, however, S. 2611 provided no additional labor protections for the estimated 200,000 temporary workers who would come into the United States each year.[179] On May 23, 2006, the Senate rejected Senator Edward Kennedy's amendment to S. 2611 that would enhance enforcement of labor protections for guestworkers and all U.S. workers.[180] These workers would be brought to the country on a three-year visa, renewable one time, to work in any sector where there are "willing employers."[181] This would greatly expand the current temporary worker programs in agriculture and high-tech industries. The congressional debate over immigration proposals in spring 2006 shows that guaranteeing labor rights for guestworkers is not a priority in any legislative proposal for immigration reform.[182] In fact, the bill the Senate passed in April 2006 calls for guestworkers in the new H-2C program to have the same "working conditions that are normal to workers similarly employed in the area of intended employment."[183]

One of the major distinctions in the various bills is whether the guestworkers will be able to petition for permanent residency on their own or whether an employer must sponsor them.[184] Guestworkers in the new H-2C program would be able to adjust their status to permanent resident after four years in the program, regardless of their employer's sponsorship.[185] Guestworkers in the program less than four years would have to petition through their employer. The H-2C program would allow workers to change to other employers within the program.[186]

Recent rulings of the NLRB also make it more difficult to organize temporary workers because they cannot be placed into the same bargaining unit as permanent workers without employer consent.[187] In 2000, the NLRB held in *M. B. Sturgis* that the Board could not certify a bargaining unit that contained both temporary and permanent workers without the employer's consent.[188] The decision was based on the wide latitude that the NLRB had in determining appropriate bargaining units under Section 9(b) of the NLRA.[189] Four years later, however, the composition of the Board changed and a majority of its five members had been appointed by President George W. Bush.[190] In 2004, the Board overruled *M.B. Sturgis* in *H.S. Care, L.L.C.*[191] The Board held that the NLRA does not allow for joint employer bargaining units without employer consent, in this case, a bargaining unit of employees of the temporary staffing agency and the regular employees of the employer using the staffing agency.[192] The decision will affect any attempts to organize guestworkers if they are matched with willing employers through international staffing companies.

In the current climate for organizing, it is unrealistic to think that guestworkers have the same rights as other workers to organize unions.

Indeed, even if they did, that would not be sufficient to have real leverage to bargain with their employers. If guestworkers are dependent on their employers to petition to change their legal status, they are likely to be unwilling to enforce labor rights that they have. Even if workers could petition for resident status in the United States, under the current Senate proposal they would have to work as guestworkers for four years before having that ability.[193] While the Senate's immigration bill would allow guestworkers to change jobs, this is not the touchstone of voice on the job, but rather exit from the job.[194] This will do little to improve conditions for other guestworkers or to prevent the same conditions from repeating themselves at a new workplace. Alternative ways of providing voice to these global temporary workers are needed.

### Alternate Models to Give Guestworkers Greater Voice at Their Workplaces

Guestworker programs may not be workable within the current system of collective bargaining, marked by long delays in the time it takes for the resolution of claims of unfair labor practices. There are new models, however, that might mitigate the negative effects of temporary status. One of these is the pact between the Farm Labor Organizing Committee in North Carolina (FLOC) and the North Carolina Growers Association. In 2004, the FLOC reached an agreement with the North Carolina Growers Association to advocate on behalf of workers in the H-2A program.[195] The pact seeks an end to alleged blacklisting against workers who seek to enforce their rights.[196] Another example is the United Farm Workers Union (UFW) pact with Global Horizons. In April 2006, the UFW entered into an agreement with Global Horizons, a Southern California labor contractor that matches temporary workers with employers.[197] The new arrangement was timely and necessary, apparently, because of an existing federal probe into Global Crossing's abuses of H-2A workers in Hawaii that resulted in a $300,000 settlement.[198]

The FLOC and UFW campaigns to represent H2-A workers highlight the important role that unions and nongovernmental organizations can play in closing the democracy deficit. These programs are incomplete, however, since much of the role of unions today is not simply to bargain for an increase in material conditions but also to involve its members in noncitizen "citizenship" activities such as demonstrations and political education.[199]

Guestworkers should utilize the NAFTA labor side agreement process and international forums to challenge the lack of worker protections and inability to exercise freedom of association. Indeed, the ILO and the North American Agreement on Labor Cooperation have recently focused more seriously on the issue of migrant workers.[200] While these forums are not ideal avenues for quick resolution, they do provide an international spotlight on labor violations that are truly international since the workers themselves are literally crossing borders to work. In this regard, as other scholars have recently written, international administrative legal structures may help to close the global democracy deficit.[201] With respect to guestworkers, there may be a need for an administrative structure specifically created to review claims against employers.

In the end, guestworkers may gain some protection and voice through agreements with nongovernmental organizations and use of international administrative structures. The temporary nature of the programs will always prevent full realization of any rights that are guaranteed. Thus, any new labor immigration program should provide unskilled workers with the option to petition for permanent residency. The expansion of temporary worker programs would only further commodify workers in the global economy through the loss of democracy both at their workplaces (through the inability to enforce their rights) and at the ballot box (through a lack of influence with legislators and government officials).

## The Road Ahead

While the prospects for immigration reform currently are very unclear in the waning days of the first Obama administration, the debate since September 11, 2001 shows that the idea of a guestworker program has broad political appeal.[202] Because of the malleability of the term "guestworker," elements of many proposed guestworker programs may appeal to a variety of different political constituencies. For many employers, guestworker programs mean a steady supply of labor.[203] For some immigrant advocates it may mean a safer, better way for immigrants to migrate to the United States.[204] These are both worthy, necessary goals, but there may be other ways to accomplish them, such as through legalizing the estimated twelve million undocumented workers already here, and through increasing the number of regular visas in all unskilled labor categories and enforcing labor standards.

Whatever the ultimate outcome of the immigration bills in Congress, it seems reasonably clear that United States' reliance on guestworker programs will continue in some form or another. If there is no new guestworker program, it is likely that the existing guestworker programs in agriculture, seasonal work, and high technology will be continued and expanded. Temporary worker programs with no chance of permanent residency in the United States should be resisted. As this chapter has shown, the expansion of guestworker programs will inevitably exacerbate the democracy deficit, lead to more worker abuses, and lead to a greater number of people without voice over the terms and conditions of their work. The lack of voice both at work and in the political process for guestworkers, and the history of labor abuses in such programs, commodifies the workers involved.

The brutal needs of persons who migrate to survive must also be considered.[205] Temporary worker programs provide some economic relief to people all over the world, even if on a temporary basis. This chapter has argued that in order for the transaction to be as fair as possible, guestworkers need to work in concert with organizations in the United States, organizations in their own countries, or both. Ideally, guestworkers would maximize their bargaining power through collective action and the clear needs of U.S. businesses for their labor. In reality, though, as in most situations where there is a surplus of labor, the hiring entities (here, American corporations utilizing immigration law) maintain a great degree of leverage and workers are left to "take it or leave it."[206] For this reason, unless guestworkers can leverage their apparent economic power to seek better conditions, temporary labor programs will ultimately commodify workers.

The free labor system guaranteed by the Thirteenth Amendment is at odds with guestworker programs. The ability to quit at any time is illusory if that means that you will be deported. Worse still, these workers are unable to exercise meaningful voice over their working conditions. Thus, guestworker programs exacerbate the democracy deficit that already exists for noncitizens and other temporary workers in the United States. Unless temporary workers have the option and ability to stay in the country, they will be unable to exercise the rights that are apparently guaranteed to them on paper. Without voice, these workers will be little more than objects of trade in the global economy.

In the wake of Hurricane Katrina in September 2005, the Bush administration took measures it believed necessary to expedite the recovery of the region. The centerpiece of these efforts was the temporary repeal of the Davis Bacon Act, a law which requires prevailing wages for workers on federally funded construction projects. Until legal and congressional pressure forced the administration to reinstate the law to include Katrina recovery projects, President Bush argued that the repeal of the Davis Bacon Act was necessary to get New Orleans "back to work." In the span of a few weeks, large numbers of temporary workers were brought into the region to work on a variety of federal projects.

Throughout the debate over new guestworker programs, the common refrain was that new guestworkers would be protected by the same laws that cover all other workers. Past experiences show that statutory labor and employment laws fail to protect guestworkers. This has an impact on all workers, and especially noncitizen workers. The idea of passing better laws does little to help workers who are outside the usual political processes. Although the international cases that were brought have been less than successful, the idea of bringing international human rights norms to bear seems especially appropriate in the case of guestworkers. These norms, to be discussed in more detail in the next chapter, recall the truth of Max Frisch's statement about the German experiment with guestworkers: "We asked for workers and we got people."

# 6

# A Global Understanding of
# Worker Protection

On January 29, 2009, President Barack Obama signed the first piece of legislation to cross his desk—the Lilly Ledbetter Fair Pay Act. Ledbetter, who stood beside the president at the signing ceremony, had been the victim of pay discrimination as a manager at Goodyear Tire and Rubber in Gadsden, Alabama. Ledbetter found a pay schedule in her mailbox at work one day which plainly revealed that she had been paid less than her male colleagues for nearly 20 years. At the White House signing ceremony, Ledbetter said, "When I filed my claim against Goodyear with the EEOC 10 years ago, never—never—did I imagine the path that it would lead me down."[1]

Ledbetter's journey to notoriety began with filing a charge in the Equal Employment Opportunity Commission (EEOC) under Title VII of the Civil Rights Act. As discussed in earlier chapters, Title VII prohibits discrimination in working conditions, including pay, on the basis of sex, race, and other factors specified in the statute. Discrimination in pay on the basis of gender would also violate the Equal Pay Act of 1963. Ledbetter, like all Alabama residents, had 180 days to file her charge (in 42 other states the deadline would be 300 days) from the discrete act of discrimination to have the right to sue in court. For nearly a decade, the EEOC had followed a "paycheck rule," which restarts the statute of limitations clock each time a discriminatory paycheck is paid. Ledbetter and her attorney apparently relied on this rule, and filed her charge within 180 days of the last paycheck after she discovered the pay discrepancy.

The U.S. Supreme Court decided that Ledbetter's claim was untimely, in an opinion written by Justice Alito for the five-member court majority. Because Title VII charges must be filed within a certain time of a "discrete act" of discrimination, the court essentially put the burden on the employee to discover pay violations. The fact that many employees do not have the ability to discover violations did not change the view of the court majority. Many employers have "pay secrecy" policies that prevent employees from discussing their salaries, which makes it difficult to discern the pay practices of the employer.[2] The result of the decision was to make it harder for equal pay plaintiffs to get their claims heard by the courts.

The Court decided that the claim should have been brought within the first 180 days after the discrimination started, which in Ledbetter's case would have been 20 years ago. The Court majority was not convinced to adopt a different rule, despite the empirical studies that show that most private-sector workers are very unlikely to find out how their salaries compare to their colleagues. Indeed, many employers have policies that prohibit the sharing of salary information, even though many of those policies may be illegal.[3] The Court put the burden on the employee to discover pay discrepancies. The Ledbetter Act reinstated the paycheck rule and the idea that the statute of limitations restarts with each discriminatory paycheck.

Congress responded with the Lily Ledbetter Fair Pay Act of 2009, which President Obama promptly signed. Ledbetter had campaigned on behalf of then-candidate Obama during the 2008 campaign, and appeared in an ad denouncing the Republican ticket for not supporting legislation to overturn the Supreme Court decision in her case. But there are many other parts of the labor movement's agenda that have been stalled or scaled back, including health care reform and labor law reform, and have run aground on the shoals of procedural rules like the filibuster in the U.S. Senate. Yet again, the question of how to make workplace regulation more effective through the legislative process remains unanswered.

Ledbetter's story is significant because at this writing it is the most recent major legislative change to workplace law of the Obama administration. Even with a Democratic Congress and president, the Ledbetter Act represents a limited victory in the battle for equal pay. In this chapter, I argue for ways to implement a global constitution of worker freedom in light of the legislative quagmire that currently exists for marginal workers and is likely to persist for some time. This chapter advocates for greater incorporation of international human rights into American law, and explores the ways that notions of freedom can support greater labor rights. As pointed out through the rest of this book, there are ways that marginalized workers are taking matters into their own hands in spite of the law. These activities also will be important to a strategy that attempts to deal with the limitations of law.

In the previous chapters, I have discussed the various ways in which protective labor legislation has failed to adequately protect marginal workers—particularly those that are caught between different statutory schemes. I have argued that protective labor legislation can be helpful, but is not sufficient, to protect the rights of vulnerable workers. In many of the cases that have been discussed, however, legislation has sometimes been counterproductive to the interests of marginal workers. In fact, we need to view workers' rights as more than just political footballs, but rather as fundamental human rights.

In this chapter, I will suggest how we might get to a place where labor rights are considered human rights. First, this change in thinking will not be easy, since market fundamentalism is an entrenched part of our national psyche. Market fundamentalism is the ideology that the market should be unregulated and will achieve more efficient results that way. The ideology of the market looks with suspicion at regulation. In this book, I have argued that the answer is not more regulation of the kind that we have seen. Indeed, I have tried to make the point that a change is needed in viewing workplace rights not as "regulation," but as fundamental principles of worker freedom. James Pope has discussed this in terms of "labor's constitution of freedom," or the underpinnings of the right to strike and bargain collectively found in the Constitution.[4] Because international human rights principles will play an important role in changing how we conceptualize workers' rights, I term this as a new global understanding of worker protection.

This is not to say that international law should be the upper limit of workplace rights. Part of the problem with statutory regulation is that it is too often frozen in time and is neither protective enough of labor nor flexible enough for business. This book has shown how minimum standards all too often do not apply to marginal workers. But this does not preclude new innovations that might rise above the minimums. The rights that I have been discussing go to the heart of worker freedom. The Constitution consists of a minimum set of guarantees that apply to all workers, regardless of their status. While there are many arguments about the proper level of minimum wages, there should be little argument about the fact that people who do the same job should get equal pay, regardless of gender. The *Ledbetter* case shows that court interpretation of statutory schemes can lead to the marginalization of workers.

## *Lily Ledbetter's Story*

Lily Ledbetter's story provides an example of a legislative fix that came too late. As described above, Lily Ledbetter was a supervisor at Goodyear Tire and Rubber, who worked for Goodyear for 20 years. During her career, she had been subject to various forms of sexual harassment that she had let pass in the hopes of advancement. Eventually, she was able to make it to the rank of supervisor, but as she found out near the end of her career, there was a large disparity between her pay and that of male employees in similar positions. That spurred her lawsuit.

Ledbetter's complaint contained Equal Pay Act and Title VII claims against Goodyear. She filed an EEOC charge on March 25, 1998. Although the record is not clear about the reasons, the Equal Pay Act claims were dismissed in the pretrial stage. Ledbetter went to trial to recover two years of back wages going back to March 25, 1996. The court and the jury decided that when she started on April 1, 1979, she should have been making the same as her male comparator, Terry Amberson. Nevertheless, because of years of inequity, the jury awarded Ledbetter $3.8 million. The trial judge reduced the award, under various accepted theories. Goodyear appealed the entire verdict to the 11th Circuit Court of Appeals, which ruled that Ledbetter's claim was untimely.[5] Ledbetter appealed the case to the U.S. Supreme Court.

The Supreme Court agreed with the 11th Circuit Court of Appeals that Ledbetter's claim was untimely. It rejected the application of an earlier decision, *Bazemore v. Friday*, in which the statute of limitations for actions that occurred in the past were renewed each time the employer issued a new paycheck.[6] The Court ruled that using the *Bazemore* standard for equal pay violations was contrary to the idea that employers should have repose from lawsuits after a certain period of time. Thus, it was up to the employee to discover the equal pay violations, even though many employers prevent disclosure of salary information. Over the dissent of four justices, the majority's decision effectively made most equal pay act claims impossible to win.

Ledbetter's case became a national story, which became more intense in the heat of the presidential campaign when then-candidate Barack Obama rallied to her cause. Ledbetter appeared at a number of events for Obama and also in a commercial critiquing the McCain-Palin Republican ticket for their views on equal pay. Ledbetter's advocacy may have been particularly important to encourage working women to support the

Obama-Biden Democratic option. In the end, Obama won 56 percent of the females voting, while only 49 percent of men voted for the new president.[7]

Soon after taking office, the Democrat-controlled Congress and President Obama followed through with their promises to reverse the Supreme Court decision when Obama signed the Lily Ledbetter Fair Pay Act. The Act states that "an unlawful employment practice occurs . . . when an individual is affected by the application of a discriminatory compensation decision or practice, including each time wages, benefits or other compensation is paid, resulting in whole or part from such a decision or other practice."[8] This essentially reinstates the "paycheck rule," which means that more plaintiffs will be able to bring their lawsuits.

Now that Congress has passed the Lily Ledbetter Act, we might ask whether or not equal pay plaintiffs are still "marginal workers." After all, Ledbetter had the ear of the president and the First Lady in her struggle to overturn an adverse Supreme Court decision. Ledbetter herself might not be marginalized after the bill that bears her name, but consider instead the complications for future women, or more acutely what would have been occasioned by a woman of color plaintiff. As the work of intersectionality theorists shows, women of color are often the victims of multiple forms of discrimination, yet the law fails to adequately address all of these forms of discrimination.[9]

This does not mean that the Ledbetter Act was not a worthwhile piece of legislation. What is more revealing, however, is the rest of the agenda that was not enacted. While the Ledbetter Act will preserve some cases that would otherwise have been dismissed, nearly 50 years of litigation under the Equal Pay Act has failed to completely close the pay gap. This is because of the underlying attitudes of pay discrimination which continue to permeate the workplace. The Ledbetter Fair Pay Act will not change the landscape significantly. A fundamental change of norms is needed regarding gender discrimination in this country, and a more expansive vision of pay equity. In many human rights instruments, for example, equal pay and comparable worth are foundational principles. The European Union, for example, adopts both equal pay and comparable worth into its human rights instruments.[10] While these principles may not close the gap in themselves, they provide an important set of default principles that should guide courts in favor of coverage.

The fight for comparable worth has been seen as one of the defining battles of the women's movement in the 1970s and early 1980s. Comparable worth is the principle that work of equal value, even in different jobs, should be compensated similarly. Comparable worth was one of the rallying cries of the women's movement and part of a litigation strategy to expand Title VII of the Civil Rights Act of 1964. Although one Supreme Court opinion in 1981 seemed to open the door to comparable worth claims, a decision three years later closed the door just as quickly as it had been opened.[11]

The women's movement has not yet retaken the mantle of comparable worth. Even in the favorable political climate in which the Ledbetter Act was passed, a more far-reaching piece of legislation, the Paycheck Fairness Act, did not get very far. The Paycheck Fairness Act is an effort to enhance the remedies under the equal pay act, but it does not resurrect the battle for comparable worth.[12] This shows the difficulty of making the argument through the statute in the contemporary period.

Lily Ledbetter, and her place in the 2008 presidential campaign, is emblematic of pay discrimination as a problem that affects middle-income white women workers, when in fact the pay gap for women of color is even greater than for white women. The bifurcation of race and class that was discussed in the *Emporium Capwell* case in chapter 3 is further exacerbated by gender discrimination in this case. While the statute provides good opportunities to coalesce around the issue of pay equity, deeper issues about comparable worth and the end of pay discrimination will linger, until there is a fundamental change about how we view discrimination. At the same time, there are limits to what can be accomplished through the law, as shown by Michael McCann's study of the pay equity movement. In *Rights at Work*, McCann showed that the pay equity movement used litigation as a foundation to the movement, while building solidarity.[13] Moreover, women in unions are able to utilize collective bargaining laws and grievance procedures to get more information about the employer's pay practices. These are ways that women can work around the limitations of the law.

Ledbetter's case might be considered a victory for marginal workers. After all, she was able to change the law for future cases. It did not affect the outcome in her case, and the fact that it was too difficult to get any reforms other than the statute of limitations indicates that further progress will come slowly and incrementally. Further, most victims of pay discrimination will continue to find it difficult to bring their claims because they cannot even get the data they need to do so. Thus, a change in attitudes about pay discrimination will have to occur, hopefully through social movement advocacy.

## *Social Movement Strategies*

Many other social movements besides worker movements are trying to expand rights. But the best course for workers' rights will not be the same as every other social movement seeking an expansion of rights. Gay rights, immigrants' rights, and other forms of social progress have not only been accomplished through legislation, but through a variety of other means as well. A catalyst for many of the legislative efforts in the gay rights movement were state supreme court decisions favoring the right of same sex marriage in the highest courts of Hawaii and Massachusetts. In California, the right to same sex marriage was established statewide through a state Supreme Court decision in 2006. Voters amended the Constitution to reverse that decision through a ballot initiative called Proposition 8. Now, a federal court challenge to Proposition 8 might be how California adopts same-sex marriage, assuming higher federal courts agree that the Proposition violates the federal Constitution.[14]

In the field of workers' rights, major litigation campaigns have not been part of the social movement strategy. Much like the gay rights movement, there are different ideas about whether to try judicial strategies. As discussed in chapter 2, some scholars have argued that the labor movement should mount a cohesive strategy of litigation and tactics aimed at administrative agencies and the courts.[15] As described earlier, workers may have a more difficult time making legislative changes because the interests of their coalitions are very diffuse. There is a need, then, for guiding principles, rather than simply practical politics or targeted litigation.

Because of the limitations of the law, a new way of conceptualizing workers' rights as freedom is necessary. Now, this is not an all-purpose glove to fit the hands of all the problems facing workers today, but workers' freedom provides an important underlying thread and counter-narrative to market fundamentalism. The right to unionize is undergirded by freedom—the freedom of association, as I have discussed at several points in this book. Antidiscrimination law is premised on the freedom to use one's talents and skills without regard to race, sex, disability, or other arbitrary obstacles. The Thirteenth Amendment prohibition against involuntary servitude provides constitutional protection to free labor. In many instances, freedom undergirds the foundational principles that must be at the heart of an agenda for workers' rights.

In this chapter, I identify three ways to conceptualize labor rights that transcend domestic legislation, and the legal instruments that support them. Each of these principles is already part of a new dialogue in workers' rights. Together, they form a global understanding of worker freedom. In sum, these principles are: (1) employees are workers; (2) immigrants are persons; and (3) workers' rights are human rights. I will discuss each of these in more detail, and how, together, they form a new charter for an understanding of labor rights as fundamental human rights. The strategy that I put forth requires a change in the way that workplace regulation is accomplished.

### *The International Legal System: New Hope or a Dead End?*

First, it is necessary to discuss the international legal system that provides the underpinnings of these labor rights. The International Labor Organization (ILO) was founded in 1919 on the idea that "the labor of a human being is not a commodity or an article of commerce," as stated in its founding document, the Declaration of Philadelphia. The ILO promulgates principles in the form of conventions, which ILO member countries such as the United States are encouraged to adopt. ILO Convention 87, as discussed previously, provides that workers should have the freedom of association "without any distinction whatsoever." While the precise contours of this phrase have never been exhaustively defined, it can have a much broader scope than many cases where courts have construed employee status narrowly. The breadth of these instruments has enabled the AFL-CIO to challenge unfavorable Supreme Court decisions in the ILO. This will be discussed later in this chapter.

In order to broaden the vision of labor rights in American law, the incorporation of international law into U.S. courts is the next step. But there are many obstacles to fully incorporating international human rights. First, many of the treaties and international instruments to which the United States is a signatory are not self-executing. This means that they cannot be sued upon in court without congressional legislation. In this respect, there may be a need for legislation, but there is very little likelihood that this legislation will ever be passed because it would also enable lawsuits against the government for failing to protect the rights of its citizens. However, in the absence of the right to sue, there are other ways of bringing human rights into the courtroom. The Alien Tort Claims Act, a federal statute from 1791 originally intended to combat piracy at sea, can be used to sue for labor violations by aliens whose rights are violated in the United States, as well as those whose rights are violated abroad. The statute requires the court to ascertain "the law of nations," which the Court may do by reference to the international principles, even when they are not self-executing treaties.

This approach has its critics. Many charge that this is an anti-democratic "workaround" of the congressional role of implementing treaties. These international instruments often have been ratified as treaties with the full force of law in any case. Their only limitation is that they do not provide a "private right of action," or the right to sue violators in court. Nevertheless, some scholars and judges have been skeptical of the place of international law in U.S. courts. United States Supreme Court Justice Antonin Scalia has railed against the importation of international law in a number of cases, ranging from affirmative action, to gay rights, to the death penalty for juveniles. In *Roper v. Simmons*, the Court struck down the juvenile death penalty in part because of the international consensus arrayed against it. In dissent, Justice Scalia stated, "the basic premise of the Court's argument: that American law should conform to the laws of the rest of the world—ought to be rejected out of hand."[16]

Even some within the labor movement are skeptical of the full promise of the international legal system. Jay Youngdahl, for example, argues that the focus should be on solidarity and not on rights. Most labor lawyers, including me when I was in practice, never cite international law in briefs to the courts. Thus, the inability to see the human rights dimensions of workplace law also includes labor lawyers and practitioners in the field. This should change. Nevertheless, there is more activity by nongovernmental organizations using human rights in the labor law field. One of the primary groups mobilizing these challenges was the International Labor Rights Fund, now known as the International Labor Rights Forum.

The International Labor Rights Fund was founded in 1988 to bring litigation to redress global human rights. The organization was founded with the assistance of the labor movement and co-counseled with various major labor law firms, including the respected labor union firm Bredhoff and Kaiser. The ILRF was one of the first public interest organizations to bring cases under the Alien Tort Claims Act alleging that U.S. companies and their agents had violated the international labor rights of workers in their employ in other countries. The Alien Tort Claims Act, by its terms, allows for noncitizens to sue for injuries committed against them in violation of the law of nations. Starting in the 1990s, the ILRF brought lawsuits against major corporations for human rights abuses in other countries.

These lawsuits are sometimes criticized on the grounds that they are harming foreign relations and perhaps also harming employment opportunities for workers in those countries.

All of these might be legitimate concerns. But another legitimate concern is that the cause of workers' rights will continue to stagnate in the political process. Human rights will always be an evolving concept, but the international law system provides a baseline and reference point that is a good starting point. Although many international rights are hard to enforce, domestic rights are also difficult to enforce. As a lawyer, I litigated many cases where the fact that there was a statute prohibiting behavior neither deterred employers from engaging in that behavior nor changed the minds of those employers. These limitations of the law are present in both domestic and international systems in the protection of workers' rights.

The Alien Tort Claims Act (ATCA) has been used in a number of cases in foreign countries to hold corporations accountable. For example, in an effort to prevent the ongoing murder of trade unionists in Colombia, ATCA suits were brought on the theory that paramilitaries were in league with corporations like Coca-Cola and Drummond Coal to keep unions out of the factories. If U.S. corporations are found to be complicit in the systematic targeting of union activists, they may be sued in federal civil court for damages for torts committed in violation of the "law of nations." In at least one of these cases, a federal court held that the ILO Conventions on freedom of association and collective bargaining were implicated by the targeting of union members and were thus actionable in the United States.[17] The court held that the ILO Conventions, even though not adopted by the United States, were sufficiently fundamental to give the plaintiffs standing to sue private parties in the United States. Although the decision is somewhat isolated, it can be the leading edge of similar suits, including those brought by aliens in the United States who are denied the right to organize. Noncitizen workers such as José Castro, the fired worker in *Hoffman Plastic Compounds* described at the beginning of chapter 1, are able to bring ATCA suits, which may be more successful than NLRB administrative proceedings.

How will a "labor rights as human rights" orientation change minds? The answer may be found in the civil rights movement. Resistance to the advancement of minorities seemed permanently ingrained to many observers. But through the perseverance and tenacity of countless individuals, the mood of the country became more tolerant of civil rights.

Certainly, there has been plenty of backlash to various aspects of the civil rights agenda. Eventually, however, there has been greater acceptance of civil rights. The same can happen for workers' rights, which were once accepted as articles of faith, but are now seen as, at best, obstacles to be avoided, and at worst, destructive to the nation.

We might see instances like those that occur in Colombia and other foreign countries as aberrations, or more likely as examples of how much better off workers are in the United States. Instead, I argue that these incidents show how far some are willing to go in the name of market fundamentalism. Indeed, while unionists in the United States are not the targets of assassination, the pull of market fundamentalism means that employers will spare little effort to stifle organizing at their businesses. In both cases, the underlying human right is freedom of association.

What about the freedom of employers to speak? There is nothing inconsistent with allowing employers to oppose unionization and speak to their employees. But the extreme coercive tactics used by employers are inconsistent with according human rights and dignity to employees' interests in freedom of association and collective bargaining.

## Public Values in Private Places

Further, it is necessary to bring public values into private places. As discussed earlier, much of the strategy against collective bargaining and antidiscrimination laws is an appeal to these advances as being a threat to freedom. Freedom has a powerful pull as a public value in American society. Collective bargaining is viewed as an interference with the freedom of capital. Some even argue that laws against racially or sexually centered environments impinge upon freedom of speech, and the ban on discriminatory hiring itself is a restriction on the freedom of contract. But there is another vision of freedom that can be advanced. The Worker Freedom Act passed by the Oregon Legislature in 2008 is a case in point. The legislation was intended to give workers the right to "opt out" of captive audience meetings. Employer groups challenged the law as being preempted by the NLRA and a violation of the First Amendment. While not an unexpected line of argument for the employers in these types of cases, the employer freedom over workers continues to be played out. The employees' freedom to not listen to anti-union speeches is pitted against the employers' freedom to speak their opinions to their employees. When balancing these two freedoms, it must be remembered that the employee's freedom is already severely restricted by the practical inability to leave.

Under the market fundamentalist view, the freedom of workers is minimal. The standard liberal notion is that an employee is free to look for other work if the employer discourages collective bargaining or discriminates. This is illusory. While there may be employers not willing to discriminate even in the absence of regulation, many employers see resistance to unionization as fundamental to their rights as market actors. Thus, market fundamentalist ideology is pitted against legislated rights, which are seen as the product of political compromise and log rolling. The Democratic Party is seen as captive to the unions, and so any pro-labor legislation is viewed as illegitimate, whereas market fundamentalism is viewed as an indisputable part of the fabric of American society.

Workers' rights advocates must present a counter-narrative of worker freedom to the narrative of market fundamentalism. The ethic of freedom can be problematic, just as overreliance on rights can be a double-edged sword. Freedom has been misused as an explanation for foreign policies. "They hate our freedom" as an explanation for terrorism, and "spreading freedom" as a justification for U.S. military intervention were part of the Bush administration's standard talking points. However, the idea of freedom should not be discarded because it is misused. Indeed, freedom is the animating ideal in the fundamental labor rights featured in this book. Freedom of association is the basis for the right to organize and bargain collectively. Freedom from arbitrary discrimination, and the concomitant freedom for minorities to integrate into society, is at the heart of civil rights law. And of course, the freedom from involuntary servitude is guaranteed in the Thirteenth Amendment of the Constitution.

While most can agree on freedom as an abstract ideal, the contours of freedom will likely remain essentially contested. There will remain a need for interpretation and regulation. Interpretations of workplace regulation should proceed from the starting point that favors worker protection. This should be the starting point for courts which are adjudicating workers' rights.

But this alone will not change the level of protection for workers. There will need to be litigation and further legislation. The focus of much of the litigation will be immigrants, since the Alien Tort Claims Act applies only to aliens, i.e., noncitizens. But the Alien Tort Claims Act might provide a crack in the door for other interventions of human rights for all citizens.

As discussed, many of the human rights principles that form the basis of a global freedom have been assumed as treaty obligations by the United States. Not all of these rights are self-executing, so the way that many of these principles will be brought in is through advocates reminding courts of these default principles. They can also be brought to bear using the holding of *The Charming Betsy*, an early Supreme Court case which held that statutes should be interpreted in keeping with international law. Scholars have recently begun using the *Charming Betsy* doctrine to argue for expansive interpretations of the NLRA.[18]

### *"Employees" Are Workers*

All of the cases I have discussed in this book deal with statutory "employees"—where there is no dispute that the plaintiffs are covered by the law. Employee status is the dividing line between being covered by protective labor statutes and being completely marginalized, such as farmworkers and domestic workers in states where there are no state law protections. There are also situations when employees are misclassified as independent contractors, though not addressed here. This does not mean that misclassification is not a problem. In fact, the federal General Accounting Office in August 2009 published a study that pointed to the findings of another study which put the amount of misclassification at between 10 percent and 30 percent of the workforce.[19] Besides the obvious impact on government tax revenues, misclassification also leaves many workers without any protection.

By comparison to workers who are outside the regulatory system, the workers discussed in this book have multiple sources of protection. Women of color, for example, are able to bring claims under both race and sex discrimination protections, but it is not clear that that makes them more successful in pursuing discrimination claims. Indeed, a study of government data by sociologists Lauren Edelman and Rachel Best shows that those with "intersectional" claims, drawing upon more than one characteristic for protection, are more likely to be *un*successful in their claims than those bringing claims on either race or sex grounds.[20] This piece of empirical evidence confirms the existence of intersectional disadvantages that critical race and feminist theorists have been discussing for years. This is another illustration of the paradox of statutory protections—the more grounds of protection there are for workers, the more likely it is that these protections will not actually result in more protection. This has been shown in the cases that I have discussed in each chapter of this book, but the Edelman and Best study is one of the first empirical explorations of these phenomena.[21]

As discussed, statutory protection by its nature is politically contingent and focused on particular classes of workers. For example, the minimum wage and overtime laws contain a number of exemptions for workers that hold administrative, executive, or professional positions. The process of putting workers in different categories loses focus on a living wage for all workers. The focus on minimum wages has also taken away from other nonwage benefits that all workers might need, such as paid time off and vacation. It also prevents workers from seeing common interests.

Employee status may be an important dividing line for many purposes, since there are some clear examples of contractors—such as plumbers, performers, and painters— who are often employed by contract. Many of the rights that would apply to contractors would also apply to employees. Nevertheless, the distinction creates many opportunities for mischief. The more distinctions that employers can exploit, the more divided the workplace will be. This makes it harder for workers to see their common interests. Denying the right to unionize to undocumented workers has affected the ability of other workers to unionize. The lack of protection for noncitizens may embolden employers to use citizenship policies to discriminate against people of color with impunity. Having all of these divisions makes it harder for people to see their common interests.

The distinctions between employees and supervisors also destroy some positive collaboration that might benefit all workers. The dividing line between employees and supervisors also makes sense for some purposes, such as in the division between labor and management for the purposes of collective bargaining. But the courts have taken the distinction too far, as the U.S. Supreme Court did in *Kentucky River Community Care, Inc. v. NLRB*.[22] The Court there held that charge nurses were not employees under the statute, and thus not protected by the law of union organizing. Interestingly, in the early years of the National Labor Relations Act (NLRA) there was no distinction between employees and supervisors—both were protected by the Act. There is another section of the Act which makes company unions illegal, which would probably deal with most of the mischief that would result if supervisors were given protection of the NLRA.

Now, after *Kentucky River*, there will be a number of battles over who is a supervisor or not. With so many people made supervisors in the workplace these days, there is much less chance that solidarity will result in the workplace. Thus, statutes and their categories tend to divide workers against what they might see as their common interests. For example, even though managers cannot get overtime under the statute, there may be common interests between exempt and nonexempt employees in involuntary and unreasonable overtime. There is no international human rights standard on overtime or minimum wage. Yet, there are commonalities that all workers share in fair treatment with regard to wages and hours. Statutory categorization is not the way to find these commonalities.

If employees, supervisors, and independent contractors are seen first as "workers," better protection for all who work should ensue. Even if better protection did not ensue, workers might see common interests if statutory distinctions were less important. This might lead to better legislative protection as well. In some countries, employee status is even more expansive. In Mexico, for example, Article 8 of the Mexican Constitution says that a worker is "anyone who does subordinate work for another individual or legal person."[23] This broad definition could capture a greater number of people in the United States within the category of "workers."

It is not an accident that the international instruments protecting labor rights are meant to apply to "workers." While there has been no singular definition of worker in international law, there is reason to think that it is broader than the definition in many statutes. ILO Convention 87, for example, states that workers should have the freedom to associate "without any distinction whatsoever." This shows a preference in international law for broad coverage. Further, there may be value in a more unified standard of applying protections more uniformly to workers. The definition I would propose is that certain rights, such as the freedom to associate and the right to be free from discrimination, should apply to all who work, and not just employees.

Throughout its history, the International Labor Organization has promulgated conventions for its member nations to adopt. Not all of the member nations have adopted them, nor did they always result in better labor standards in the countries that adopted them. China, for example, has adopted Conventions 87 and 98, while the United States has not adopted either.[24] Thus, not all of the member countries ratified enough of the declarations, while those that did ratify did not always live up to the letter and spirit of the Conventions. In 1998, the ILO took a step toward fundamental labor rights when it set forth its Declaration of Fundamental

Principles and Rights at Work, which aimed to make fundamental, four of the rights embedded in various Conventions. These are:

1. The Freedom of Association and the Effective Recognition of Collective Bargaining[25]
2. The Elimination of All Forms of Compulsory Labor[26]
3. The Effective Abolition of Child Labor[27]
4. Elimination of Discrimination With Respect to Employment or Occupation[28]

There are many other Conventions that affect a multiplicity of different work situations, but the ILO felt that these four principles should be binding on all governments that are members, even if they have not ratified the individual conventions that underlie these principles.[29]

The Declaration provides a useful starting point for the theme underlying many of the principles in this book. It is a starting point—not the end of the discussion. Yet, there is controversy about the application of these principles to governments that have not adopted them. The ILO has responded that membership in the organization and in the world community requires adherence to these basic principles. The problem with the ILO has been: who decides when a country is not in compliance?

Other critics would say that U.S. law should not be captive to the decisions of a global body. First, it must be remembered that many of these principles are already part of U.S. law. Second, I am not abdicating the role that American courts play in determining American law. I am arguing that they should take human rights principles into account in making their decisions. The Supreme Court has used international instruments as guiding, rather than controlling, authority in cases involving the juvenile death penalty, affirmative action, and anti-sodomy laws.[30] Thus, it is not new that international law principles have been used in legal decisions.

The strategy that I advocate in this book places a heavy emphasis on the Constitution and international law. This raises a quandary of democratic theory—the countermajoritarian thesis.[31] Legislatures are the central feature of representative democracy, but even legislative bodies are held in check by courts. The countermajoritarian thesis holds that courts should see their roles as limited because in most cases judges are not elected. International law is seen as even more problematic from the perspective of representative democracy. International labor standards are promulgated by organizations that are made up of member states for which the citizenry of various countries had no say in the composition of the members.

These objections miss the representative and deliberative nature of many international bodies, as well as the explicit incorporation of many norms into U.S. law, such as the Alien Tort Claims Act (ATCA), which has been discussed earlier in this chapter. The ATCA provides federal court jurisdiction for violations of international law committed against noncitizens. Federal courts in recent cases have found freedom of association and involuntary servitude to be protected under the statute. In *Doe v. Unocal*, the plaintiffs were Burmese villagers who were forced into labor by the government, allegedly at the behest of a French company and the Unocal Corporation.[32]

Why do the same standards not apply to all persons within the jurisdiction of the United States? The question is answered specifically by the patchwork of statutes that this book has critiqued. The ATCA was passed in 1789 to redress piracy on the high seas, not for the protection of workers. But since the terms of the statute apply generally to "aliens," a number of cases have been brought for violations of international labor law in other countries. These cases have done much to further the kind of labor rights that I have been discussing in this book, but their principles need to be extended to the rest of the workforce.

### *"Immigrants" Are "Persons"*

As previously described, immigrants, both legal and undocumented, are often caught between the margins of law, and rendered invisible to the law in the process. In chapter 1, we saw that undocumented worker José Castro was denied the remedies that other workers would receive, even though he suffered the same injury. These inequities may have constitutional dimensions. Although there is no viable equal protection claim that Castro could bring because of his status, there is a basic inequity in the rights of Castro as compared to other workers. With respect to the ability to attend public elementary and secondary schools, the Supreme Court has held that a student's undocumented status has no relevance to his or her constitutional right to attend school. The Court decided that education was too important to be rationed based on immigration status. "[E]ducation provides the basic tools by which individuals might lead economically productive lives which benefit us all. In sum, education has a pivotal role in maintaining the fabric of our society."[33] Because of this interest, the State of Texas could not deny funding to schools that enrolled undocumented students, consistent with the Equal Protection Clause of the Fourteenth Amendment, which covers not simply citizens or legal residents, but all "persons within the jurisdiction of the United States."

The importance of equal rights in the workplace can be analogized to the importance of education. More importantly, the right to organize unions is another of those "basic tools" to building an economically productive society, and the right of some people to freely organize unions may also benefit us all. Nevertheless, there might be less sympathy for José Castro than for undocumented students trying to get an education. While the children may indeed be more sympathetic figures, the public policies they further are equally strong. There may be many differences between school children and workers, but constitutionally speaking, they are both undocumented.

Recall that in *Hoffman Plastic Compounds, Inc. v. NLRB*, the Supreme Court held that undocumented employees were not entitled to the same remedies as other employees were for retaliatory firing. An undocumented worker cannot receive reinstatement (since employing the worker would be illegal), and the *Hoffman* court held that the pay that Castro would have earned had he not been fired was in conflict with immigration law. Thus, Castro was caught in the margins of these two bodies of law.

The aftermath of *Hoffman* also shows us something about the differences between labor rights in the United States and the international stage. After the decision, the AFL-CIO filed a complaint with the Committee on Freedom of Association of the International Labor Organization alleging that the decision violated ILO Convention 87 requiring governments to protect the freedom of association "without any distinction whatsoever."[34] Convention 98 requires governments to protect the right to bargain collectively. Both of these conventions were cited in the AFL-CIO's petition to the Committee of Freedom of Association (CFA) after the Supreme Court handed down its *Hoffman* decision. The CFA decided that the Hoffman decision did not comport with Convention 87's requirement that governments protect freedom of association "without any distinction whatsoever."

The U.S. government responds that it is not obliged to follow Conventions 87 and 98 because they have not been ratified and accepted by the

Senate like other treaties. Member states in the ILO are not obliged to adopt every convention promulgated by the Organization. In 1998, however, the ILO promulgated the Fundamental Declaration, which held four rights to be fundamental—the right to associate for the purpose of collective bargaining, the right to be free from discrimination, the end of all child labor, and freedom from involuntary servitude. The ILO holds that all member countries should adhere to these principles regardless of whether they have ratified the convention at issue. Further, the United States claims that its law already meets the standards set by international law.

As I discussed in chapter 4, there are many instances in which the Constitution applies to immigrants, whether they are in the United States legally or not. This is because the Constitution's text applies to "persons," and not just citizens. The text of the Fifth and Fourteenth Amendments does not distinguish between those who are here legally or illegally, only those within the jurisdiction of the United States. Thus, personhood, rather than immigration status, is the touchstone for due process and equal protection rights.

When applied to situations in which the government is the employer, as discussed in chapter 6, the application of due process and equal protection rights is clear. As applied to private employers, there are Thirteenth Amendment implications for conditions that arise to the level of involuntary servitude. There are various situations dealing with guestworkers that were discussed in chapter 5 which might rise to the level of involuntary servitude. Undocumented workers also often labor in conditions that approach involuntary servitude, and the Amendment does not distinguish between citizens and noncitizens. It also applies to private entities. Thus, there should be more cases brought by immigrants under the Thirteenth Amendment.

As discussed in earlier chapters, there are a number of ways in which even noncitizens can engage in citizenship activity at work. Jennifer Gordon, documenting her time at the workplace project in Long Island, called the activity "noncitizen citizenship."[35] This included lobbying the New York legislature for stronger remedies in wage and hour law. Also, every year on May Day, large numbers of immigrants march in the streets of many U.S. cities for immigration reform even though many of them are risking deportation. Full personhood allows for a voice in the debates of the day, especially when it relates to the ability to participate as economic citizens.

## Labor Rights Are Human Rights

The debate about whether labor rights are human rights raises other questions about how to best further the interests of workers. Many of the theories advanced in this book self-consciously situate the locus of workers' rights from the legislatures to the courts. Constitutional rights and rights under international law need to be enforced through court action. Many have been skeptical of relying too much on constitutional rights in the courts to create social change. In his influential book *The Hollow Hope: Can the Courts Bring About Social Change?* Gerald Rosenberg argued that as for civil rights, court decisions were not as effective as legislation. Rosenberg's thesis has attracted praise and criticism, but its applicability to workplace law is a lingering question. Perhaps civil rights is something that people can get on board with more easily than labor rights, but in practice there should not be a difference between the two.[36]

There are reasons why some rights should transcend domestic political processes. Political scientists have long discussed the imperfections of the legislative process. Workers are diffuse with competing interests and constituencies. Labor unions traditionally served to marshal these interests as part of coalitions in order to pass civil rights and minimum wage legislation. Now that unions do not represent as large a share of the economy as they did in the past, it is much more difficult to pass legislation.

Critical realism, as I discuss it here, is an orientation that takes a skeptical view of the law's ability to accomplish change. At the same time, critical realism seeks to be realistic about the chances for reform. Particularly in this polarized political environment, it is unlikely that major legislative reform packages will pass. Thus, to effect change, proponents of workers' rights must look to other methods besides the legislative process. These methods will include court litigation, filings in international fora, and the linkage of trade standards with labor standards. While this work will not immediately bear fruit, it is needed to change the dialogue about the centrality of several minimum workers' rights principles. More than particular processes that have to change, there are a number of attitudes that must change as well.

## Changing Conceptions of Freedom

Much of this book outlines a strategy for advocacy in the courts. Nevertheless, long-lasting change will not occur until employers are less resistant to workers' rights. One measure of this resistance has been the proclivity of employers to thwart unionization. A recent study by the Center for Economic and Policy Research found that one of every five union organizers or activists were likely to be fired during union election campaigns.[37] Thus, it is necessary to change attitudes about workers' rights in American culture. While my vision is necessarily American, there may be consonance with human rights campaigns in other countries.

At stake is a vision of freedom and self-realization. As George Lakoff writes, "If the idea of freedom changes radically, then freedom as we have known it is lost."[38] His argument is that this is not a battle over semantics, but a battle for norms, behaviors, and ideals. Opposition to workers' rights has for too long been couched in terms of "freedom of contract," and capital's freedom to move. But these are not the only visions of freedom.

Freedom has for too long been the province of the libertarian right. Ayn Rand and her adherents made freedom from regulation and labor unions the centerpiece of their philosophy.[39] The freedom of capital to move with unfettered abandon is also seen as the cornerstone of American democracy. The freedom of workers to associate, or as President Franklin Delano Roosevelt put it more directly, the freedom from want and the freedom from fear, should be part of the American workplace.

Unfortunately, in many workplaces, there is an abundance of both want and fear. It may not be possible to eliminate want from all workplaces, but it may be possible for employers to strive for a certain minimum level of dignity, in other words, a "living wage" is something that unions have guaranteed and that has been part of movements for the working poor. It may not be possible for every employer to be unionized, but it may be possible to end employer coercion in the employee's choice of bargaining representatives. These two reforms would go a long way to enhancing the freedom from want and freedom from fear.

But statutory minimums, living wage ordinances, and collective bargaining laws have failed to provide adequate wages and benefits to large segments of the population. Thus, the centrality of these rights to enhanced labor freedom must be emphasized. In his essay "Two Concepts of Freedom," Isaiah Berlin noted that freedom from government or other interference is merely the flip side of the freedom "to live up to your full potential and flourish."[40] In the work context, this freedom is necessary for a fully actualized work life.

We must not forget that freedom of association is also specifically referenced in labor law. The National Labor Relations Act, in its prefatory legislative findings drafted and enacted by Congress in 1934, states that the Act should protect the "exercise by workers of full freedom of association, self-organization, designation of representatives of their own choosing for the purpose of negotiating terms and conditions of employment and other mutual aid or other mutual aid or protection." The actual rules of the statute, such as Section 7's protection of concerted activity, are supposed to be interpreted in keeping with that preamble, even if that has not always been the case. Nevertheless, this is one of the few places in a labor law statute where freedom is actually referenced.

Two years earlier, in 1932, Congress expressly repudiated the Supreme Court's freedom of contracts jurisprudence in the Norris-LaGuardia Act. The preamble states that the "individual unorganized worker is commonly helpless to exercise actual liberty of contract to protect his freedom of labor and thereby to obtain acceptable conditions of employment."[41] The Act also expressly outlaws the yellow dog contracts that the Supreme Court approved in its 1915 *Coppage v. Kansas* decision, where an employee agrees at the beginning of his or her employment not to join a union. This new vision of freedom was enshrined in statute.

But somewhere along the way, freedom has lost its way. In a liberal at-will environment, freedom is the freedom to leave if you do not like the conditions you are offered. What the drafters of the Norris La Guardia and Wagner Acts realized was that true freedom was not obtained by just walking out the door in the face of a bad deal. True freedom, as Franklin Roosevelt would tell Congress in his 1941 State of the Union address, is "freedom from want, and freedom from fear," which, translated for the workplace, means having the will to seek to improve working conditions through persuasion, fortitude, and dignity. This is why the principles discussed in this book are framed in terms of freedom, because workers need to be free to associate, to be free from servitude, to be free from arbitrary discrimination, and to be free from retaliation for asserting rights.

## The Role of Unions

The language of freedom has been co-opted to mean "freedom from unions," "free to be an independent contractor," or "freedom to speak about sex in the workplace."[42] "Freedom from unions" is the primary reason employers use to try to persuade their employees against joining a union. Labor law cases are replete with examples of employers saying that the union would "not permit you to talk to us; would come in between us." Supreme Court cases like *Emporium Capwell*, discussed in chapter 3, tend to further that opinion, even if such campaigns do not really use Supreme Court opinions. As also discussed in chapter 3, however, having a union does not mean that employers are prohibited from discussing any matters with employees. Instead, there are a number of ways in which the statute allows some communication between the employees and management, including the proviso to Section 7 and court interpretations of the prohibition of "company unionism" that allows teamwork between labor and management.

The courts have been more willing to recognize some visions of freedom over others. For example, the right of workers to dissent or "not to associate" from their union has been confirmed in cases such as *Chicago Teachers Association v. Hudson* and *Communications Workers of America v. Beck*. In these cases, the Supreme Court couched the right to be a Beck dissenter in the First Amendment, because the union is certified by the government. Although this is a broader notion of state action than accepted in many constitutional cases, it accepts the notion that there are some quasi-constitutional freedoms in the workplace. As such, we can ask if other governmental acts, such as the accepting of government funds, should also impose constitutional norms on employers. These are the kinds of envelopes that need to be pushed to make labor's constitution of freedom a reality.

The right wing has been very effective in couching the opposition to workers' rights in the language of freedom. The First Amendment rights of employers have been used as a bludgeon to the advancement of worker rights. This has allowed employers to hold captive audience meetings and say outrageous things in order to prevent their employees from unionizing. Although collective bargaining has failed workers in particular situations, it is important not to minimize the role that unions play in the lives of marginalized workers. There are numerous examples when unions provided support for immigrants, women, and people of color. These minority groups have enjoyed advantages in wages and benefits. Indeed, a recent survey has shown that union workers in several states have better wages and benefits.[43] The problem is that it will be a long time, if ever, before unions will again be a force in the economy.

The labor movement has put much stock and capital in the political process as a way to return to postwar strength in the economy. This investment has indeed paid dividends to the unorganized workforce, and also to organized labor for setting the foundation for wages and benefits. In the end, stronger and more effective unions are necessary for better worker protection. Unions are a procedural protection that obviates the need for many protective labor statutes, but for unions to be more prevalent, employer resistance must change.

### Recognizing and Framing Worker Rights

How will the values of employers be changed? Although there is no easy answer to this question, we know that employers often see the right to organize as a challenge to their domination of the workplace. Although many employers might see union organizing in their interests, a good number of employers might feel differently about their workforce organizing if it was viewed as a human right. Recent modeling by cognitive psychologists such as cognitive scientist George Lakoff shows that minds can be changed if frames of reference are changed.[44] Lakoff's work has described the need for a dialogue that reframes issues such as global warming as "the climate crisis," and health care reform as "health insurance reform." This may be necessary to change the entrenched interests that resist change in the environmental and health realms.

There has been less attention to the ways that workers' rights have been framed by corporate interests. While this happens on an ongoing basis in union election campaigns every day, it is useful to think about how workers' rights have been framed as "special interests" and for the benefit of "union bosses." Typical employer arguments include how the union will take all of the employees' wages and give them nothing in return. They also argue that the union is simply trying to ruin the employer for its own ends. Despite the illogic of these statements, they are sometimes effective at reversing support for the union.

The framing of unions as greedy self-interested parties has also become the dominant trope in contemporary politics. Strikes are often depicted as an affront by well-taken care of union workers to other employees in the economy who do not have as much. Like many other high-profile strikes, the Southern California grocery strike of 2002 had many non-union workers complaining that the striking grocery workers were selfish to try to maintain their health care coverage without co-pays in this economy. Many workers outside the grocery industry complained to the media, "I have to pay for my health care; I don't see why they shouldn't." Public employees are also seen as a "special interest" in Sacramento and many other state capitals.

These public perceptions make it harder for the labor movement to lobby for improvements to labor law which might benefit all working people. Public employee unions, for example, are often pilloried in politics as the "prison guards who run the state." Although the corrections officers are a powerful union in California and other states, it does not follow that all public employee unions wield the same kind of power. Teachers, school employees, and transit workers, to name a few, have less power than the image of public employees in the media raiding the public fisc.

Nothing here is meant to limit the recognition of other human rights at work. For example, health and safety is also a human right. We could spend a long time talking about the failings of the Occupational Safety and Health Administration of 1970 (OSHA). There are many ways in which the statutory system has failed marginal workers. First, the statute does not provide for a private right of action, and instead relies on administrative enforcement. Second, even if an employee is the victim of retaliation for making a complaint about a health and safety issue, he or she must rely on the U.S. Department of Labor to file a lawsuit.

There are a number of ways that the statutory process could be considered inadequate. Indeed, health and safety are international human rights under a number of different international instruments. The principles that I have discussed are applicable to a wide range of issues in the modern workplace.

## Nonlegislative Options

The fact that legislative change has failed to produce much change for workers may lead to other options, such as executive actions. This route has been tried in the battle for labor law reform. When the attempt to get a striker replacement bill in Congress failed in the 1990s, the labor movement turned to President Clinton to at least obtain an executive order to ban private contractors from using striker replacements when they get government contracts. President Clinton ultimately did pass the executive order, but it was successfully challenged in court by the Chamber of

Commerce on the grounds that it was preempted by federal labor law.[45] These episodes have suggested that even unilateral action to protect workers' rights has not been successful. This is in part because of the heavily politicized environment in which much of the activity is contained.

### *Equal Pay: An Incomplete Agenda*

The Ledbetter Act was an incremental improvement in the long struggle for equal pay. But that was only part of a larger litigation agenda aimed at closing the pay gap. 45 years after the passage of the Equal Pay Act, the pay gap has failed to fully close, especially for women of color. This is why the Paycheck Fairness Act was proposed at the same time. This act would make a variety of changes to put the Equal Pay Act on the same footing as Title VII, by allowing winning plaintiffs to obtain compensatory and punitive damages.[46]

While these improvements may someday be enacted into law, in the meantime there will be many lesser known plaintiffs than Lily Ledbetter that fall through the margins. Many of these plaintiffs will be women of color, only further compounding the disadvantage that these women face in the workplace. The fact that there is still a significant disparity between the wages of women of color and white women shows that legislation has failed to change the gap. As with many of the problems that I have discussed in this book, law is necessary but not sufficient to deal the problems of marginal workers. Attitudinal changes are necessary as well.

### *Conclusion: The Failure of Politics to Protect Marginal Workers*

When it was first proposed during the Bush administration, the Employee Free Choice Act (EFCA) was seen as the last great hope to revive the labor movement. Whether the legislation will ever pass is something that cannot be answered right now. Even if EFCA does pass, a question will remain as to why it was ever necessary. As discussed in chapter 3, many of the rights included in the EFCA are already in the Act. The right for a union to be recognized upon a "showing of majority support" within the bargaining unit is within the text of the statute. But as described in chapter 2, the right of the employer to demand a secret ballot election is not in the statute itself, but was something that was created as a litigation strategy to get another right (bargaining orders for unfair labor practices).

The Employee Free Choice Act aims to change the hardened view that an election is always needed to get a union in the workplace. It also seeks to increase penalties for unfair labor practices and make bargaining a first contract easier. The forces opposing the law have made the debate about democracy and freedom. Yet, the proponents of the law have not made the case for freedom of association as a fundamental right. Most observers now agree that federal labor law reform is not going to happen anytime soon.

One of the other stated policy goals of the Obama administration has been immigration reform. This agenda met stiff resistance and has at various times looked in grave doubt. Even if it does pass, there is little to no chance that "comprehensive immigration reform" will include enhanced labor and employment protections for immigrants, whether they are documented or not. While Latinos/as might have the political capital necessary to get some immigration reform legislation passed, business support is needed to pass immigration reform. It is very unlikely that the Chamber of Commerce and other business lobbyists will be interested in supporting immigration reform if it includes greater labor protections for immigrant workers.

As a result of the labor movement's collapse, the back stop of statutory rights must remain robust. But while the Obama administration has accomplished several things by executive order, such as the expansion of leave for domestic partners, there is much that cannot be done, even by executive order. For example, two of President Barack Obama's nominees faced the politics of the anti-labor movement head on. Errol Southers was picked by the president to lead the Transportation Security Administration (TSA). Southers's nomination looked to be approved until he seemed to support the right of TSA workers to unionize. This led Republicans to oppose his nomination and hold the nomination. The fight to confirm Southers was not helped by the nominee's missteps in the application process. Nevertheless, the willingness of the Republicans in Congress to leave the position vacant in order to ensure that TSA officers did not get the right to unionize shows the lengths that many who oppose labor rights will go to ensure that they are not expanded.

Similar rancor surrounded the nomination of Craig Becker to the National Labor Relations Board. Becker, a former law professor and lawyer for the Service Employees International Union, was nominated by President Obama in July 2009 to be part of the five-member body that interprets the National Labor Relations Act, even though the Board had been operating since 2007 with only two members. Becker's nomination had been held by Senator John McCain (R-AZ), who with other Senate Republicans was concerned that Becker would implement the proposed Employee Free Choice Act through administrative fiat. Despite the practical impossibility of that happening, senators continued to make it hard to confirm the nominee. Many wondered whether Becker's main disqualifying characteristic was that he was a union lawyer, rather than simply being a Democrat, since there is a tradition for each party to have some nominees on the Board. When Democrats are in power, for example the majority of the Board members (including the Chair) are Democratic appointees, but two slots are reserved for Republicans. Becker's nomination languished in the Senate, unable to break a filibuster, which included two Democratic senators voting with the Republicans to prevent Becker from getting a majority vote on the Senate floor.

The fact that two well-qualified nominees like Becker and Southers could not get Senate approval shows the big task facing those who would argue, as I have in this book, for expanded worker rights. That task will not be an easy one. But I think these heavily politicized examples show that the legislative arena is unlikely to produce real change for marginal workers. Because many Democrats supported the continued filibuster of Becker's nomination, or failed to rally around Southers and other nominees, suggests that labor rights may not be their highest priority. The Employee Free Choice Act is another example of the inability to count on the political party of the legislator to predict support for their legislation.

The remaking of the workplace through law is incomplete. Although statutory change has improved the lot of many workers, there also have been negative effects from legislation. The answer is not necessarily the end of legislation, but a more holistic approach to lawmaking that is more protective of workers. Courts too should construe statutes in keeping with the fundamental human rights norms that protect workers. But it is hard to put faith in these institutions when they have come up short in many previous instances. Thus, much of the change we need to see in the protection of workers is change in the way we view workers' rights. Instead of seeing workers' rights as politically contingent on who is in control of the government, a human rights orientation says that some baselines are nonnegotiable—that no one should be kept in a condition of servitude, that people should have the freedom of association and be free from arbitrary discrimination. There is a common thread running through these principles—worker protection and the freedom that comes with it. And while protection is an essentially contested concept, it is well past time that the ideology of market freedom was countered with a philosophy of labor freedom.

The examples of marginal workers that I have discussed here have been among the most vulnerable members of our society: including undocumented workers, noncitizens, and racial minorities. Nevertheless, their lack of protection affects all workers, or at least those who wish to take a stand in the workplace, who wish to redress workplace discrimination or to change workplace law. Taken together, that accounts for a very large portion of the workforce. Once we start seeing the connections between different groups of workers, real change for all workers has a fighting chance.

# Notes

PREFACE

1. See, e.g., Stuart Scheingold and Austin Sarat, *Cause Lawyers and Social Movements* (Stanford: Stanford University Press, 2006).

2. See Thomas Geoghean, *Which Side Are You On? Trying to Be for Labor When It's Flat on Its Back* (New York: Farrar, Straus, and Giroux, 1991).

3. The study was published in 54 *Hastings Law Journal* 71 (2002).

4. Kathleen M. Erskine and Judy Marblestone, "The Movement Takes the Lead: The Role of Lawyers in the Struggle for a Living Wage in Santa Monica, California," in Sarat and Scheingold, *Cause Lawyers and Social Movements*, 249 (describing the role of lawyers in the Santa Monica living wage campaign). See also Stephanie Luce, *Fighting for a Living Wage* (Ithaca, NY: Cornell University Press, 2004).

5. See Noah Zatz, "The Minimum Wage as a Civil Rights Protection: An Alternative to Anti-Poverty Arguments?" *University of Chicago Legal Forum* 1 (2002).


CHAPTER 1

1. Catherine L. Fisk and Michael Wishnie, "The Story of *Hoffman Plastic Compounds, Inc. v. NLRB*: Labor Rights Without Remedies for Undocumented Immigrants," in Laura J. Cooper and Catherine L. Fisk, eds., *Labor Law Stories* (New York: Foundation Press, 2005).

2. Ibid.

3. See Hector L. Delgado, *New Immigrants, Old Unions: Organizing Undocumented Workers in Los Angeles* (Philadelphia: Temple University Press, 1994); Ruth Milkman, *L.A. Story: Immigrant Workers and the Future of the U.S. Labor Movement* (New York: Russell Sage, 2006), 85, table 2.1.

4. *Hoffman Plastic Compounds, Inc. v. NLRB*, 535 U.S. 137, 151 (2002).

5. U.S. Immigration and Customs Enforcement, ICE Fiscal Year 2007, Annual Report at 8.

6. See *Transcript of Oral Argument, Hoffman Plastic Compounds v. NLRB*, 2002, WL 77224 at 17.

7. *Hoffman Plastic Compounds, Inc. v. NLRB*, 535 U.S. at 152.

8. See, e.g., James B. Atleson, *Values and Assumptions in American Labor Law* (Amherst: University of Massachusetts Press, 1983); Karl E. Klare, "Critical Theory and Labor Law," in David Kairys, *The Politics of Law: A Progressive Critique*, 2d ed. (New York: Basic Books, 1993).

9. See Marley Weiss, *"Kentucky River* at the Intersection Between Professional and Supervisory Status—Fertile Crescent or Bermuda Triangle," in Laura M. Cooper and Catherine L. Fisk, eds., *Labor Law Stories* (New York: Foundation Press, 2005), 353.

10. See Kevin R. Johnson, *Opening the Floodgates: Why America Needs to Rethink Its Borders and Immigration Laws* (New York: New York University Press, 2007); Victor Romero, *Alienated: Immigrant Rights, the Constitution and Equality in America* (New York: New York University Press, 2005).

11. Milkman, *L.A. Story*; Hector Delgado, *New Immigrants, Old Unions* (Greenwood, CO: Edgewood Press, 1986).

12. For example, realist forefather Felix Frankfurter wrote the definitive work on the Labor Injunction in 1930. His book formed the research for the Norris-La Guardia Act, passed by Congress in 1932.

13. See, e.g., *Vegelhan v. Guntner,* 167 Mass. 92, 44 N.E. 1077 (1896).

14. See William E. Forbath, *Law and the Shaping of the American Labor Movement* (Cambridge, MA: Harvard University Press, 1991).

15. *Coppage v. Kansas,* 236 U.S. 1 (1915).

16. See Alexander Tsesis, *The Thirteenth Amendment and American Freedom: A Legal History* (New York: New York University Press, 2004), 7; James G. Pope, "The Thirteenth Amendment versus the Commerce Clause: Labor and the Shaping of American Constitutional Law, 1921–1957," 102 *Columbia Law Review* 1 (2002); Risa L. Goluboff, *The Lost Promise of Civil Rights* (Cambridge, MA: Harvard University Press, 2007).

17. See *N.L.R.B. v. Jones & Laughlin Steel Corp.,* 301 U.S. 1 (1937).

18. See Cynthia Estlund, "The Ossification of American Labor Law," 102 *Columbia Law Review* 1527 (2002).

19. See Paul C. Weiler, *Governing the Workplace: The Future of Labor and Employment Law* (Cambridge, MA: Harvard University Press, 1990).

20. See Ellen J. Dannin, *Taking Back the Workers' Law: How to Fight the Assault on Labor Rights* (Ithaca, NY: Cornell ILR Press, 2006).

21. Klare, "Critical Theory and Labor Relations Law"; and Atleson, *Values and Assumptions in American Labor Law.*

22. *Citizens United v. Federal Election Commission,* Feb. 3, 2010, Slip. Op.

23. Beth Shulman, *The Betrayal of Work: How Low-Wage Jobs Fail More Than 30 Million Americans* (New York: New Press, 2003).

24. Peter Gosselin, *High Wire: The Precarious Financial Lives of American Families* (New York: Basic Books, 2008), 3 (describing how the United States as a whole became richer while many families became poorer).

25. See General Accounting Office Report, "Wage and Hour Division's Complaint Intake and Investigative Processes Leave Low Wage Workers Vulnerable to Wage Theft," March 25, 2009; see also Kim Bobo, *Wage Theft in America: Why Millions of Working Americans Are Not Getting Paid and What We Can Do About It* (New York: New Press, 2009).

26. Robert Pollin and Stephanie Luce, *The Living Wage Movement* (Ithaca, NY: Cornell/ILR Press, 2005); Eileen Applebaum, Annette D. Bernhardt, and Richard J. Murnane, *Low Wage America: How Employers Are Reshaping Opportunity in the Workplace* (New York: Russell Sage, 2006), 1 ("In 2001, about 27.5 million Americans, 23.9

percent of the work force, earned less than $8.70 an hour." (citing Mishel, Bernstein, and Boushey, *The State of Working America* (Washington, DC, 2003), table 2.9).

27. Similar prevailing wage statutes such as the Davis-Bacon Act which apply to federal government contractors also represent a small subset of employers.

28. *Ricci v. DeStefano*, 530 F.3d 87 (2d Cir. 2008) *rev'd.* 129 S.Ct. 894 (2009).

29. Stuart Scheingold, *The Politics of Rights: Lawyers, Public Policy and Political Change*, 2d ed. (Ann Arbor: University of Michigan Press, 2004); Mark Tushnet, "An Essay on Rights," 62 *Texas Law Review* 1363 (1984); Kimberlé W. Crenshaw, "Race, Reform and Retrenchment: Transformation, Legitimation in Antidiscrimination Law," 101 *Harvard Law Review* 1363 (1988).

30. See Richard Delgado and Jean Stefancic, *Critical Race Theory: An Introduction* (New York: New York University Press, 2002).

31. See, e.g., Teresa A. Sullivan, *Marginal Workers, Marginal Jobs: The Underutilization of American Workers* (Austin: University of Texas Press, 1978).

32. For a recent book articulating a coherent framework to workplace regulation, see Stephen W. Befort and John W. Budd, *Invisible Hands, Invisible Objectives: Bringing Workplace Law and Public Policy Into Focus* (Stanford, CA: Stanford University Press, 2009).

33. Jennifer Jihye Chun, Organizing at the Margins: The Symbolic Politics of Labor in the United States and Korea (Ithaca, NY: Cornell University Press, 2009).

34. Bob Dylan, *100 Songs: Words and Pictures* (London: Omnibus Press, 2010).

CHAPTER 2

1. Mark Tushnet, "An Essay on Rights," 62 *Texas Law Review* 1363 (1984).

2. Mary Ann Glendon, *Rights Talk: The Impoverishment of Political Discourse* (New York: Free Press, 1983).

3. Ibid., at 115.

4. See *Pattern Makers League of North America, AFL-CIO v. NLRB*, 473 U.S. 95 (1985) (union members can resign during a strike); *Communications Workers of America v. Beck*, 487 U.S. 735 (1988) (union members can change their status to "agency fee payers" and be responsible only for the costs of grievance administration and collective bargaining).

5. See James A. Gross, ed., *Worker Rights As Human Rights* (Ithaca, NY: Cornell University Press, 2003); Lance A. Compa and Stephen E. Diamond, *Human Rights, Labor Rights, and International Trade* (Philadelphia: University of Pennsylvania Press, 1996).

6. Jay Youngdahl, "Solidarity First: Labor Rights Are Not the Same as Human Rights," 18 *New Labor Forum* 31 (Winter 2009).

7. Lance Compa, "Solidarity and Human Rights," 18 *New Labor Forum* 39 (Winter 2009); see also Patricia J. Williams, *The Alchemy of Race and Rights: Diary of a Law Professor* (Cambridge, MA: Harvard University Press, 1990).

8. For a modern take on this, see Maria L. Ontiveros, "Labor Union Coalition Challenges to Governmental Action: Defending the Civil Rights of Low-Wage Workers," 2009 *University of Chicago Legal Forum* 103.

9. James G. Pope, "The Thirteenth Amendment versus the Commerce Clause: Labor and the Shaping of American Constitutional Law, 1921–1957," 102 *Columbia Law Review* 1 (2002).

10. See *West Coast Hotel v. Parrish*, 300 U.S. 379, *N.L.R.B. v. Jones & Laughlin Steel Corp.*, 301 U.S. 1 (1937).

11. "Immigrant Rights and the Thirteenth Amendment," 16 (2) *New Labor Forum* 26 (2007); "Noncitizen Immigrant Labor and the Thirteenth Amendment: Challenging Guest Worker Programs" (Symposium: A New Birth of Freedom: The Thirteenth Amendment—Past, Present and Future), 38 *University of Toledo Law Review* 923 (2007)."Immigrant Workers' Rights in a Post-Hoffman World: Organizing Around the Thirteenth Amendment," 18 *Georgetown Immigration Law Journal* 651 (2004).

12. Walter Olson, *The Excuse Factory, How Employment Law Is Paralyzing the American Workplace* (New York: Free Press, 1997).

13. Kevin M. Clermont and Stewart J. Schwab, "Employment Discrimination Plaintiffs in Federal Court: From Bad to Worse," 3 *Harvard Journal of Law and Public Policy* 103 (2009).

14. Thomas Geoghegan, *See You in Court: How the Right Made America a Lawsuit Nation* (New York: New Press, 2009).

15. *NLRB v. Jones & Laughlin Steel Corp.* 301 U.S. (1937).

16. David E. Bernstein, *Only One Place of Redress: African Americans, Labor Regulation and the Courts, From Reconstruction to the New Deal* (Durham, NC: Duke University Press, 2001).

17. Paul Frymer, *Black and Blue: African Americans, the Labor Movement and the Decline of the Democratic Party* (Princeton, NJ: Princeton University Press, 2007), 77.

18. Ellen Dannin, *Taking Back the Workers' Law: How to Fight the Assault of Labor Rights* (Ithaca, NY: Cornell University Press, 2007).

19. See Richard Delgado and Jean Stefancic, *Critical Race Theory: An Introduction* (New York: New York University Press, 2001).

20. Lewis Maltby, *Can They Do That? Retaking Our Fundamental Rights in the Workplace* (London: Portfolio Group, 2009).

21. 29 U.S.C. S 158c, emphasis added.

22. See Dannin, *Taking Back the Workers' Law*, at 109–10; Paul Secunda, "Toward the Viability of State-Based Legislation to Address Workplace Captive Audience Meetings in the United States," 29 *Comparative Labor Law and Policy Journal* 125–27 (2008).

23. See *Chamber of Commerce v. Brown*, 128 S.Ct. 2408 (2006).

24. Peter Gabel, "The Phenomenonology of Rights-Consciousness and the Pact of the Withdrawn Selves," 62 *Texas Law Review* 1563 (1984).

25. Angela Harris, "Foreword: Jurisprudence of Reconstruction," 82 California Law Review 741 (1994).

26. See Deborah C. Malamud, "The Story of *Steele v. Louisville & Nashville Railroad Co.*: White Unions, Black Unions and the Struggle for Racial Justice on the Rails," in *Labor Law Stories*, Laura M. Cooper and Catherine L. Fisk, eds. (New York: Foundation Press, 2005), 55.

27. Richard Delgado, "A Comment on Rosenberg's New Edition of *The Hollow Hope*," 103 *Northwestern University Law Review Colloquy* 147 (2008).

28. Gross, *Workers' Rights as Human Rights*.

29. Rebecca E. Zietlow, *Enforcing Equality: Congress, the Constitution, and the Protection of Individual Rights* (New York: New York University Press, 2006).

30. See Christopher R. Martin, *Framed! Labor and the Corporate Media* (Ithaca, NY: Cornell University Press, 2004), 12; Michael Parenti, *Inventing Reality: The Politics of Mass Media* (New York: St. Martin's Press, 1986), 85–86.

31. See, e.g., Sylvia Allegretto, Ary Amerikaner, and Steven Pitts, Data Brief, Black Unemployment in June 2010, U.C. Berkeley Labor Center, July 2, 2010.

32. Roger David Waldinger and Michael Ira Lichter, *How the Other Half Works: Immigration and the Social Organization of Labor* (Berkeley: University of California Press, 2003); Leticia Saucedo, "Addressing Segregation in the Brown Collar Workplace: Toward a Solution for the Inexorable 100%," 41 *University of Michigan Journal of Law Reform* (2008).

33. See Ruben J. Garcia, "Toward Fundamental Change for the Protection of Low-Wage Workers: The 'Labor Rights are Human Rights' Debate in the Age of Obama," *University of Chicago Legal Forum* 421 (2009).

34. Michael Zweig, *What's Class Got to Do with It?* (Ithaca, NY: Cornell University Press, 2004).

35. 304 U.S. 308, 332–33 (1938).

36. See Dannin, *Taking Back the Workers' Law*, 87–88; Clyde Summers, quoted at Dannin, p. 88.

37. Dannin, *Taking Back the Workers' Law*, 87.

38. Julius G. Getman and Thomas C. Kohler, "The Story of *NLRB v. Mackay Radio & Telegraph Co.*: The High Cost of Solidarity" (2006), in *Labor Law Stories*, supra, at p. 50.

39. Ibid., n. 80.

40. See Julius G. Getman, *The Betrayal of Local 14* (Ithaca, NY: Cornell University Press, 1999), 103.

41. Ibid.

42. Ibid., quoting Executive Order 12954, 60 Fed. Reg. 13023 (1995).

43. *Chamber of Commerce v. Reich*, 74 F.3d 1322 (D.C. Cir. 1996).

44. See *Edward J. DeBartolo Corp. v. Fla. Gulf Coast Bldg. & Constr. Trades Council*, 485 U.S. 569 (1988); *United States v. Granderson*, 511 U.S. 39 (1994).

45. Karl Llewllyn, "Remarks on the Theory of Appellate Decision and the Rules Canons of about How Statutes Are to Be Construed," 3 *Vanderbilt Law Review* 395 (1950).

46. Steve Greenhouse, "U.S. Cracks Down on 'Contractors' as a Tax Dodge," *New York Times*, Feb. 18, 2010, at A1, A3.

47. See Peggie Smith, "The Publicization of Home-Based Care Work in State Labor Law," 92 *Minnesota Law Review* 1390 (2007); Noah D. Zatz, "Working Beyond the Reach and Grasp of Employment Law," in *The Gloves-Off Economy: Workplace Standards at the Bottom of America's Labor Market*, Annette Bernhardt et al., eds. (Ithaca, NY: Cornell University Press, 2007), 31–64.

48. Christopher Brown, "Union Speaker Says Worker Misclassification Attracting Interest from Enforcers," *Daily Labor Report* (BNA), July 9, 2010.

49. See George Lakoff, *Whose Freedom? The Battle over America's Most Important Idea* (New York: Farrar, Straus, and Giroux, 2005).

50. See Cass R. Sunstein, *FDR's Unfinished Revolution and Why We Need It More Than Ever* (New York: Basic Books, 2004), ix.

## CHAPTER 3

1. Tables Containing Record Counts Generated from the Southeast Asian Combat Area Casualties Current File (CACF), http://www.archives.gov/research/vietnam-war/casualty-statistics.html#year.

2. 420 U.S. at 51.

3. Elizabeth M. Iglesias, "Structures of Subordination: Women of Color at the Intersection of the NLRA and Title VII. Not!" 28 *Harvard Civil Rights and Civil Liberties Law Review* 395–503 (1993); Marion Crain, "Whitewashed Labor Law, Skinwalking Unions," 23 *Berkeley Journal of Employment and Labor Law* 211 (2002).

4. Karl Klare, "Critical Theory and Labor Relations Law, in *The Politics of Law: A Progressive Critique* (New York: Pantheon Books, 1982).

5. *Boys Markets v. Retail Clerks Local 770*, 398 U.S. 235 (1970).

6. 361 U.S. 477, 511 (1960).

7. See, e.g., Philip S. Foner, *Organized Labor and the Black Worker, 1619–1973* (New York: International Publishers, 1974); *Labor Divided: Race and Ethnicity in United States Labor Struggles, 1835–1960* (New York: SUNY Press, 1989) (Robert Asher and Charles Stephenson, eds., 1990); David Roediger, *The Wages of Whiteness: Race and the Making of the American Working Class* (New York and London: Verso, 1991).

8. See Paul Frymer, *Black and Blue: Race, African Americans and the Democracy* (Princeton, NJ: Princeton University Press, 2009).

9. Dan Georgakas and Marvin Surkin, *Detroit: I Do Mind Dying* (Cambridge: South End Press, 1999), 43.

10. Herbert Hill, "Black Workers, Organized Labor and Title VII of the 1964 Civil Rights Act: Legislative History and Legislative Record," in *Race in America: The Struggle for Equality*, Herbert Hill and James E. Jones Jr., eds. (Madison: University of Wisconsin Press, 1993), 263, 289; Charles Denby, *Autocracy and Insurgency in Organized Labor* (Edison, NJ: Transaction Publishers, 1972).

11. Georgakas and Surkin, *Detroit*, at 43, 51.

12. 323 U.S. 192 (1944).

13. See Frymer, *Black and Blue*, 19.

14. 29 U.S.C. § 159(e)(1).

15. Adrienne E. Eaton and Jill Kriesky, "Union Organizing Under Neutrality and Card Check Agreements," 55 *Industrial and Labor Relations Review* 42 (2001).

16. Larry Tye, *Rising from the Rails: Pullman Porters and the Making of the Black Middle Class* (New York: Henry Holt, 2004), 233.

17. *Emporium Capwell*, 420 U.S. at 61.

18. 485 F.2d 917 (D.C. Cir. 1973).

19. 485 F.2d at 932 (Wyzanski, dissenting).

20. 420 U.S. at 61 n.12.

21. Ibid.

22. *NLRB v. Washington Aluminum Co.*, 370 U.S. 9 (1962).

23. 370 U.S. at 12.

24. *NLRB v. Local 1229, International Brotherhood of Electrical Workers* (Jefferson Standard), 346 U.S. 464 (1953).

25. *Western Addition Cmty. Org v. NLRB*, 485 F.2d 917 (D.C. Cir 1973), rev'd, *Emporium Capwell Co.*, 420 U.S. 50 (1975).

26. 420 U.S. 73.

27. Charles J. Morris, *The Blue Eagle at Work: Reclaiming Democratic Rights in the Workplace* (Ithaca, NY: Cornell University Press, 2008).

28. Susan J. McGolrick, *Forty-Six Labor Law Professors Urge NLRB to Issue Rule on Members-Only Bargaining*, 113 DLR A-1, June 15, 2010.

29. 62 *Minnesota Law Review* 1049, 1978.

30. Gail Collins, *When Everything Changed: The Amazing Journey of American Women from 1960 to the Present* (New York: Little, Brown, 2009), 219–20.

31. Ibid., 220.

32. Marion G. Crain, "Whitewashed Labor Law, Skinwalking Unions," 23 *Berkeley Journal of Employment and Labor Law* 211 (2002).

33. International Labour Organizations Conv. 111.

34. Marion G. Crain, Calvin Sharpe, and Reuel Schiller, "The Story of Emporium Capwell: Civil Rights, Collective Action, and the Constraints of Union Power," in *Labor Law Stories* (New York: Foundation Press, 2005).

35. David Benjamin Oppenheimer, "The Story of *McDonnell Douglas v. Green*," in Joel Wm. Friedman, ed., *Employment Discrimination Stories* (New York: Foundation Press, 2006), 1.

36. Ibid., at 25.

37. Frymer, *Black and Blue*, at 34.

38. Zaragosa Vargas, *Labor Rights Are Civil Rights* (Princeton, NJ: Princeton University Press, 2005).

39. Mary Dudziak, *Cold War Civil Rights: Race and the Image of American Democracy* (Princeton, NJ: Princeton University Press, 2000).

40. www.opensecrets.org/news/2009/02/labor-and-business-spend-big-0.html.

41. William B. Gould IV, "New Labor Law Reform Variations on an Old Theme: Is the Employee Free Choice Act the Answer?" 79 *Louisiana Law Review* 1 (2009).

42. Richard B. Freeman and Joel Rogers, *What Workers Want* (Ithaca, NY: Cornell University Press, 1999).

43. AFL-CIO Report, Based on a Survey by Peter D. Hart Research Associates, Workers Rights in America: What Workers Think About Their Jobs and Employers 28 (Sept. 2001); see also Gregory Defreitas, "Unionization Among Racial and Ethnic Minorities," 46 *Industrial and Labor Relations Review* 284 (1993).

44. Ruth Milkman, ed., *Organizing Immigrants: The Challenge for Unions in Contemporary California* (Ithaca, NY: Cornell University Press, 2000).

45. See Dennis A. DeSlippe, *"Rights, Not Roses": Unions and the Rise of Working-Class Feminism, 1945–1980* (Champaign: University of Illinois Press, 2000), 25.

46. Nancy F. Gabin, *Feminism in the Labor Movement: Women and the United Auto Workers, 1935–1975* (Ithaca, NY: Cornell University Press, 1990), 225.

47. DeSlippe, *"Rights, Not Roses,"* at 193.

48. Ibid.

49. See Dorothy Sue Cobble, *Dishing It Out: Waitresses and Their Unions in the Twentieth Century* (Urbana: University of Illinois Press, 1991), 186, 200.

50. Claire Bingham and Laura Leedy Glanser, *Class Action: The Story of Lois Jensen and the Landmark Case That Transformed Sexual Harassment Law* (New York: Anchor Books, 2002).

51. Ibid. at 123.

52. See Calvin Sharpe, "'By Any Means Necessary': Unprotected Conduct and Decisional Discretion Under the National Labor Relations Act," 20 *Berkeley Journal of Labor and Employment Law* 293 (1999).

CHAPTER 4

1. *Farah v. Espinoza*, 462 F.2d 331 (5th Cir. 1972).

2. *Espinoza v. Farah*, 343 F. Supp. 1205 (D. Tex. 1971).

3. Carlos Saltero, *Latinos and the Law: Landmark Supreme Court Cases* (Austin: University of Texas Press, 2006), 95.

4. Kimberlé W. Crenshaw, "Demarginalizing the Intersection of Race and Sex: A Black Feminist Critique of Antidiscrimination Doctrine, Feminist Theory and Antiracist Politics," 1989 *University of Chicago Legal Forum* 139.

5. See generally Elizabeth M. Iglesias, "Structures of Subordination: Women of Color at the Intersection of Title VII and the NLRA. Not!" 28 Harvard Civil Rights–Civil Liberties Law Review 395 (1993).

6. See, e.g., *United States v. Makowski*, 120 F.3d 1078 (9th Cir. 1997); *Erebia v. Chrysler Plastic Prod. Corp.*, 772 F.2d 1250 (6th Cir. 1985); Miller v. Kenworth of Dothan, Inc., 82 F. Supp. 2d 1299 (M.D. Ala. 2000).

7. *Nieto v. United Auto Workers Local 598*, 672 F. Supp. 987, 989 (E.D. Mich. 1987).

8. See Zapata v. IBP, Inc., No. CIV.A. 93-2366-EEO, 1998 WL 717677 (D. Kan. Sept. 29, 1998) (finding "wetback" epithet used against plaintiff and other Mexicans was evidence of race, national origin, and ancestry discrimination). See also Kevin Johnson, "The Case Against Race Profiling in Immigration Enforcement," 78 Washington University Law Quarterly 675, 716–28 (2000) (discussing how exceptions to Fourth Amendment protections for immigrants harms Latinos/as and other nonwhites).

9. Interpretive Memorandum, 110 Cong. Rec. 7212, 7213 (1964)

10. 42 U.S.C. § 2000e-2 (a)(1) (2000).

11. 343 F.Supp.1205 (D. Tex. 1970).

12. U.S. Census Bureau, Race and Hispanic Origin of the Foreign Born Population in the United States: 2007, January 2010 http://www.census.gov/prod/2010pubs/acs-11.pdf.

13. I use the term "immigrant" in this chapter rather than the legal term "alien" because: (1) there are negative stereotypes attached to "alien," and (2) my exploration of "immigrant" involves more than a legal status, not as in the dichotomous citizen/alien legal framework, but as an identity that can live on even after citizenship is obtained. See, e.g., Kevin R. Johnson, "'Aliens' and the U.S. Immigration Laws: The Social and Legal Construction of Non-Persons," 28 *University of Miami Inter-American Law Review* 263 (1997); Victor C. Romero, "The Domestic Fourth Amendment

Rights of Undocumented Immigrants: On Gutierrez and the Tort Law/Immigration Law," 35 Harvard Civil Rights–Civil Liberties Law Review 57, 59 n.12 (2000).

14. Eric Schmitt, "Census Data Show a Sharp Increase in Living Standard," *New York Times*, Aug. 6, 2001, at 1 (stating, "immigrants make up 11 percent of the country's population, the largest share since the 1930s"); U.S. Department of Commerce, Economics and Statistics Administration, Bureau of the Census, *We the American ... Foreign Born*, Sept. 1993, at 2; Cindy Rodriguez, "Impact of the Undocumented: Study Cites Boom in the Job Rolls," *Boston Globe*, Feb. 6, 2001 at A01.

15. See generally Ruben J. Garcia, "Critical Race Theory and Proposition 187: The Racial Politics of Immigration Law," 17 Chicano-Latino Law Review 118 (1995); Kevin R. Johnson, "Race Matters: Immigration Law and Policy Scholarship, Law in the Ivory Tower, and the Legal Indifference of the Race Critique," 2000 University of Illinois Law Review 525.

16. 42 U.S.C. § 2000e-2 (a)(1) (2000) states, "It shall be an unlawful employment practice for an employer (1) to fail or refuse to hire or to discharge any individual, or otherwise to discriminate against any individual with respect to his compensation, terms, conditions, or privileges of employment, because of such individual's race, color, religion, sex, or national origin."

17. See generally Espinoza, 414 U.S. at 86.

18. See generally Gloria Sandrino-Glasser, "Los Confundidos: De-Conflating Latinos/as' Race and Ethnicity," 19 Chicano-Latino Law Review 69 (1998) (critiquing the conflation of Latinos/as' race and nationality in national origin jurisprudence). The conflation of immigrant status, race, and national origin that I discuss here is similar to Sandrino-Glasser's exploration of the conflation of race and nationality. I do not believe that legal recognition of immigrant status under antidiscrimination law will mark an end to the conflation that Sandrino-Glasser describes. As I argue below, I believe, however, that de-conflation of race, national origin, and immigration status would better reflect social realities than current doctrines.

19. David Bacon, "Labor Fights for Immigrants: The Stage Is Set for a Showdown Over the Fate of Undocumented Workers," *Nation*, May 21, 2001 (noting the importance of immigrant workers to the survival of the labor movement).

20. On undocumented immigrants' basic coverage under Title VII, see *Rios v. Enterprise Ass'n Steamfitters Local Union 638, of U.A.*, 860 F.2d 1168, 1173 (2d Cir. 1988); see also EEOC v. Hacienda Hotel, 881 F.2d 1504, 1516–17 (9th Cir. 1989); Patel v. Quality Inn S., 846 F.2d 700 (11th Cir. 1988) (undocumented immigrants entitled to minimum wages and overtime pay by the Fair Labor Standards Act), *cert. denied*, 489 U.S. 1011 (1989). On the inadequacy of remedies, see Maria L. Ontiveros, "To Help Those Most in Need: Undocumented Workers' Rights and Remedies Under Title VII," New York University Review of Law and Social Change 607 (1993).

21. *NLRB v. A.P.R.A. Fuel Oil Buyers Group, Inc.*, 134 F.3d 50, 53 (2d Cir. 1997) (employer may require reinstated worker to provide proof of authorization to work in the United States); see also NLRB General Counsel Memorandum 98-15 (Dec. 4, 1998) (directing agency lawyers that reinstatement should be sought without regard to immigration status, but that the employer then can refuse to reinstate the employee if the employee cannot show the legal ability to work in the United States). But see *Del Rey Tortilleria, Inc. v. NLRB*, 976 F.2d 1115 (7th Cir. 1992) (questioning, in

dicta, whether undocumented workers should be covered by the NLRA at all in light of IRCA).

22. 122 S. Ct. 1275 (2002).

23. On undocumented immigrants' basic coverage under Title VII, see *Rios v. Enterprise Ass'n Steamfitters Local Union 638, of U.A.*, 860 F.2d 1168, 1173 (2d Cir. 1988); see also *EEOC v. Hacienda Hotel*, 881 F.2d 1504, 1516–17 (9th Cir. 1989); *Patel v. Quality Inn S.*, 846 F.2d 700 (11th Cir. 1988) (undocumented immigrants entitled to minimum wages and overtime pay by the Fair Labor Standards Act), *cert. denied*, 489 U.S. 1011 (1989). On the inadequacy of remedies, see Maria L. Ontiveros, "To Help Those Most in Need."

24. In *Hoffman*, the Court decided only whether back pay would be available to undocumented immigrants under the NLRA. Ibid. at 1278. The Court acknowledged that the undocumented would continue to be covered by the NLRA, but denied back pay on the following grounds: "The [NLRB] asks that we overlook [the worker's undocumented status] and allow it to award back pay to an illegal alien for years of work not performed, for wages that could not lawfully have been earned, and for a job obtained in the first instance by a criminal fraud." Ibid. at 1283.

This rationale for denying back pay, which overlooks the illegality of the employer's actions and potential deterrence factors, could be used to deny remedies *and* basic coverage to undocumented immigrants under a variety of protective labor laws, such as Title VII and the Fair Labor Standards Act.

25. 414 U.S. 86 (1973).

26. Ibid. at 87.

27. Ibid. at 95. In his dissent, Justice Douglas argued that the employer's policy had a disparate impact on the Latino/a plaintiffs, and that discrimination based on birth outside the United States is necessarily discrimination based on national origin. Ibid. at 96 (Douglas, J., dissenting).

28. See generally Gloria Sandrino-Glasser, "Los Confundidos: De-Conflating Latinos/as' Race and Ethnicity" (critiquing the conflation of Latinos/as' race and nationality in national origin jurisprudence).

29. See, e.g., Nieto v. United Auto Workers Local 598, 672 F. Supp. 987 (E.D. Mich. 1987). In *Nieto*, the court stated: "[A]lthough the verbal harassment [suffered by plaintiff] was replete with references to green cards, boats, wetbacks and border patrols suggesting national origin discrimination, this is racial discrimination within the meaning of section 1981." Ibid. at 989.

30. See, e.g., United States v. Makowski, 120 F.3d 1078 (9th Cir. 1997); Erebia v. Chrysler Plastic Prod. Corp., 772 F.2d 1250 (6th Cir. 1985); Miller v. Kenworth of Dothan, Inc., 82 F. Supp. 2d 1299 (M.D. Ala. 2000).

31. Immigrants have been successful in establishing the right to public education. See, e.g., *Plyer v. Doe*, 457 U.S. 202 (1982) (children of undocumented immigrants are entitled to public education).

32. See 8 U.S.C. § 1324b(a)(1) (2000). The aggrieved individual must make a complaint with the Office of Special Counsel (OSC) for Immigration Related Unfair Employment Practices in the Civil Rights Division of the U.S. Department of Justice. Ibid. § 1324b(b)(1). If the OSC finds that the complaint has merit, an administrative law judge, whose decision can then be enforced or appealed in the United States Court of Appeals, will hear the complaint. Ibid. § 1324b(d)(1), (i)(1).

33. http://www.justice.gov/opa/pr/2000/March/110cr.htm.

34. http://www.justice.gov/opa/pr/2001/August/372osc.htm.

35. http://www.justice.gov/opa/pr/2004/April/04_crt_251.htm.

36. Charlie Savage, "Report Examines Civil Rights Enforcement During Bush Years," *New York Times*, Dec. 3, 2009 at A26.

37. Newsletter of the Office of Special Counsel, Fall 2006, available at http://www.justice.gov/crt/osc/pdf/oscupdate_nov_06.pdf page 8.

38. Bruce Springsteen, "Across the Borders," on *The Ghost of Tom Joad* (Columbia Records, 1995).

39. This is because of the different jurisdictional requirements of the two statutes. IRCA only applies to national origin claims against employers having four to fourteen employees; Title VII applies to employers with fifteen or more employees. Ibid. § 1324b(a)(2)(B), (b)(2).

40. See generally ibid. § 1324b(a)(2)(B), (b)(2).

41. 42 U.S.C. § 2000e(b) (2000) (defining "employer" as a "person engaged in an industry affecting commerce who has fifteen or more employees for each working day in each of twenty or more calendar weeks in the current or proceeding calendar year").

42. Leticia Saucedo, "Three Theories of Discrimination in the Brown Collar Workforce," 2009 *University of Chicago Legal Forum* 345 (2009); Leticia Saucedo, "The Employer Preference for the Subservient Workforce and the Making of the Brown Collar Workforce," 67 *Ohio State Law Journal* 961 (2006).

43. *Espinoza v. Farah* (dissenting opinion of Justice Douglas).

44. John C. Eastman, "Born in the U.S.A.? Reassessing Birthright Citizenship in the Wake of 9/11," 42 *Richmond Law Review* 955 (2008).

45. *Wong Kim Ark v. United States*, 169 U.S. 649 (1898).

46. See, e.g., Josh Price, "Difficult Maneuvers in Discourse Against Latina Immigrants in the United States," 7 Cardozo Journal of International and Comparative Law 277, 287–89 (1999) (discussing Indian immigrant identity in the context of domestic violence); Dorothy E. Roberts, "BlackCrit Theory and the Problem of Essentialism," 53 *University of Miami Law Review* 855, 861–62 (1999) (discussing Roberts's choice and ability to identify both as the daughter of a Jamaican immigrant and a descendant of slaves from the Southern United States). Drucilla Cornell describes immigrant identity as "one that has fluid parameters because many different social and historical forces constitute it." Drucilla Cornell and William W. Bratton, "Deadweight Costs and Intrinsic Wrongs of Nativism: Economics, Freedom, and Legal Suppression of Spanish," 84 Cornell Law Review 595, 684 (1999); see also Leslie Espinoza, "A Vision Towards Liberation," 19 Chicano-Latino Law Review 193 (1998).

47. The 1996 Personal Responsibility and Work Opportunity Reconciliation Act, Pub. L. 104-193, 110 Stat. 2105 (1996) (codified as amended in various sections of Title 42, U.S. Code) ended many federal government benefits for noncitizens, whether "legal" or not. Some of these benefits were later restored, but merely as grandfather clauses. (See Noncitizen Benefit Clarification and Other Technical Amendments of 1998, Pub. L. No. 105-306, 112 Stat. 2926 (1998) (codified as amended at 8 U.S.C. § 1611(b)(5)); see also *Lewis v. Thompson*, 252 F.3d 567, 582–88 (2d Cir. 2001) (denying prenatal care to children of undocumented immigrants was not a violation of equal protection.)

48. See Elvia R. Arriola, "Foreword: March!" 19 *Chicano-Latino Law Review* 1, 30 (1998).

49. 454 U.S. 432 (1982).

50. 403 U.S. 365 (1971).

51. 432 U.S. 7 (1977).

52. *Foley v. Connelie*, 435 U.S. 291 (1978) (New York's citizenship requirement for police officers upheld); *Cabell v. Chavez-Salido*, 454 U.S. 432 (1982) (upholding California's ability to prevent aliens from serving as deputy probation officers); see also *Ambach v. Norwick*, 441 U.S. 68 (1979) (allowing New York to bar aliens from becoming public school teachers); Victor C. Romero, "Expanding the Circle of Membership by Reconstructing the 'Alien': Lessons from Social Psychology and the 'Promise Enforcement' Cases," 32 University of Michigan Journal of Law Reform 1 (1998) (describing how the court-stripping provisions of the Illegal Immigration Reform and Immigrant Responsibility Act of 1996 strip immigrants of membership in the polity).

53. See I.N.A. § 1101(a)(15)(A-V) (containing 22 statutory definitions of "immigrant").

54. New York City Commission on Human Rights, See "Discrimination Against Muslims, Arabs, and South Asians in New York City Since 9/11" (Summer, 2003).

55. Richard Thompson Ford, "Race as Culture: Why Not?" 47 *UCLA Law Review* 1803 (2000).

56. Ibid.

57. See ibid., note 8, at 1803 (an ideologically left-wing critique of the attempt to extend civil rights protection to cultural differences or identity correlated traits). For a proposal for greater legal protection of "foreignness," see Natsu Saito, "Alien and Non-Alien Alike: Citizenship, 'Foreignness', and Racial Hierarchy in American Law," 76 Oregon Law Review 261 (1997).

58. See generally Espinoza, 414 U.S. at 86.

59. Linda Chavez, *Out of the Barrio: Toward a New Politics of Hispanic Assimilation* (New York: Basic Books, 1992).

60. International Labor Organization Convention 111, Elimination of Discrimination.

61. Ibid.

62. 42 U.S.C. § 1981(a).

63. *Anderson v. Conboy*, 156 F.3d 167, 169–70 (2d Cir. 1998) (holding union requirement that its employees be citizens of the United States is actionable private discrimination on the basis of alienage under 42 U.S.C. § 1981), cert. granted sub. nom., *United Bhd. of Carpenters v. Anderson*, 526 U.S. 1086 (1999), cert. dismissed, 527 U.S. 1030 (1999). But see *Bhandari v. First Nat'l Bank of Commerce*, 887 F.2d 609 (5th Cir. 1989) (en banc) (holding section 1981 does not prohibit discrimination based on alienage by private actors), cert. denied, 494 U.S. 1061 (1990).

64. See Ruth Colker, *Hybrid: Bisexuals, Multiracials, and Other Misfits Under American Law* (New York: New York University Press, 1996).

65. See, e.g., *Bhandari v. First Nat. Bank*, 808 F.2d 1082 (5th Cir. 1987).

66. Jennifer Gordon and Robin A. Lenhardt, "Rethinking Work and Citizenship," 55 *UCLA Law Review* 1611 (2008).

67. "Smithfield wins a union after a 16-year struggle," *Labor Notes*, Nicole Fulmore, Mischa Gaus, http://www.labornotes.org/node/2003 *Labor Notes*, Dec. 24 2008

(discussing the increased solidarity of African American workers after the election of President Obama).

68. Peter Rachleff, "A Union of Immigrants Wins Minneapolis Hotel Strike," *Labor Notes*, Aug. 2000, at 1, 14 (describing the union's outreach in 17 different languages during strike); Terry Fiedler, "Hotel Workers OK Five-Year Contract on Eve of Convention," *Minnesota-St. Paul Star Tribune*, June 29, 2000, at 1A (describing the union's membership consisting of Somali, Tibetan, and Latino/a immigrants); Peter Racheleff, "Workers Who Understand Struggle," *Dollars and Sense*, Sept. 2000, at 21 (interview with Jaye Rykunyk, Local 17's principal officer, stating that the union was successful in the negotiations because immigrant workers "understand struggle").

69. Kimberly Hayes Taylor, "Illegal Workers Get to Stay in the U.S.," *Minnesota-St. Paul Star Tribune*, Apr. 26, 2000, at 1B (reporting that the INS gave seven undocumented immigrants who tried to form a union at a downtown Minneapolis hotel "deferred-action" status for two years; the eighth was deported immediately because he had been caught entering the United States without documents once before in 1998). There are, of course, examples where competing notions of immigrant identity cause division. See, e.g., Timothy Aeppel, "Long Strike Breeds Immigrant Factions," *Wall Street Journal*, June 12, 2001, at B1, B4 (describing divisions between Bosnians and Laotians at a strike in Des Moines, Iowa).

70. David Bacon, *Illegal People: How Globalization Creates Migration and Criminalizes Immigrants* (Boston: Beacon Press, 2008).

71. 499 U.S. 244 (1991).

72. 499 U.S. at 256.

73. See also 42 U.S.C. § 2000e(f); 42 U.S.C. § 2000e-1(a) (inapplicability of Title VII to certain alien employees).

CHAPTER 5

1. Bittersweet Harvest, Smithsonian Institution Exhibit, Washington, DC; http://www.sites.si.edu/exhibitions/exhibits/bracero_project/main.htm.

2. See Evelyn Nakano Glenn, *Unequal Freedom: How Race and Gender Shaped American Citizenship and Labor* (Cambridge, MA: Harvard University Press, 2002), 190–96 (Japanese and Haoles in Hawaii were treated strictly as laborers, not as settlers and potential citizens. At first, the policy for Asian workers favored single men free of family ties—this minimized housing costs, and indeed the housing conditions were very bad—Japanese were brought in as temporary workers from 1870–1930); see also Shannon Leigh Vivian, "Be Our Guest: A Review of the Legal and Regulatory History of U.S. Immigration Policy Toward Mexico and Recommendations for Combating Employer Exploitation of Nonimmigrant and Undocumented Workers," 30 *Seton Hall Legislative Journal* 189, 196–98 (2005).

3. Camille J. Bosworth, "Guest Worker Policy: A Critical Analysis of President Bush's Proposed Reform," 56 Hastings Law Journal 1095, 1095–120 (2005).

4. Kitty Calavita, *U.S. Immigration Law and the Control of Labor 1820–1924* (London: Academic Press, 1984).

5. Justin Akers Chacón and Mike Davis, *No One Is Illegal: Fighting Racism and State Violence on the U.S.-Mexico Border* (Chicago: Haymarket Books, 2006), 139–47.

6. Ibid.

7. Cruz v. United States, 219 F. Supp. 2d 1027, 1051 (N.D. Cal. 2005).

8. Cruz v. United States, 2003 WL 21518119 (N.D. Cal. 2003), reconsideration granted in part, 219 F. Supp. 2d 1027 (N.D. Cal. 2005).

9. Ibid. at 1031–33.

10. Ibid. at 1032.

11. Cal. Civ. Proc. Code § 354.7 (West 2006).

12. See Bill Ong Hing, *Deporting Our Souls: Values, Morality and Immigration Policy* (New York: Cambridge University Press, 2006), 10–11 (describing H.R. 4437 and the Senate bill that included a guestworker program); Edward J. W. Park and John S. W. Park, *Probationary Americans: Contemporary Immigration Policies and the Shaping of Asian American Communities* (New York and London: Routledge, 2004, 108–14 (describing current guestworker proposals, balancing flexibility with efficiency).

13. See Bittersweet Harvest, the Bracero Program 1942–1964, http://americanhistory.si.edu/exhibitions/small_exhibitions.cfm?key=1267&exkey=770&pagekey=777.

14. See George Lakoff and Sam Ferguson, *The Framing of Immigration* (2006), http://www.rockridgeinstitute.org/research/rockridge/immigration (describing the "framing" of immigration). Of course, the proponents of more liberal immigration policies also use language liberally in pushing "earned legalization" rather than "amnesty." See Edwin Meese III, "An Amnesty by Any Other Name," *New York Times*, May 24, 2006, at A27.

15. Highly skilled temporary workers face potential exploitation and lack of bargaining power, but they generally have more bargaining power than low-skilled workers. For this reason, I am limiting my analysis to unskilled temporary workers, including those currently working legally in the United States under such programs as the H-2A and H-2B programs.

16. *Webster's* dictionary defines "commodity" as an "article of commerce … something useful or valued" *Merriam-Webster Dictionary* (1998), 106.

17. See David Ricardo, "The Principles of Political Economy and Taxation," in *The Works and Correspondence of David Ricardo*, pp. 11–20.

18. See Thomas L. Friedman, *The World Is Flat: A Brief History of the Twenty-First Century* (New York: Farrar, Straus and Giroux, 2005), 225–27 (concluding that Ricardo is right about the theory of comparative advantage).

19. See Charles Whelan, *Naked Economics: Undressing the Dismal Science* (New York: Norton, 2010), at 21.

20. Intellectual labor, in particular, is becoming more valuable in the global economy. See David Dante Troutt, "A Portrait of the Trademark as a Black Man: Intellectual Property, Commodification, and Redescription," 38 *U.C. Davis Law Review* 1141, 1143–45 (2005) (describing the sometimes close connection between race and commodification, even in the intellectual property domain); see also Anthony Paul Farley, "The Apogee of the Commodity," 53 *DePaul Law Review* 1229, 1230 (2004) (describing the connection between labor and commodification). Traditional contract law doctrine has been utilized more frequently in high-tech settings by employers seeking to protect their "investment" in certain workers. See Alan Hyde, *Working in Silicon*

*Valley: An Economic and Legal Analysis of a High Velocity Labor Market* (Armonk, NY: M. E. Sharpe, 2003), 27–40.

21. See Richard Abel, "General Damages Are Incoherent, Incalculable, Incommensurable, and Inegalitarian (But Otherwise a Great Idea)," 55 *DePaul Law Review* 253, 282–91 (2006); Mary Anne Case, "Pets or Meat," 80 *Chicago-Kent Law Review* 1129 (2005) (discussing the commodification of affection for pets); Mary Lyndon Shanley, "Collaboration and Commodification in Assisted Procreation: Reflections on an Open Market and Anonymous Donation in Human Sperm and Eggs," 36 *Law and Society Review* 257, 258 (2002) (discussing commodification of human sperm and eggs).

22. For example, the Clayton Act of 1914 explicitly stated that "the labor of a human being is not a commodity or an article of commerce." Clayton Antitrust Act, 15 U.S.C. § 17 (1914) The National Labor Relations Act, enacted twenty-one years later in 1935, gave legal protection to collective bargaining, thus providing voice to workers. National Labor Relations Act, Section 7, 29 U.S.C. § 151 (1935).

23. See generally Beth Shulman, *The Betrayal of Work: How Low Wage Jobs Fail 30 Million Americans and Their Families* (New York: New Press, 2003); Andy Stern, *A Country That Works: Getting America Back on Track* (New York: Free Press, 2006).

24. See David Ricardo, "On the Principles of Political Economy and Taxation," in *The Works and Correspondence of David Ricardo*, Piero Saffa and M. H. Dobb, eds. (Indianapolis: Liberty Fund, 2005), vol. 1.

25. As Carlos Fuentes wrote in his fictional novel, *The Crystal Frontier*, "Mexico [is] exporting more labor than cement or tomatoes." (New York: Farrar, Straus and Giroux, 1997), 166, 167.

26. See Eric Tucker, "'Great Expectations' Defeated? The Trajectory of Collective Bargaining Regimes in Canada and the United States Post-NAFTA," 26 Comparative Labor Law and Policy Journal 97, 104–5 (2004); see also Sanford E. Gaines, "NAFTA as a Symbol on the Border," 51 UCLA Law Review 143, 167–70 (2003).

27. See Marc R. Rosenblum, *The Transnational Politics of U.S. Immigration Policy* (Boulder, CO: Lynne Rienner, 2004). The author conceptualizes migration policy-making as a two-stage, two-level game. "In the first stage, Congress and the president negotiate over legislation, with the president playing a subordinate but significant role by introducing legislation, shaping the public debate, and potentially vetoing bills. . . . In addition, migrant-sending states may influence policymaking at either stage, including through traditional lobbying efforts, by influencing migration outcomes directly, and/or by linking U.S. policy to other bilateral issues." Ibid.

28. Alfred C. Aman, Jr., *The Democracy Deficit: Taming Globalization Through Law Reform* (New York and London: New York University Press 2004), 129–82 (discussing the implications of the globalizing state for law reform).

29. See Friedman, *The World Is Flat*, 373–74 (discussing "technological determinism").

30. See Aman, *The Democracy Deficit*, at 129–81 (arguing for an administrative law solution to globalization problems); Daniel C. Esty, "Good Governance at the Supra-national Scale: Globalizing Administrative Law," 115 *Yale Law Journal* 1490, 1523–41 (2006) (proposing a new administrative law framework for global problems).

31. See generally Judith Golub, "Immigration Reform Post 9/11," 13 U.S.-Mexico Law Journal 9 (2005).

32. See William B. Gould IV, "Labor Law for a Global Economy: The Uneasy Case for International Labor Standards," 80 *Nebraska Law Review* 715, 750–51 (2001); Katherine Van Wezel Stone, "Labor and the Global Economy: Four Approaches to Transnational Labor Regulation," 16 *Michigan Journal of International Law* 987, 996–98 (1995).

33. See generally James Atleson, *Values and Assumptions in American Labor Law* (Amherst: University of Massachusetts Press, 1983); Howard Kimeldorf, *Battling for American Labor: Wobblies, Craft Workers, and the Making of the Union Movement* (Berkeley: University of California Press, 1999).

34. See generally Nelson Lichtenstein, *State of the Union: A Century of American Labor* (Princeton, NJ: Princeton University Press, 2003).

35. While the number of workers organized in unions has been falling in recent years, the number of statutes protecting worker rights has actually increased. This has been particularly true at the state level, such as in California. See, e.g., Private Attorneys General Act of 2004, Cal. Lab. Code § 2698 (2006) (allowing workers to sue for violations of the labor laws).

36. See Lance Compa, *Human Rights Watch, Unfair Advantage: Workers' Freedom of Association in the United States Under International Human Rights Standards*, 2d ed. (Ithaca, NY: Cornell University Press, 2004), 7 (citing reports documenting the rise in violations of workers' rights in the 1980s).

37. See Crain, "Transformation of the Professional Workforce," at 601. See generally Albert O. Hirschmann, *Exit, Voice & Loyalty: Responses to the Decline in Firms, Organizations and States* (Cambridge, MA: Harvard University Press, 1970) (explaining how voice is sometimes a more effective mechanism than exit in changing organizations).

38. See Milkman, *L.A. Story* (citing Hirsch and Macpherson's compilations for the figure that union membership has decreased in the private sector from 24 percent in 1973 to 8 percent in 2005). For more statistics on union membership over the past 20 years, see Unionstats.com, Union Membership and Coverage Database From the CPS (Documentation), available at http://www.trinity.edu/bhirsch/unionstats (last visited Jan. 26, 2007).

39. See David K. Shipler, *The Working Poor: Invisible in America* (New York: Vintage Books, 2005), 113–14 ("Being undocumented is precarious. Fearing deportation, you will think twice about contesting your wages or working conditions").

40. See The Economic Policy Institute, *The State of Working America 2006/2007*, (2006), available at http://www.stateofworkingamerica.org/intro_ exec.html (discussing the stagnation of wages in the United States since 2000). This stagnation affects the wages of all workers, as argued by the AFL-CIO in its petition with the U.S. Trade Representative over labor rights violations in China. Petition of the AFL-CIO with the U.S. Trade Representative, at 89–90, available at http://www.aflcio.org/issues/jobseconomy/globaleconomy/upload/china_petition.pdf.

41. One example of the broad support for guestworker programs is the advocacy of Tamar Jacoby of the Manhattan Institute, a traditionally conservative think tank. See Tamar Jacoby, "Immigration Nation," *Foreign Affairs*, Nov./Dec. 2006, at 50.

42. U.S. Const. art. I.

43. U.S. Const. amend. XIII.

44. The Clayton Antitrust Act, 15 U.S.C. § 17 (1914).

45. See *Brown v. Pro Football League*, 518 U.S. 231, 253 (1996) (Stevens, J., dissenting) ("The policy behind the statutory labor exemption protects the right of workers to act collectively to seek better wages ....").

46. National Labor Relations Act, 29 U.S.C. § 151cmt. 16 (1935). On the labor exemption, see Brown, 518 U.S. at 253 (1996).

47. International Labour Organization, Declaration of Philadelphia (1944), available at http:// www.ilo.org/public/english/bureau/inf/download/brochure/pdf/page5. pdf ("Labour is not a commodity.").

48. See Joseph E. Stiglitz, *Globalization and Its Discontents* (New York: Norton, 2002), 25 (describing the challenge, upon assuming the presidency of the World Bank in 1997, of "1.2 billion people around the world living on less than a dollar a day," and "2.8 billion people living on less than $2 a day").

49. See Dean Hubbard, "What Kind of Globalization? Organizing for Workers' Human Rights," 9 *WorkingUSA* 315, 318 (2006).

50. See Steven R. Weisman, "Financial Leaders Gather, A Bit Tensely," *New York Times*, Sept. 16, 2006, at C9 (describing a proposal to include more input from countries such as China, Mexico, and Turkey).

51. See Sandra Polaski, "Protecting Labor Rights Through Trade Agreements: An Analytical Guide," 10 *U.C. Davis Journal of International Law and Policy* 13, 14 (2003) (describing trade agreements between the United States and Chile, the United States and Singapore). Examples of recent trade agreements include the United States-Chile Free Trade Agreement, U.S.-Chile, June 6, 2003, 117 Stat. 909; United States-Singapore Free Trade Agreement, U.S.-Sing., May 6, 2003, 117 Stat. 948.

52. See Michael D. Yates, *Naming the System: Inequality and Work in the Global Economy* (New York: Monthly Review Press, 2003), 21–22 (describing how free trade policies can lead to economic insecurity among a majority of the world's population).

53. See Friedman, *The World Is Flat*, at 22–28.

54. Ibid. at 21–28.

55. The H1-B program for technology workers offers some ability to petition for residency with the help of an employer, but that program has been plagued by delays and limitations. Workers in that program, because of the need to be tied to one employer, lack the full mobility that Friedman touts. David N. Pellow and Glenna Matthews, "Immigrant Workers in Two Eras: Struggles and Successes in Silicon Valley," in *Challenging the Chip: Labor Rights and Environmental Justice in the Global Electronics Industry* (Philadelphia: Temple University Press, 2006), 129 (describing the difficulties of organizing in Silicon Valley because of the largely temporary workforce).

56. National Labor Relations Act (NLRA), 29 U.S.C. § 151 et seq. (2000).

57. 29 U.S.C. § 158(a)(5) (2000).

58. Fair Labor Standards Act (FLSA), 29 U.S.C. §§ 201–19 (2000).

59. Stephen B. Moldof, "The Application of U.S. Labor Laws to Activities and Employees outside the United States," 17 *Labor Lawyer* 417, 423 (2002).

60. Lance Compa, *Human Rights Watch, Unfair Advantage: Workers' Freedom of Association in the United States under International Human Rights Standards* (Ithaca, NY: Cornell University Press, 2004), 44–46 (describing the ILO framework).

61. Sarah Paoletti, "Making Visible the Invisible: Globalization's Impact on Workers in the United States," 13 *Indiana Journal of Global Legal Studies* 105, 126 (2006).

62. Congress recently passed the Central American Free Trade Agreement (CAFTA-DR), which focuses on the countries south of Mexico and north of Panama, as well as the Dominican Republic. In the last 15 years, the United States has also entered into a number of bilateral free trade agreements (FTAs) such as the U.S-Chile FTA and the U.S.-Jordan FTA. See Sandra Polaski, "Protecting Labor Rights through Trade Agreements," at 14.

63. North American Agreement on Labor Cooperation, U.S.-Can.-Mex., principle 11, Sept. 14, 1993, 32, I.L.M. 1499 [hereinafter NAALC].

64. For example, when the Immigration Reform and Control Act (IRCA) was enacted in 1986, an estimated 3.6 million people were legalized under the amnesty provisions of that law. The number of people who might qualify for legalization under the proposal considered by the Senate in 2006 would be closer to 10–12 million people, based on numbers provided by the Pew Hispanic Center. According to Pew, unauthorized migrant families were comprised of 13.9 million people in 2004, of which 4.7 million were children. Of the 4.7 million children, 3.1 million were U.S. citizens. Pew Hispanic Center, Unauthorized Migrants: Numbers and Characteristics (2006), available at http:// pewhispanic.org/files/reports/46.pdf.

65. See Jennifer M. Chacon, "Misery and Myopia: Understanding the Failures of U.S. Efforts to Stop Human Trafficking," 74 *Fordham Law Review* 2977, 2981–82 (2006); Ivy C. Lee and Mie Lewis, "Human Trafficking from a Legal Advocate's Perspective: History, Legal Framework and Current Anti-Trafficking Efforts," 10 *U.C. Davis Journal of International Law and Policy* 169, 188–93 (2003); Dennis Wagner, "Phoenix's Hidden $2 Billion Industry; Human Smuggling; Vicious Organizations Move Thousands of Immigrants Through Valley Every Day," *Arizona Republic*, July 23, 2006, at 1 (describing human smuggling as a $2 billion a year business); Bernice Yeung, "Trafficked: How Three Attorneys Rescued a Former Sex Slave from Deportation," *California Lawyer*, Dec. 2004, at 31 (telling the story of a trafficking victim).

66. Condoleeza Rice, U.S. Secretary of State, Remarks upon the Release of the Sixth Annual Trafficking in Persons Report (June 5, 2006), available at http://www.state.gov/secretary/rm/2006/67551.htm ("Defeating human trafficking is a great moral calling of our time and under President Bush's leadership the United States is leading a new abolitionist movement to end the sordid trade in human beings").

67. Trafficking Victims Protection Act, 22 U.S.C. § 7103 (2000).

68. See infra text accompanying notes 115–16 (the complaints alleging violations of the NAFTA labor-side agreement).

69. Ibid.

70. See, e.g., Philip Martin, "There Is Nothing More Permanent Than Temporary Foreign Workers," Center for Immigration Studies Backgrounder, Apr. 2001, available at http://www.cis.org/articles/2001/back501.html ("Importing guest workers—some of whom will settle—in such a situation is analogous to importing mine workers just before the ore runs out"); Ruben Navarette, "Here We Go Again," *USA Today*, Apr. 4, 2006, at 13A ("I'm talking about importing hundreds of thousands of new foreign workers from a country such as Mexico to work in farming, construction, hotels or

restaurants"); Robert J. Samuelson, "We Don't Need 'Guest Workers,'" *Washington Post*, Mar. 21, 2006, at A21.

71. S. Rep. No. 106–24, at 32 (1999), available at http:// frwebgate.access.gpo.gov/ cgi-bin/getdoc.cgi?dbname=106_cong_ reports&docid=f:sr204.106.pdf ("The INA reflects the American tradition of employing U.S. workers in private sector jobs that promote the growth of a middle class, rather than importing and exploiting a rolling stream of alien workers, without permanent immigrant status or family ties, in low-paid permanent positions, most to be kept almost all the time on their employers' premises").

72. See Joseph E. Stiglitz, *Making Globalization Work* (New York: Norton, 2006) (describing democratic deficits).

73. Jamin Raskin, "Lawful Disenfranchisement: America's Structural Democracy Deficit," 32 *Human Rights Magazine* 12 (Spring 2005), available at http://www.abanet. org/irr/hr/spring05/lawful.html (describing the disenfranchisement of ex-felons).

74. For more information about the ILO structure, see International Labour Organisation, Structure of the ILO, http:// www.ilo.org/public/english/depts/fact. htm (last visited Jan. 28, 2006); see also Ed Lorenz, "Bringing Law to Globalization Through ILO Conventions: A Labor Perspective on the Core Labor Standards," 11 *Michigan State University–Detroit College of Law Journal of International Law* 101, 103 (2002) (describing the ILO "tri-partied system of governance").

75. "BLS Reports Percentage of Workers in Unions Still 12.5 Percent, But Overall Numbers Up," *Daily Labor Report* (BNA) No. 14, at AA-1 (Jan. 23, 2006). The latest Bureau of Labor Statistics data show a continually worsening trend. See "Union Membership Falls to 12 Percent," *San Diego Union –Tribune*, Jan. 26, 2007, at 4 (noting that union membership was 35 percent in the mid-1950s).

76. "Hundreds of Thousands Rally Nationwide for Immigrant Rights, Path to Citizenship," *Daily Labor Report* (BNA), no. 70, Apr. 12, 2006, at A-2.

77. Maureen B. Cavanaugh, "Democracy, Equality, and Taxes," 54 *Alabama Law Review* 415, 430–35 (2003) (discussing consent as the revolutionary claim for independence).

78. Enrique De La Garza Toledo, "Free Trade and Labor Relations in Mexico," in *International Labor Standards: Globalization, Trade, and Public Policy*, Robert J. Flanagan and William B. Gould IV, eds. (Palo Alto, CA: Stanford University Press, 2003), 227.

79. See Roger Blanpain et al., *The Global Workplace: International and Comparative Employment Law: Cases and Materials* (Cambridge: Cambridge University Press, 2007), 211–12.

80. Shereen Hertel, *Unexpected Power: Conflict and Change Among Transactional Activists* (Ithaca, NY: ILR Press, 2006), 101–03 (describing the changes proposed by President Fox's labor secretary Ralph Absacal that would make Mexican labor law more business-friendly).

81. Kim Barry, "Home and Away: The Construction of Citizenship in an Emigration Context," 81 *NYU Law Review* 1 (2006); Ruth Rubio-Marin, "Transnational Politics and the Democratic Nation-State: Normative Challenges of Expatriate Voting and Nationality Retention of Emigrants," 81 *NYU Law Review* 117, 126–28 (2006).

82. See Randal C. Archibold, "Immigrants Take to U.S. Streets in a Show of Strength," *New York Times*, May 2, 2006, at A1 (discussing marches that took place nationwide on May 1); "Immigrants, Supporters Rally May 1 For Rights, Comprehensive Legislation," *Daily Labor Report* (BNA) No. 84, May 2, 2006, at A11.

83. See Rubio-Marin, "Transnational Politics and the Democratic Nation-State," at 126–28.

84. Jeremy Waldron, "Deliberation, Disagreement and Voting," in *Deliberative Democracy and Human Rights*, Harold Hongju Koh and Ronald C. Slye, eds. (New Haven, CT: Yale University Press, 1999), 210.

85. The Fifteenth Amendment to the Constitution protects the right of citizens to vote. U.S. Const. amend. XV. In some cases, however, the right to vote is available to noncitizens. For example, Mexicans living in the United States can cast ballots in Mexican elections. Noncitizens living in certain jurisdictions, such as Takoma Park, Maryland, can vote in local school board elections. Jamin B. Raskin, "Legal Aliens, Local Citizens: The Historical, Constitutional and Legal Meanings of Alien Suffrage," 141 *University of Pennsylvania Law Review* 1391, 1463 (1993) (describing how the city of Takoma Park, Maryland, extended the right to vote in local school board elections to noncitizens).

86. See generally Michael R. Triplett, "White House Outlines Immigration Reforms, Including Guestworker Programs, Worker IDs," *Daily Labor Report* (BNA) No. 15, Jan. 24, 2007, at A-13.

87. Linda Bosniak, *The Citizen and the Alien: Dilemmas of Contemporary Membership* (Princeton, NJ: Princeton University Press, 2006), 122–40 (discussing theorists that separate "membership" in a community from "citizenship").

88. See "Cap Reached for H-2B Visas, Homeland Security Says," *Daily Labor Report* (BNA) No. 67, at A-11 (Apr. 7, 2006) (discussing how quickly the H-2B visa cap is reached).

89. Jennifer Gordon, "Transnational Labor Citizenship," 80 *Southern California Law Review* 503 (2007); Jennifer Gordon, "Workers Without Borders," *New York Times*, Mar. 10, 2009 at A 27.

90. See, e.g., George W. Bush, U.S. President, Remarks by the President on Immigration Policy (Jan. 7, 2004), available at http:// www.whitehouse.gov/news/ releases/2004/01/20040107-3.html. Bush took care to distinguish his proposal from an "amnesty." Ibid. "Those who make th[e] choice [to apply for citizenship] will be allowed to apply in the normal way. . . . I oppose amnesty, placing undocumented workers on the automatic path to citizenship. Granting amnesty encourages the violation of our laws, and perpetuates illegal immigration." Ibid.

91. Eric Lekus, "Senate Votes to Restore Language Allowing Guestworkers to Self-Petition for Green Cards," *Daily Labor Report* (BNA) No. 97, May 19, 2006, at AA-1.

92. See Milkman, *L.A. Stories*, at 129 (immigrants have shown more interest in unions than native-born workers, as shown by a study conducted by the University of California Institute for Labor and Employment).

93. See 8 U.S.C. § 1184(c) (2000) (describing the petition process of the "importing employer").

94. See Shannon Leigh Vivian, "Be Our Guest: A Review of the Legal and Regulatory History of U.S. Immigration Policy Toward Mexico and Recommendations for

Combating Employer Exploitation of Nonimmigrant and Undocumented Workers," 30 Seton Hall Legislative Journal 189, 196–98 (2005).

95. Bosworth, "Guest Worker Policy," 1095–1120.

96. Calavita, *U.S. Immigration Law and the Control of Labor.*

97. Chacón and Davis, *No One Is Illegal*, 139–47.

98. Ibid.

99. Cruz v. United States, 219 F. Supp. 2d 1027, 1051 (N.D. Cal. 2005).

100. Cruz v. United States, 2003 WL 21518119 (N.D. Cal. 2003), reconsideration granted in part, 219 F. Supp. 2d 1027 (N.D. Cal. 2005).

101. Ibid. at 1031–33.

102. Ibid. at 1032.

103. Cal. Civ. Proc. Code § 354.7 (West 2006).

104. Perhaps because of the problems they experienced with the Bracero Program, many ex-Braceros who have been interviewed believe that current guest-worker proposals should ensure higher wages and long-term contracts. Anna Gorman, "Ex-Braceros Back Senate Plan, But With Upgrades," *L.A. Times*, June 18, 2006, at B1.

105. Saskia Sassen, *Guests and Aliens* (New York: The New Press, 1999), 144–45.

106. Immigration and Nationality Act of 1965, §§ 101(a)(15)(H)(i)(b), 101(a)(15)(H)(ii)(a), 101(a)(15)(H)(ii)(b) (2006).

107. See generally 8 U.S.C. § 1188 (2000).

108. See Compa, *Human Rights Watch*, at 36–38.

109. Of course, some guestworker programs in technology can lead to the worker staying permanently, if the employer sponsors the worker and has an ongoing need for the labor. See Roger Daniels, *Guarding the Golden Door: American Immigration Policy and Immigrants Since 1882* (New York: Hill and Wang, 2004), at 256–57.

110. See Chacón and Davis, *No One Is Illegal*, at 139–47 (discussing the Bracero program).

111. Philip L. Martin and Michael Teitelbaum, "The Mirage of Guest Workers," *Foreign Affairs*, Nov.–Dec. 2001, at 117, 129.

112. Immigration and Nationality Act of 1965, §§ 101(a)(15)(H)(i)(b), 101(a)(15)(H)(ii)(a), 101(a)(15)(H)(ii)(b).

113. David Tajgman and Karen Curtis, *Freedom of Association: A User's Guide* (International Labour Office ed., 2000).

114. See U.S. Department of Labor, Status of Submissions Under the North American Agreement on Labor Cooperation (NAALC) (2006), http:// www.dol.gov/ ilab/programs/nao/status.htm#iib8 (last visited Feb. 3, 2007) (describing the status of Mexico NAO Submission 2003-1 (North Carolina)).

115. Petition to the National Administrative Office of Mexico Under the North American Agreement on Labor Cooperation, submitted by the Central Independiente de Obreros Agricolas y Campesinos and Farmworker Justice Fund, Inc. (2003) (on file with the *Journal of Gender, Race & Justice*).

116. The current status of NAFTA petitions can be found at U.S. Department of Labor, Status of Submissions Under the North American Agreement on Labor Cooperation (NAALC), http://www.dol.gov/ilab/programs/nao/status.htm #iib8 (last visited January 24, 2007).

117. But see Tamara Kay, "Labor Transnationalism and Global Governance: The Impact of NAFTA on Transnational Labor Relationships in North America," 111 *American Journal of Sociology* 715, 742–44 (2005) (discussing the success of global governance institutions such as NAFTA). See also Tamara Kay, *NAFTA and the Politics of Labor Transnationalism* (Cambridge: Cambridge University Press, 2011).

118. See Mathew Schafer, "The Role of Nongovernmental Organizations in Canada-U.S. Relations," 30 Canada-U.S. Law Journal 69, 79 (2004) (describing the labor side complaint process and its shortcomings).

119. See U.S. Department of Labor, Responses to Questions Submitted by Mexico (on file with author).

120. Section 152(3) of the National Labor Relations Act excludes agricultural workers from the definition of "employee," 29 U.S.C. § 152(2) 1935.

121. See generally Alejandro V. Cortes, "The H-2A Farmworker: The Latest Incarnation of the Judicially Handicapped and Why the Use of Mediation to Resolve Employment Disputes Will Improve Their Rights," 21 Ohio State Journal on Dispute Resolution 409 (2006).

122. See Lance Compa, *The North American Free Trade Agreement (NAFTA) and the North American Agreement on Labor Cooperation (NAALC)* (The Netherlands and London: Kluwer Law International, 2001), 37–58.

123. North American Agreement on Labor Cooperation, U.S.-Can.-Mex., Sept. 14, 1993, 32 I.L.M. 1499.

124. Ibid.

125. For example, guestworkers in the United States would have the opportunity to file an action under the Alien Torts Claims Act of 1789, 28 U.S.C. § 1391 (2000). For a discussion on how these actions could be brought, see Michael J. Wishnie, "Immigrant Workers and the Domestic Enforcement of International Labor Rights," 4 University of Pennsylvania Journal of Labor and Employment Law 529, 533–43 (2001).

126. U.S. Department of Labor, Memorandum in Support of Petition on Labor Law Matters Arising in the United States (Apr. 13, 2005), available at http://dol.gov/ilab/media/reports/nao/submissions/2005-01memo.htm.

127. See Consolidated Appropriations Act of 2005, Pub. L. 108-447, 118 Stat. 2809 ("None of the funds appropriated in this Act to the Legal Services Corporation shall be expended for any purpose prohibited or limited by, or contrary to any of the provisions of, sections 501, 502, 503, 504, 505, and 506 of Public Law 105-119 ..."); 45 C.F.R. § 1626 (2006) (recipients of federal legal assistance funds may "provide legal assistance only to citizens of the United States and eligible aliens").

128. For status on the complaint, see U.S. Department of Labor, Status of Submissions Under the North American Agreement on Labor Cooperation (NAALC), http://www.dol.gov/ilab/programs/nao/status.htm#iib7 (last visited Jan. 26, 2007).

129. For complaint summaries, see Southern Poverty Law Center, *Hector Luna, et al. v. Del Monte Fresh Produce* (Southeast), Inc., http:// www.splcenter.org/legal/docket/files.jsp?cdrID=57&sortID=0 (last visited Jan. 28, 2007) (alleging wage violations by Del Monte); Southern Poverty Law Center, *Federico Salinas-Rodriguez v. Alpha Services, Inc.*, http:// www.splcenter.org/legal/docket/files.jsp?cdrID=48&sortID=3 (last visited Jan. 28, 2007) (discussing "minimum wage

and overtime protections, and other violations of the Migrant and Seasonal Agricultural Worker Protection Act"); Southern Poverty Law Center, *Rosiles-Perez, et al. v. Superior Forestry Service, Inc.*, http://www.splcenter.org/legal/docket/files.jsp? cdrID=56&sortID=0SPL (last visited Jan. 28, 2007) (discussing the Fair Labor Standards Act and Migrant and Seasonal Workers Protection Act).

130. Southern Poverty Law Center, *Beneath the Pines: Stories of Migrant Tree Planters* 14–15 (2005) available at http://www.splcenter.org/images/dynamic/main/ijp_beneaththepines_web.pdf.

131. Ibid.

132. Lexis Congressional Service, Bill Tracking Report, 110th Congress, 2nd Session, S. 2094, introduced September 26, 2007.

133. See Newsletter of the Northwest Workers Justice Project, Senator Bernard Sanders Introduces H-2B Reform Bill, winter 2008 at p. 3.

134. For example, guestworkers in the H-2B program must be paid the prevailing wage. See 8 U.S.C. § 1101(a)(15)(H)(ii)(b) (2000) (the H-2B provision); 8 C.F.R. § 214.2(h)(6)(iv) (2006).

135. Kevin Bales and Ron Soodalter, *The Slave Next Door: Human Trafficking and Slavery in America Today* (Berkeley: University of California Press, 2009), 68–77.

136. "Harvest of Shame" (CBS television broadcast 1960).

137. For a further discussion of the moral objections to guestworker programs, see Stephanie Franklin, "'Jobs that Americans Won't Do' Filled By Desperate Migrants," *Chicago Tribune*, Jan. 17, 2005, p. 1.

138. See Samuelson, "We Don't Need Guestworkers" (arguing against expanded guestworker programs).

139. See Michael R. Triplett, "White House Outlines Immigration Reforms, Including Guestworker Programs, Worker IDs," *Daily Labor Report* (BNA) No. 15, Jan. 24, 2007, at A-13.

140. See, e.g., Samuelson, "We Don't Need Guestworkers"; Martin and Teitelbaum,"The Mirage of Guestworkers."

141. Ibid.

142. See Lauren Gilbert, "Fields of Hope, Fields of Despair: Legisprudential and Historic Perspectives on the AgJobs Bill of 2003," 42 *Harvard Journal on Legislature* 417 (2005) (describing how the legislative debate over the AgJobs Bill of 2003, seeking to increase the number of workers in agriculture, failed to meet the needs of both farmworkers and growers).

143. See Philip Martin, Manolo Abella, and Christine Kuptsch, *Managing Labor Migration in the Twenty-First Century* (New Haven, CT: Yale University Press, 2006), 55–82 (describing highly skilled guestworker programs); Philip L. Martin, *Promise Unfulfilled: Unions, Immigration and the Farm Workers* (Ithaca, NY: ILR Press, 2003), 53–54 (describing how the political power of agriculture lead to temporary worker programs).

144. See Elisabeth Bumiller, "Bush Would Give Illegal Workers Broad New Rights," *New York Times*, Jan. 7, 2004, at 1; H. G. Reza, "Bush Plan No Migrant Lure," *L.A. Times*, Feb. 15, 2004, at 1; Leonel Sanchez, "Latinos Split on Bush's Immigration Plan, Citing Repatriation Provision," *San Diego Union-Tribune*, Jan. 30, 2004, at A3; Alan

Zarembo, "Garment Laborers Say Bush Guest-Worker Plan an Ill Fit," *L.A. Times*, Feb. 8, 2004, at A1.

145. Chacón and Davis, *No One Is Illegal*, 146–47.

146. Daniels, *Guarding the Golden Door*, 256–57 (showing that the H-1B cap was increased for fiscal years 1999 and 2000).

147. U.S. Const. amend. XIII.

148. See Maria L. Ontiveros, "Immigrant Workers' Rights in a Post-Hoffman World—Organizing Around the Thirteenth Amendment," 18 *Georgetown Immigration Law Journal* 651, 671–74 (2004) (arguing that the conditions of undocumented workers in the United States may be violations of the Thirteenth Amendment).

149. Ibid.

150. See ibid.; Tobias Barrington Wolff, "The Thirteenth Amendment and Slavery in the Global Economy, 102 Columbia Law Review 973, 1047–49 (2002) (arguing that the conditions of workers employed by U.S. companies abroad may be a violation of the Thirteenth Amendment).

151. See Alexander Tsesis, *The Thirteenth Amendment and American Freedom* (New York: New York University Press, 2004), 51–52, 79–80 (discussing the application of the Thirteenth Amendment to labor rights).

152. See James Gray Pope, "Labor's Constitution of Freedom," 106 Yale Law Journal 941 (1997) (detailing the history of labor's use of the Constitution before the passage of the National Labor Relations Act).

153. See Josiah Bartlett Lambert, *"If the Workers Took a Notion": The Right to Strike and American Political Development* (Ithaca, NY: ILR Press, 2005), 195–96 (grounding the right to strike in the Thirteenth Amendment). See James Gray Pope, "The Thirteenth Amendment Versus the Commerce Clause: Labor and the Shaping of American Constitutional Law, 1921–1957," 102 *Columbia Law Review* 1 (2002) (arguing for an expanded use of the Thirteenth Amendment, as opposed to the Commerce Clause, to enforce labor and human rights).

154. See Pope, "The Thirteenth Amendment," at 7 (discussing the debate over whether to ground the NLRA in the Thirteenth Amendment or the Commerce Clause).

155. United States v. Kozminski, 487 U.S. 931, 952 (1988) (holding that the employer's ability to frustrate the employees' immigration application was not involuntary servitude under the Thirteenth Amendment).

156. See Ontiveros, *Organizing Around the Thirteenth Amendment*, at 679–80.

157. See Carens, *Culture, Citizenship, and Community*, at 106.

158. See Hing, *Deporting Our Souls*, at 9.

159. See Comprehensive Immigration Reform Act of 2006, S. 2611, 109th Cong. (2d. Sess. 2006); see also Immigration and the 2006 Election, Backgrounder (Nat'l Immigration Forum, Washington, DC), available at http:// www.immigrationforum. org/documents/TheDebate/CivicParticipation/2006VoteAnalysis.pdf (last visited February 2, 2007).

160. See Jennifer Gordon, *Suburban Sweatshops: The Fight for Immigrant Rights* 268–73 (2005); Jennifer Gordon, "Transnational Labor Citizenship," 80 *Southern California Law Review* 503 ( 2007); Edward Rubin, "Getting Past Democracy," 149 *University of Pennsylvania Law Review* 711, 724 (2001) (analyzing different forms of democratic participation).

161. Leslie Berenstein, "Border Deaths on Record Pace," *San Diego Union-Tribune*, July 22, 2006, at A1 ("During fiscal year 2005, 472 people are known to have died attempting to cross the border illegally, making it the deadliest year on record").

162. Hing, *Deporting Our Souls*, at 3.

163. For a list of International Labour Organization member countries, which includes the United States and Mexico, see http:// www.ilo.org/public/english/standards/relm/country.htm (Oct. 5, 2006).

164. International Labor Organization, Fundamental Principles and Rights at Work, http://www.ilo.org/dyn/declaris/DECLARATIONWEB.INDEXPAGE?var_language=EN (last visited Nov. 17, 2006).

165. See International Labor Organization Convention No. 87, Concerning Freedom of Association and Protection of the Right to Organize, July 9, 1948, 68 U.N.T.S. 17; see also International Labor Organization Convention No. 98, Concerning the Application of the Principles of the Right to Organize, July 1, 1949, 96 U.N.T.S. 257.

166. See International Labor Organization, Ratifications of ILO Convention 87, http://www.ilo.org/ilolex/cgi-lex/ratifce.pl?C087 (last visited Dec. 19, 2006).

167. International Covenant on Civil and Political Rights, art. 22, § 1, Dec. 16, 1966, 999 U.N.T.S. 171, available at http:// www.ohchr.org/english/law/ccpr.htm; Maria Pabon Lopez, "The Intersection of Immigration Law and Civil Rights Law: Noncitizen Workers and the International Human Rights Paradigm," 44 Brandeis Law Journal 611, 628 (2006) (applying International Labour Organization principles to noncitizen workers' rights).

168. North American Agreement on Labor Cooperation, U.S.-Mex.-Can., Annex 1, Sept. 14, 1993, 32 I.L.M. 1499 [hereinafter NAALC].

169. Ibid. at art. 11(1)(3).

170. George W. Bush, U.S. President, Remarks on a New Temporary Guestworker Program (Jan. 7, 2004), available at http:// www.whitehouse.gov/news/releases/2004/01/20040107-3.html.

171. See infra Part III.A.

172. Fawn Johnson, "House Passes Enforcement Only Bill Containing No Guestworker Language," *Daily Labor Report* (BNA), Dec. 20, 2005, at AA-1.

173. Report Supplement, Legislation, Lawmakers to Revisit Unfinished Business, Pension, Business, Immigration, *Daily Labor Report* (BNA) No. 243, Jan. 17, 2006, at S-5 [hereinafter Report Supplement].

174. See Johnson, "House Passes Enforcement Only Bill."

175. See Hing, *Deporting Our Souls*, at 9.

176. See Report Supplement, Legislation, Lawmakers to Revisit Unfinished Business.

177. See ibid., at 37–38.

178. Fawn Johnson, "In Signing Border Security Measure, Bush Calls for Guestworker Program," *Daily Labor Report* (BNA) No. 193, Oct. 5, 2006, at A-10 (explaining how a comprehensive immigration bill was blocked by House Republicans in favor of the border fence bill).

179. Comprehensive Immigration Reform Act of 2006, S. 2611, 109th Cong. (2d. Sess. 2006).

180. See "Republican Policy Committee Urges Removal of Wage Language," *Daily Labor Report* (BNA) No. 13, at A-11 (July 17, 2006) (referring to a proposal on enhanced wage protections that was rejected in the final bill).

181. See "With Caveats, House Hearing Witnesses Express Support for Guest-workers," *Daily Labor Report* (BNA) No. 139, at A-1 (July 19, 2006).

182. See Eric Lekus, "Senate Approves Plan to Create System Requiring Electronic Verification of New Hires," *Daily Labor Report* (BNA) No. 100, May 24, 2006, at AA-1 (discussing the defeat of Senator Kennedy's amendment to the Senate Bill 2611, which would have required increased labor protections for guestworkers brought to the United States under the bill).

183. Comprehensive Immigration Reform Act of 2006, S.2611, 109th Cong. (2d Sess. 2006).

184. Hing, *Deporting Our Souls*, at 36.

185. See ibid. at 38 (discussing S. 2611).

186. See ibid. at 31 (discussing S. 2611).

187. Recent decisions of the NLRB have constricted the definition of "employee." See Brown University, 342 N.L.R.B. No. 42 (2004) (graduate students are not employees eligible for collective bargaining); Oakwood Healthcare, Inc., Case 348 N.L.R.B. No. 37 (2006) (one of the "Kentucky River cases" which held that charge nurses are not employees).

188. 331 N.L.R.B. 1298 (2000).

189. See 29 U.S.C. § 159(b) (1935).

190. See National Labor Relations Board: NLRB Board Members, http://www.nlrb. gov/about_us/overview/board/index.aspx (click on board member to display biography).

191. H.S. Care, L.L.C., 343 NLRB No. 76 (2004).

192. Ibid.

193. See Eric Lekus and Heather M. Rothman, "Senate Votes to Keep Path to Citizenship in Proposed H-2C Temporary Visa Program," *Daily Labor Report* (BNA) No. 98, May 22, 2006, at AA-1.

194. See Hirschmann, *Exit, Voice & Loyalty*, 33–34, 55 (arguing that in many cases voice is a more effective mechanism than exit).

195. Steven Greenhouse, "Growers' Group Signs First Union Contract with Guest-workers," *New York Times*, Sept. 17, 2004, at A6.

196. Ibid.

197. Steven Greenhouse, "Farmworkers' Union Is Set to Announce First National Contract for Guest Workers," *New York Times*, Apr. 11, 2006, at A17; Jerry Hirsch, "Farm Labor Contractor, Union in Pact," *L.A. Times*, Apr. 12, 2006, at C2.

198. "Labor Firm to Pay Nearly $300,000 to Settle DOL Back Pay Claims for Thai Farmworkers," *Daily Labor Report* (BNA) No. 101, at A-1 (May 25, 2006).

199. See Gordon, *Suburban Sweatshops*; Paul Johnston, "Citizenship Movement Unionism: For the Defense of Local Communities in the Global Age," in *Unions in a Globalized Environment: Changing Borders, Organizational Boundaries, and Social Roles*, Bruce Nissen, ed. (Armonk, NY: M.E. Sharpe, 2002), 236.

200. Lee Swepston, "Closing the Gap Between International Labor Law and U.S. Law," in *Workers' Rights as Human Rights*, James A. Gross, ed. (Ithaca, NY: ILR Press, 2003), 53, 64.

201. See Daniel C. Esty, "Good Governance at the Supranational Scale: Globalizing Administrative Law," 115 *Yale Law Journal* 1490, 1494 (2006).

202. See Hing, *Deporting Our Souls*, at 17 (describing the broad appeal of a "guest-worker" program).

203. See Manolo I. Abella, *Int'l Labour Organization, Sending Workers Abroad: A Manual for Low- and Middle-Income Countries* (Geneva: International Labour Organization, 1997), 5–12 (examining the institutional and policy implications of the role played by the government and the private sector in facilitating the migration of workers).

204. See David Bacon, "Workers, Not Guests," *The Nation*, Feb. 19, 2007, at 5, 8 (discussing the alliance of the labor federation Change to Win with the Essential Worker Immigrant Coalition to lobby for a guestworker program).

205. See generally Martha F. Davis, *Brutal Need: Lawyers and the Welfare Rights Movement, 1960–1973* (New Haven, CT: Yale University Press, 1993).

206. See Michael J. Mayerle, "Proposed Guest Worker Statutes: An Unsatisfactory Answer to a Difficult, If Not Impossible, Question," 6 *Journal of Small and Emerging Business Law* 559, 578 (2002) (discussing the fear many temporary workers have of challenging their employer's practices, resulting in depressed wages and poor working conditions).

CHAPTER 6

1. Remarks of Lilly Ledbetter at White House signing ceremony, January 29, 2009 http://www.whitehouse.gov/blog/issues/Civil-Rights?page=2.

2. See Rafael Gely, "An Empirical Examination of Pay Secrecy Laws, Pay Secrecy/ Confidentiality Rules and the National Labor Relations Act," *University of Pennsylvania Journal of Labor and Employment Law* (2003).

3. 29 U.S.C. § 157 provides protection for employees to discuss "wages, hours and other terms and conditions of employment."

4. James Gray Pope, "Labor's Constitution of Freedom," 106 *Yale Law Journal* 941 (1997).

5. 421 F.3d 1169 (11th Cir. 2005); 550 U.S. 618 (2007).

6. *Bazemore v. Friday*, 478 U.S. 435.

7. See Institute for Women's Policy Research, www.iwpr.org.

8. Pub. L. No. 111-2 § 3, 123 Stat. 5, 5–6.

9. See Kimberlé W. Crenshaw, "Demarginalizing the Intersection of Race and Class," 1989 *University of Chicago Legal Forum* 139–67 (1989).

10. EU Treaty Article 141; EU Equal Pay Directive 75/117.

11. *County of Washington v. Gunther*, 452 U.S. 161 (1981).

12. But see Robin E. Shea et al., *The Impact of the Lilly Ledbetter Fair Pay Act, 2009 ASPIA* 17 (2009).

13. Michael W. McCann, *Rights at Work: Pay Equity Reform and the Politics of Legal Mobilization* (Chicago: University of Chicago Press, 1994).

14. See Margaret Talbot, "A Risky Proposal: Is It Too Soon to Petition the Court on Gay Marriage?" *The New Yorker*, Jan. 18, 2010.

15. Ellen Dannin, *Taking Back the Workers' Law: How to Fight the Assault on Labor Rights* (Ithaca, NY: Cornell University Press, 2008).

16. *Roper v. Simmons*, 543 U.S. 551 (2005).

17. *Estate of Rodriguez v. Drummond Coal*, 256 F. Supp. 2d 1250 (N.D. Ala. 2003).

18. See Charles J. Morris, *The Blue Eagle at Work: Reclaiming Democratic Rights in the Workplace* (Ithaca, NY: Cornell University Press, 2008).

19. General Accounting Office Report, *Employee Misclassification: Improved Coordination, Outreach and Targeting Could Better Ensure Detection and Prevention.*

20. Lauren Edelman and Rachel Best, Multiple Disadvantages: An Empirical Test of Intersectionality Theory Using EEO Data, forthcoming 2011 *Law and Society Review.*

21. Ibid.

22. 523 U.S. 706 (2001).

23. See Roger Blanpain et al., *The Global Workplace: International and Comparative Employment Law Cases and Materials* (Cambridge: Cambridge University Press, 2006), 220.

24. Hilary K. Josephs, *Labor Law in China*, 2d ed. (Huntington, NY: Juris Publishing, 2003), 71.

25. International Labor Organization Conventions, 87, 98.

26. International Labor Organization Convention, 105.

27. International Labor Organization Convention, 182.

28. International Labor Organization Convention, 111.

29. www.ilo.org/declaration.

30. *Roper v. Simmons*, 543 U.S. 551 (2005); *Grutter v. Bollinger* 539 U.S. 306 (2003); *Lawrence v. Texas*, 539 U.S. 558 (2003).

31. Robert Dahl, "Decision Making in a Democracy: The Supreme Court as a National Policymaker," *Journal of Public Law*, 6 (Fall 1957), 279–95.

32. *Doe v. Unocal*, 403 F.3d 708 (9th Cir. 2005).

33. 457 U.S. 202, 222 (1982).

34. International Labor Organization Convention 87, *Freedom of Association* (Washington, DC: ILO, 1919).

35. Jennifer Gordon, *Suburban Sweatshops: The Fight for Immigrant Rights* (Cambridge, MA: Harvard University Press, 2006).

36. Gerald Rosenberg, *The Hollow Hope: Can the Courts Bring About Social Change*, 2d ed. (Chicago: University of Chicago Press, 2008).

37. John Schmitt and Ben Zipperer, "Dropping the Ax: Illegal Firings During Union Election Campaigns, 1951–2007" (Center for Economic and Policy Research Report, March 2009). Available at www.cper.net/index.php/publications /reports/ dropping-the-ax-update.

38. George Lakoff, *Whose Freedom: The Battle Over America's Most Important Idea* (New York: Farrar, Strauss and Giroux, 2006).

39. See Ayn Rand, *Atlas Shrugged* (New York, Random House, 1957); *The Fountainhead* (New York: Bobbs Merrill, 1943).

40. Isaiah Berlin, *Four Essays on Liberty* (Oxford: Oxford University Press, 1969; New York: Random House, 1957).

41. 29 U.S.C. § 102.

42. Kingsley Browne, "Workplace Censorship," Rutgers Law Review 579 (1995); Eugene Volokh, Comment: "Freedom of Speech and Workplace Harassment," 39 *UCLA Law Review* 1791 (1992).

43. John Schmitt, Center for Economic and Policy Research, "The Union Wage Advantage for Low-Wage Workers," May 2008.

44. Lakoff, *Whose Freedom?*

45. *Chamber of Commerce v. Reich*, 57 F. 3d 1099 (D.C. Cir. 1995).

46. See Rhonda McMillion, "Payday Equality: ABA Urges Congress to Bolster Laws Curing Gender Based Wage Discrimination," *ABA Journal*, May 2010, p. 67.

# Index

# About the Author

RUBEN J. GARCIA is Professor of Law at the William S. Boyd School of Law, University of Nevada, Las Vegas.